Online Reputation Management

FOR DUMMIES®

by Lori Randall Stradtman

WILEY

John Wiley & Sons, Inc.

Online Reputation Management For Dummies®

Published by
John Wiley & Sons, Inc.
111 River Street
Hoboken, NJ 07030-5774

www.wiley.com

WILEY

About the Author

Lori Randall Stradtman has been a passionate fan of social media and blogging since 2005, when she first went back to school at the University of Georgia to earn a degree in Communications.

After graduating from college in May 2008, Lori started Social Media Design and soon after began guest posting on Social Media Examiner, BlogWorld, and SmartBrief, and has been quoted in *Huffington Post*.

Lori loves the idea of training business owners and C-level employees on the power of a strong and positive online reputation.

Dedication

This book is dedicated to my kids, Phil, Sally, and Josh, who have always inspired me to be strong and to do things that feel impossible in the moment. Seeing myself reflected in their eyes motivates me more than any amount of money or accolades.

I also want to dedicate this book to my hubby, Chris Stradtman, without whose patience and support I could never have interviewed all the experts and engaged in so much research. He's also been known to take me out for awesome dinners during my writing frenzies, shameful places with food no trainer would approve of. I love him for it all.

Author's Acknowledgments

Ever since I witnessed firsthand a new friend's misery and fear connected with her online privacy and reputation, something transformed inside of me and I couldn't just do social media design anymore. My life changed as I listened to her plight, enlarged with a rapidly evolving sense of purpose. I knew I had to help people to take control of their lives online.

I've spent the last year interviewing heroes and villains, quiet SEO & analytics geeks and celebrities, white- and black-hat hackers, defamation litigators and neuroscientists, and world-class online reputation management leaders and bloggers, as well as the people who work for social media departments, everywhere from start-up size to the biggest brands online for the information I share with you in this book.

I've even been lucky enough to interview world-class Internet Security experts and two actual founders of the Internet, Karl Auerbach and David J. Steele.

I wish I could give credit here to every expert and every person named in a case study. As it is, I can only list people according to how pivotal their contribution was. I'm also overwhelmingly grateful to L. Lin Wood, celebrity defamation litigator; Lin Milano, celebrity online reputation expert; Andrew Bates, Social SEO analyst extraordinaire; Shashi Bellmakonda, and more.

And most inspiring, most patient, loved most of all are my hubby and kids. They are like breath to me.

Publisher's Acknowledgments

We're proud of this book; please send us your comments at http://dummies.custhelp.com. For other comments, please contact our Customer Care Department within the U.S. at 877-762-2974, outside the U.S. at 317-572-3993, or fax 317-572-4002.

Some of the people who helped bring this book to market include the following:

Acquisitions and Editorial

Senior Project Editor: Christopher Morris

Acquisitions Editor: Amy Fandrei

Copy Editor: Debbye Butler

Technical Editor: Andrea Vahl

Editorial Manager: Kevin Kirschner

Editorial Assistant: Leslie Saxman

Sr. Editorial Assistant: Cherie Case

Cover Photo: © Lane Oakley/GettyImages

Cartoons: Rich Tennant (www.the5thwave.com)

Composition Services

Project Coordinator: Patrick Redmond

Layout and Graphics: Jennifer Creasey, Joyce Haughey, Corrie Niehaus

Proofreader: Toni Settle

Indexer: BIM Indexing & Proofreading Services

Publishing and Editorial for Technology Dummies

Richard Swadley, Vice President and Executive Group Publisher

Andy Cummings, Vice President and Publisher

Mary Bednarek, Executive Acquisitions Director

Mary C. Corder, Editorial Director

Publishing for Consumer Dummies

Kathleen Nebenhaus, Vice President and Executive Publisher

Composition Services

Debbie Stailey, Director of Composition Services

Contents at a Glance

Table of Contents

Introduction

· ·

*N*othing is more valuable than your good name . . . online! Think about it. You've worked hard all your life to build a reputation for yourself so that you can:

- ✔ Get a good job
- ✔ Keep that good job
- ✔ Make your family proud
- ✔ Feel good about yourself
- ✔ Make a good impression
- ✔ Leave a legacy your loved ones can be proud of

At some point way back in the last millennium, you could establish a name for yourself or your business based on the long-term relationships you cultivated within a localized geographic area, and you never needed to care about the things people halfway around the world were saying about you. And when people slandered or libeled your good name, you had legal protection.

Back then, nearly all channels of communication from the customer back to the brand were stiffly controlled by the brand. It was a largely one-way communication model. Brands would broadcast ads via mass media but wouldn't listen to the things people said about their brands. They relied on bottom-line numbers, which can be deceptive and can ill-prepare management for future market shocks.

Today, the Internet has changed everything. It's changed the playing field for the legal system, and it's changed the way people communicate as individuals and en masse. Two-way communication dominates over one-way communication, and ordinary people can have engaged audiences of thousands online. The benefits are great, but so are the risks. The easier it is for customers to disseminate information to an increasingly large audience, the greater the threat to a brand's reputation. Nowadays people's reputations get damaged often and easily. There's little anybody can do about it, except to be prepared. That's why I'm here.

About This Book

I'm excited to be able to step you through creating a scalable system for your online reputation management (ORM) that will see you through both good and tough times online, and also help you create solid and rewarding relationships with more people than you ever imagined.

Countless people encounter amazing opportunities by maintaining a solid reputation online. In today's world, it almost doesn't matter where you live. If you can contribute something useful online from right where you are, you have the potential to reach millions.

Here are a few reasons why I'm so excited to be able to share this crucial information with you:

- ✔ Every few seconds, somebody's identity is stolen online, often resulting in financial loss and terrible upheaval. I get to help make sure this doesn't happen to you.

- ✔ Every few seconds, somebody's Facebook account is hacked, causing embarrassment and loss. I get to help make sure this doesn't happen to you.

- ✔ Within a few hours, a huge corporation's reputation is damaged to such an extent that it can take months, if not years to recover. I'm excited to be able to show you how to craft a strategy that prevents and minimizes damage, and converts negative energy into positive reviews.

- ✔ Fringe groups organize online and stage attacks from all parts of the globe to gain attention for their causes, often at the expense of any business that stands in their way. I get to show you how to negotiate these choppy waters and reestablish smooth sailing.

Expecting the best and preparing for the worst

Together you and I create a preparedness system just like the fire drills you used to do in elementary school, except that I'm not going to ring a really loud bell or boss you around and you don't have to go outside unless you want to. Just bring your book and keep reading!

I like a fire drill metaphor because when negative messages flame up via social media they tend to explode with intensity, and heated remarks start popping up everywhere online. A gripe can start on Twitter and quickly migrate to Facebook or YouTube if it isn't addressed quickly enough where it started. Trying to control the flow of countless people commenting is like fighting a wildfire. Your very best solution is prevention, which involves creating a strong social platform and a well-designed crisis plan.

Touring online reputation management together

Please think of me as your best friend in another city who is taking you around to see all the best hangouts, cafes, and natural wonders that only a real local knows about. You'll love some of the places I show you and want to spend most of your time there. Other places will be more like learning how to get in touch with the fire or police departments. They aren't places you want to call every day, but they're priceless when you really need them. I'm honored to take you on this journey through online communication as it relates to your precious, one-of-a-kind reputation.

You have in your hands a guidebook to creating your very own customized ORM system that will protect and serve you if crisis strikes, and boost your genuine influence and sales online. You'll make lots of new friends along the way and understand social media in an entirely new light. Please bear in mind that this isn't just crisis prevention. It's your new media makeover.

Conventions Used in This Book

Consistency can make things easier to understand. In this book, those consistent elements are *conventions.* In fact, I use italics to identify and define new terms. I also put search terms and keywords in italics.

Also, I put anything you need to type in **bold** so it's easy to see.

Foolish Assumptions

I'm assuming that you are someone interested in ethical Internet marketing, a brand manager, a CEO, or just an everyday Joe who has been bullied online or had his good name tarnished and wants to re-establish his reputation online so that this is less likely to ever happen again.

Many people (and professional service providers) assume that online reputation management means monitoring for your brand's name and pushing out good publicity to cover up any bad reviews or, if possible, getting the people publishing negative reviews or false information to retract their comments made online. Don't assume that online reputation management is simply another term for damage control. It's a system of behavior that actually creates positive opportunities for your business that never would have existed unless you made the effort to put your best foot forward online.

Still, in this book I make a number of foolish assumptions about you, including:

- ✔ You want to take care of your online reputation management or are a professional brand manager. Even if you've just opened your own photography studio, you need to manage your brand online in order to boost your business and keep those positive reviews right where everybody will be looking for them: online!

- ✔ You are interested in the long-term health of your name and your brand online.

- ✔ You don't want to suddenly have to become continuously active on every social network known to humankind and consequently marry your smartphone because that's all you have time for anymore. I show you how to craft a simple, scalable system that works for your needs right now and when you have hundreds of employees and are on the NYSE. You never know!

- ✔ You'll want to research more on your own. I show you the most relevant tools and approaches for a modern online reputation management system and share resources for you to explore more deeply if you find a topic (like social media analytics) that really grabs your attention

- ✔ You're interested in saving time and money in every possible way as I step you through this process. This book is designed to cater to everyone from solo entrepreneurs to Fortune 100 companies, so some tools with expensive licenses may be much more than you need to function efficiently.

- ✔ Once you have created your online reputation management strategy, you will set aside a little time every month to stay current or optimize your system .

- ✔ You're a big fan of the KISS principle. (Keep It Simple, Stupid.) These days, nearly every message you see online capitalizes on your fear of missing out on something important. I help you to craft your own strategy and stand strong.

How This Book Is Organized

I show you many networks or tools here (such as Facebook and search engine optimization, or SEO, keywords) from different practical perspectives. They're so interwoven and deserve a For Dummies book all on their own, but I show you relevant tips and tricks to use in your own successful ORM system. Here's a high-level description of what you'll find in each part.

Part I: Getting Started with Online Reputation Management

Part I is all about what online reputation management is — and is not. Here I introduce you to the various goals and approaches you can use to create your online reputation management system. It gets you started by sharing clear goals that you need to consider and what's involved with them.

Part II: Organizing Your Teams

Part II shows you how to create and organize your online reputation management teams and introduces you to different kinds of social media and technical professionals who can assist.

Part III: Listening Is Love

Part III is the foundation of every great online reputation management strategy: listening to what people are saying about you and your brand. I show you how to choose the best tools, how to research your most effective (and surprising) SEO keywords, and how to set up your listening tools.

Part IV: Establishing Your Reputation

Part IV facilitates engaging smoothly within social media networks, claiming your brand online, creating great messages, learning how to tap in to focused interest groups, blogging, articles, press releases, live broadcasting, and choosing visuals that will impact and inspire your followers to share and develop relationships with influential people online.

Part V: Responding to Crisis: Your Step-by-Step Plan

Part V takes you through the essentials of managing social media emergencies, qualifying and responding to situations as they appear on your listening radar, promoting good will, and turning proverbial lemons into lemonade. Yes, you really can!

Part VI: The Part of Tens

This tends to be my favorite part of every For Dummies book! Part VI gives you ten online reputation management tips for special events, ten ways to "faceplant" your online reputation, and ends with ten ways to create a happy fan base.

Icons Used in This Book

The little images (called icons) you see in the margins throughout this book emphasize a point to remember, a danger to be aware of, or information that I think you may find helpful or that will make a task easier. Here's what each of those icons means:

When you see this icon, take special note of the information so that you . . . uh . . . remember it later.

Tips are bits of information that you may find useful or that make something you need to do easier.

I use this icon to point out situations that can get you into trouble. Heed these warnings!

Where to Go from Here

The next page, of course. I recommend heading for Chapter 1. And use the material in this book to make your online reputation the best it ever was.

Online Reputation Management For Dummies is designed so that you can read a chapter or section out of order, depending on what subjects you're most interested in. Although it's true that some topics later in the book use concepts described more fully in earlier chapters, don't feel obligated to read every chapter, particularly if you feel you already have a good handle on that subject. Where you go from here is entirely up to you!

Occasionally, we have updates to our technology books. If this book does have any technical updates, they'll be posted at www.dummies.com/ onlinerepmanagementfdupdates.

Part I
Getting Started with Online Reputation Management

The 5th Wave   By Rich Tennant

"I'd respond to this person's comment on Twitter, but I'm a former Marine, Bernard, and a Marine never retweets."

In this part . . .

In Part I, I introduce you to the basic concepts of online reputation management, including the ideas and methods that will help you protect your reputation online. After all, nothing is more valuable than your good name! In Chapter 1, I give you the foundations of online reputation management and show you how to begin taking care of your online rep. When you move on to Chapter 2, you'll find I show you how to develop an approach to online reputation management that best suits you or your organization. Let's get started!

Chapter 1

Understanding Online Reputation Management

*W*hen Facebook requested permission to get its initial public offering, the company didn't put electronics or shoes as its product. It listed information about our personalized preferences as a commodity to sell to advertisers. Google uses the topics people search on to target demographics and sell advertising.

These days your identity is more than just your personality or your vital statistics. It's a valuable commodity. It can be bought and sold, damaged, tarnished, or even hijacked. It's good advice to post nothing online that you don't want your grandma to read, but make one little mistake and all the privacy settings in the world won't do you any good.

That's why people all over the world are talking about online reputation management and, in particular, online privacy. Technology is moving far faster than legislation, however. The United States has taken the least amount of action in getting social networks to limit the amount of information they get from you and how long they store it.

In this book, I share important ways for you to protect your privacy as well as craft a strategy that promotes and protects both your personal and private brand names online.

Throughout this book, I share war stories, anecdotes, and tips for keeping your name safe and well respected, as long as you don't publish those ferret juggling pictures from last year's New Year's Eve party.

What Is Online Reputation Management?

Online reputation management is the process of ensuring that the right information appears when people look you (or the name of your brand) up in search engines like Google, Bing, or Yahoo!, or on social networks like Facebook, Twitter, or LinkedIn. The idea is to minimize negative content and to promote flattering content.

To achieve this goal, you must monitor search engines and social network and do what you can to mitigate negative comments. When you find negative content, you decrease its visibility by creating enough positive content so that the negative content appears to go away. Or sometimes you can get the relevant webmaster to remove offensive content.

But the best way to eliminate negative content is to make sure it never appears in the first place. In fact, in this book I present a system of online reputation management that focuses on building a positive and proactive fan base before a crisis ever happens.

Effective online reputation management means getting involved with social networks, monitoring those networks closely (rather than just depending on automated monitoring systems like Google Alerts), and responding as quickly as possible in the event of great breaking news or a crisis.

Being proactive

Once upon a time online, before social media networks became mainstream, brands could address negative comments by tracking links and performing damage control. Today, if a crisis isn't handled correctly, a brand's image can be brought down in a matter of hours, (yes, hours!) and take months, if not years to recover.

These days, people do most of their socializing (and talking about brands) on social networks like Facebook, Twitter, LinkedIn, Pinterest, YouTube, and Tumblr, to name a few. Your best bet is to be positive and proactive. Start by:

- ✔ Claiming your brand on these networks
- ✔ Posting quality information and/or entertaining content periodically
- ✔ Monitoring networks
- ✔ Responding warmly to visitors

Social media strategy is this simple on a day-to-day basis. Having a crisis strategy and team in place makes dealing with any issue that may arise ten times easier.

Don't limit yourself to Google Alerts!

Google Alerts is a way to stay informed whenever your name, brand name, or some key terms you specify are discovered via search engines online. (I show you how to set them up in Chapter 5, as well as teach you a few tricks for using Google Alerts more efficiently.) Most people think that Google Alerts covers every mention of your name online, including mentions on social networks. Not so! However, you can use monitoring tools to catch every mention. I show you how to do this in Chapter 5, too.

In this book, I show you how to pay attention to what people are saying about you online so you can address *why* they're saying it, rather than simply covering it up with positive information.

Maintaining a strong and healthy reputation online makes you more resilient to viral attacks (pun intended).

As new media evolves, the strongest brands will be those that listen closely to what people are saying and who respond quickly with messages that show they are listening and that they understand. Such a response can go a long way. Validating the commenter's point of view can even build a lasting, durable relationship.

People expect to be heard and understood online more than ever. Smart brands recognize this growing trend and make room for it in their approaches to online reputation management.

Transparency is for brands, not people

Before the dawn of the Information Age, companies used to be able to shield themselves from scrutiny via receptionists and PR departments. No longer! The public today expects organizations to be as transparent as possible in all their dealings, especially financial.

This doesn't apply to everyone, however. The public expects transparent communication online — but only for brands. This may sound strange, but it's true. The public demands openness from brands, but still respects the privacy of the individual.

Individuals, then — even entrepreneurs or celebrities who may consider themselves to be a brand — don't have to be transparent. In fact, for individuals, being transparent is a bad idea. Don't confuse "authenticity" with being transparent. Keep your common sense online.

I suggest you identify three areas you're willing to be open about online; the rest can be just for you and your close friends. Limiting your public identity in this way is less confusing for people trying to understand your message. And besides, a little mystique can be very appealing!

Dealing with negativity

Ideally, anyone searching online for you will see warm, glowing comments about you and fascinating articles that demonstrate your expertise. Often, however, this is not the case. Occasionally problems can arise that cloud how your name looks online. Here are some real-life examples, in escalating order:

- ✔ **Remarks from disgruntled friends or business associates.** It's a fact. You can't please everybody all the time and you'll go crazy trying to. Some people just aren't going to be happy no matter what anybody does to try and make it better. Some of them may voice out online.

- ✔ **Leaked personal information.** I interviewed a schoolteacher who was fired when a picture of her holding up a wine glass appeared on the Internet. It didn't matter that she only held the wine glass for a toast at a dignified, off-hours gathering of adults. Even though she wasn't drinking at school or advocating that her little kiddies in the classroom partake, school officials fired her immediately.

  Also, I interviewed a woman who got fired when the law firm she worked for discovered the photograph of her tattoo she'd posted on her "completely private" Facebook profile. It wasn't even a racy tattoo, by the way!

- ✔ **Group dynamics gone sour.** On message boards and social networks, groups can gang up on you. A close friend built a successful web forum but was kicked off when a jealous outsider succeeded in turning the group against her. The outsider hijacked the creator's own forum and kicked her out.

- ✔ **Embarrassing viral videos.** When someone gets the bright idea to upload an embarrassing video, it can make even his employer look bad. If such a video also divulges unflattering corporate secrets, it can inspire viral outrage.

- ✔ **Disaster strikes.** During the BP oil spill crisis, online outrage gushed as hard as the leak did — and for much longer. You can bet BP has a solid online reputation management policy in place now, but things would have been much better if the company had been prepared for such a crisis ahead of time.

Beware of Yelp!

Many people believe that they can minimize negative comments by writing positive comments and reviews that look like real customers posting to online forums or review sites like Yelp. It isn't quite that easy. Most sites are well aware of fake user comments and use screening measures to keep their sites relevant and reliable.

Monitoring with Aggregators

If you're responsible for managing your own reputation, as well as that of a brand online, social aggregators will save you a surprising amount of time and energy.

What are aggregators? Glad you asked! In simple terms, aggregators monitor and measure social media.

The thing to remember is that aggregators make your life more convenient by collecting your social network activity information all in one place so that you can monitor all your major networks easily.

Here are the commonly monitored social media channels:

✔ Facebook profile

✔ Facebook brand page(s)

✔ Twitter

✔ LinkedIn

An API (application programming interface) application integrates your primary social network accounts for you. For the API to be able to access a user's actions from another platform, the user (you) has to give permission to the social aggregation platform, like Facebook, by specifying your user ID and password for the social media to be syndicated. This built-in security keeps someone else — like your competitors — from creating an account with an aggregator and obtaining all your information.

Social network aggregation services allow you to organize or simplify your social networking experience. With them you can finally stop logging on and off from Facebook, Twitter, and LinkedIn all the time and start managing them all in one place. Most give you the capability to schedule messages across different networks at the same time, although make sure you tailor your message to fit the personality and culture of the network — updates about Twitter, LinkedIn, and Google+, for example, tend to be a real bust on Facebook. You want to remain interesting, not become a spammer and clog the newsfeed with irrelevant information.

Figure 1-1 shows my HootSuite account. I show you lots more about setting this popular aggregator up in Chapter 5.

Figure 1-1:
HootSuite
panel.

Using Analytics

Analytics can tell you a lot about the kinds of people who are coming to visit you online and what they do when they get to your site. Analytics applications invisibly track the way visitors respond to the material on your site, including

- ✔ **What site your visitors came from:** This can be very useful information when you're aiming to redirect traffic from a specific location to your site. For example, most of my "referring traffic" comes from Facebook. This means that the work I'm doing there to raise awareness of my site is working.

- ✔ **How long visitors stayed at your site:** This is valuable because short visits may signal that you need to reconsider the appeal of your content.

- ✔ **How many pages they visited:** This also relates to how appealing your content and general message is. The more compelling your message, the longer people tend to linger at your site.

The most popular analytics service in the world is Google Analytics, because it's free, relatively easy to set up, and is supported by fantastic tutorials online. I tell you much more about Google Analytics and how to set it up in Chapter 6.

Although the information Google Analytics provides has an unbeatable price, the responsibility for interpreting that data rests largely on your shoulders. If analyzing information makes you head hurt, you may try a paid analytics service.

Generally, paid analytics services are for large businesses. These services can give you a wealth of understanding into your organization's many online activities, including

✔ Your site's web data and audience measurement

✔ Your advertising effectiveness

✔ Your social media strategy's effectiveness

Even if you're running a small business, paid services are worth a look. Often they provide some general analytics information for free.

Here are some of the more proven online marketing research sites you may consider checking out:

✔ ComScore (www.comscore.com)

✔ Compete (www.compete.com/us)

✔ Hitwise (www.experian.com/hitwise)

✔ Forrester Research (www.forrester.com)

Tracking Your Trends via Social Media Measurement Tools

On social media sites, topics "trend" daily, even hourly. On social media sites, people respond quickly to jokes or news items by adding their own voices or interpretation. During a presidential election, for example, polls, political discussions, cartoons, and jokes will trend almost constantly. *Trending* means that a topic has become — for at least a little while — extremely popular online. When a topic trends it

✔ Ranks more highly on Google

✔ Becomes a hot search term on Facebook

✔ Gets retweeted much more often

All of this means that if you can align your organization with a trending topic, you can get more attention than usual.

It's always a great idea to be current with what's going around online. Keep your eyes open for when you can associate your brand with a currently trending topic, especially when that topic is central to your business. This approach can help you to spread the word about your brand to more audiences online. Even if you're in a very conservative business, this can still work, given the right situation.

Here are some of my favorite hunting grounds — er, places where you can look for "trendspiration" — though there are too many to list here:

- ✔ **Google Trends:** You can look up multiple search items at once, which holds interesting search possibilities, such as "your brand, hot trend" to see what emerges if your brand is linked with that particular hot trend. It also offers Google Insights for Search. You can find Google Trends at www.google.com/trends.

- ✔ **What the Trend:** Helps you find out what's trending on Twitter and why. It's a busy interface, with hot topics from around the world. I like how you can just click on a country to see what's trending there right now. Check out What the Trend at www.whatthetrend.com.

- ✔ **Topsy:** Clean interface, real-time search available at www.topsy.com, where you can look up

  - • Everything

  - • Links

  - • Tweets

  - • Photos

  - • Videos

  - • Experts

  - • Trending

- ✔ **Trendistic:** Fun graphics for visualizing how many times the term you enter has been used on Twitter recently. For experimental purposes, I tweeted "femmepreneur" a few times over the past few days and then checked "femmepreneur" on Trendistic. It found all the instances I generated. You can play with this tool at www.twittereye.com/content/trendistic-0.

Taking Advantage of Memes

A *meme* (rhymes with "theme") is a specific kind of trending topic. It's a catchy jingle, slogan, icon, or ad tagline that spreads from person to person within a culture. As with trending topics, relevant memes are also brilliant choices for when you have Madison Avenue eyes but a thrift-store marketing budget.

Some different memes:

- ✔ Sometimes the most unexpected videos, such as the "Honey Badger" voice-over video, can become memes. That video spawned jokes, cartoons, and even a line of t-shirts saying "Honey badger don't care." For whatever reason, the video just hit a popular nerve. (You can check out this video, and its somewhat salty narration, at `www.youtube.com/user/czg123#g/u`.)

- ✔ Advertising slogans can morph into memes. People sometimes turn corporate ads into "culture jams" that use the ad to mock the brand's own controversial practices. In 2010, for instance, when Greenpeace activists wanted to criticize Nestle's environmental practices, they uploaded fake ads and videos modeled on Nestle's own advertisements.

- ✔ Sometimes odd or goofy behavior can itself become an online meme, such as the 2011's strange online craze for "planking" — that is, taking photographs of oneself lying down in unusual locations. "Catbreading" is another such meme, in which people take photos of cats (or other creatures) wearing headbands made of bread. Who thinks up this stuff?

You can use a trending meme to your advantage if you can figure out how to tie it in with you or your organization. For example, if your organization sells organic tuna cat treats, you may be able to work one of your cat treats into a "catbreading" photograph instead of a slice of bread.

Memes are an extremely viral way to market a brand or idea, but they can also spread negative information about that brand or idea just as quickly. In Chapters 14 and 15 I give you specifics on dealing with developing and full-blown crises. However, if you're in an industry that doesn't ruffle a lot of feathers, and if you deal with emerging problems quickly and transparently, you will most likely never have to handle this kind of issue.

Before you go wild connecting with the next hot meme, please keep in mind that once you release one out into the wild (upload it online) you can't take it back or control what else people will do with it. Handle memes wisely!

Qualifying Different Approaches

Although the same approach to online reputation management can be scaled for any size brand, you need to decide and define how you want to organize your online reputation management time and energy. Here are some common ways that companies organize their own systems.

- ✔ **Flying solo:** Most solo entrepreneurs at least need to choose a social aggregator, set up Google Alerts, and (no kidding) use a timer. I prefer kitchen timers because they're kitschy, but better yet, because they're a physical, finite signal that says "playtime" is over for the moment

- ✔ **Creating an everyday team:** Always consider how many people you need to monitor your brand online from day to day. With the right tools (see Chapter 5) and the right strategy (Chapter 2), you may be surprised how easily and affordably you can do this. I show you how to create your team in Chapter 3.

- ✔ **Organizing special teams:** You may discover that you need to have special teams in mind to support your everyday team. It's good to consider these:

  - *Crisis management team:* People who will pitch in during a crisis. May consist of everyday plus a few pinch hitters who thrive under pressure (more about this in Chapter 4).

  - *Geek group:* People who will maintain your hardware, software, and networking. You will at least need a designated geek, er, technical expert. I go into more detail about this in Chapters 3 and 4.

Chapter 2

Determining Your Online Reputation Management Approach

*O*ne of the things I love best about online reputation management is that improving your online reputation often improves other areas of your business. Knowing that your brand is more secure from negative publicity contributes to getting a great night's sleep, but promoting your reputation online can also enhance your

- ✔ **Brand reach:** Anytime more people hear good things about your brand or organization, you've extended your brand reach in a positive way.

- ✔ **Sales:** A trustworthy reputation can often help sell more of a service or product online.

- ✔ **Product development:** You have access to amazing market research right at your fingertips via social networks and blogs.

It's important for you to prioritize what you want to achieve with your online reputation management efforts and to craft your strategy accordingly. You need a realistic system that can leverage the opportunities that are most important to you. In this chapter, I show you how to begin framing your online reputation management strategy in three basic steps, with lots of helpful information in-between. I show you

- ✔ **How to assess your online reputation:** How you, your brand, and your industry look to an outsider and what to do about it.

> ✔ **Safety considerations, including personal privacy as well as your organization's social media and website account security:** This forms the basic foundation for your online reputation management strategy.
>
> ✔ **How to build on your secure foundation and further your brand's publicity:** If you are interested in taking your brand to this level of involvement.

In Chapter 3, I show you how to pull together your social media team (if need be) and daily online reputation management system so that you have everything you need for your brand to live long and prosper online. Hey, that's catchy!

Assessing Your Needs

No two people or brands are exactly alike, so no single approach to online reputation management works for everyone. To understand your own needs, you must first get a clear picture of your brand's existing reputation, and how that reputation stacks up to your competition. I tell you more about how to do this in the following sections.

As you go through these steps, carefully consider what level of involvement you desire and can afford to invest your time and resources into. Safeguarding your reputation online is a must, but it shouldn't consume all your time. Surely you have better, more important things to do. A good online reputation solution is one that takes only a little time, and allows you to get back to your business.

This means you should apply your strategy only where it does the most good. This is a great for locally based businesses that can't extend their services or products online. If you own a house painting business in Tulsa, for example, there isn't much point in advertising your business in New York City. This means you don't need to do much to promote your business beyond taking care of security and your basic online customer service. The security information I share later in this chapter, then, is most crucial to your success.

On the other hand, if you have an American-based, web design business, today's communication tools allow you to create a website for somebody in London almost as easily as for somebody in Los Angeles. You stand to gain a lot more by taking the next step by assertively promoting your reputation online, which also goes to safeguard you the more prominent your name becomes, as long as you take care of business and earn a trustworthy reputation. I introduce some ways that you can do this at the end of this chapter and go into greater detail in the rest of this book.

Discovering yourself online

No, this isn't a deep spiritual journey or a self-help psychology session. I intend to show you how other people sometimes look for you online so that you can see what the world sees and protect yourself accordingly.

1. **Go through all of your major social media accounts and blogs and check to see if you're consistently communicating**

   - Who you are

   - What you do

   - Who you do it for

   - Why you do it

2. **Perform Google searches for various combinations of the following terms:**

   - Your name

   - Your brand name

   - Your industry

After going through this exercise you should have a little better idea about what people searching for you or your business are seeing online. If you're less than delighted with how hard it was to find you or with what you found when you did your searches, don't despair. Add taking care of them to your online reputation management approach. Once it's set up properly, you only need to maintain and adjust as new developments occur. I show you how to take care of all these issues in Chapters 6 and 9.

Checking out your competition

It's a really good idea for you to check out what your competition is doing online. As in the previous section, perform Google searches for your competitors. How do their search results look? If you are able, ask around and find out how large their social media monitoring teams are. I also suggest looking them up via Twitter and checking out their Facebook pages (if they have these accounts) to see how active those sites are, how they typically respond to people, and what kinds of things they are doing to enhance their reputations.

I also suggest that you check out brands that are already where you'd like to be in the next couple of years. Look at what they're doing online and consider which of these approaches may serve as a model for what a more successful business looks like in your industry. Consider adding these adaptations to your online reputation approach.

Listening to how people feel about your brand

Social media sites and Internet searches allow you to get an immediate, fairly accurate snapshot of the way people are feeling about you, your brand, and your industry. Once you set up your monitoring tools (I tell you more these in Chapters 5 and 7) you can obtain in a few minutes amazingly detailed information that used to take months of expensive, highly involved market research.

Facebook is one of the most popular social networks for brands to use when assessing how people are feeling about them online. While it may be tempting to assume that the number of "likes" on your brand page directly correlates to exactly how people are feeling about you online, it's not true. When your numbers drop, I suggest remembering the following as you assess your engagement with people on Facebook:

- ✔ **People unclutter their feeds.** Your numbers may have dipped a little because people are simplifying their feeds by unfollowing pages. If you notice a marked pattern of people leaving, change up the kinds of updates you are making so that they're more appealing.

- ✔ **People sometimes leave Facebook.**

- ✔ **You post too much for their taste.** Posting once a day is comfortable for most people.

- ✔ **You don't post enough for their taste.** Again, posting once a day demonstrates that your brand is engaged. Experiment incrementally with what the majority of your community likes best.

- ✔ **You've changed focus and lost them along the way.** This happens as brands evolve. Check out Chapter 9 for specific branding tips so that you can present your brand consistently from now on.

- ✔ **They've changed focus and don't need your content anymore.** People move on as they learn what they need to learn from your brand unless you figure out how to keep it compelling. I show you more about how to engage easily within social networks in Chapter 8.

- ✔ **They only liked your page so you'd like theirs back and then unfollowed yours.** Yes, really. This happens with page swaps all the time, which is why I rarely recommend them. You end up with pages you aren't interested in competing for room in your news feed, which could have actually held interesting news for you.

Here are a few things you can do to get a feel for how people are responding to your brand online:

✔ **Spend some time getting to know your Facebook Page's Insights.** Now that Timeline has been extended to Brand Pages, there's a wealth of interesting, up-to-the-minute information available about your brand perception on Facebook.

✔ **Do a negative brand search.** This may sound strange, but you may be surprised by what informative trends turn up when you search for negative things about your brand.

✔ **Ask people point-blank how you're doing and what they'd like to see more of.** Sometimes the direct approach works best.

Setting clear goals

Before you develop your approach, you must first define what your goals are. After all, if you never set a clear goal, you never know whether you've reached it!

The goals you set should be business goals you can achieve with your online reputation management. I recommend you start with safety-oriented goals, but end with goals that help you generate positive publicity online. Make sure your goals are as focused and as clearly stated as possible. "Being popular online," for instance, is a poor goal because popularity is a nebulous term and can mean different things at different times and in different contexts.

Later in this chapter I show you how to take control of your personal security online and how to structure your brand's accounts so that you have full control over them and can maintain their security. This should be your number-one priority as you begin developing your online reputation management approach. After this is done you can build on your foundation by listening to what people are saying online (as I show you in much more in Chapters 5 and 7) and by responding to them via smart engagement and great content (which I describe in Chapters 10 through 13).

Consider these example goals:

✔ Protecting your name and brand from identity theft (1 in 10 of every U.S. consumer *has already* been victimized by identity theft).

✔ Increasing your brand awareness (you can have the goose that lays golden eggs, but if nobody knows about it . . .)

✔ Acquiring new customers.

✔ Boosting business outcomes.

✔ Responding to customer service questions and concerns in a more personal way than the call centers that customers have grown to dislike.

> ✔ Positioning your brand where your target audiences are. A brand in the publishing industry may avoid MySpace, for example, because it's more of a draw for music industry contacts.
>
> ✔ Improving public relations.
>
> ✔ Identifying your organization as the go-to brand online for your particular service or product line. Why wait for the competition to beat you there? Early adopters are always rewarded if a network becomes popular.

Catching a trend while it's building and finding a clever way to tie your own brand to it can feel a little like flying your kite on an awesome, breezy afternoon. I share trend-spotting tools in Chapter 1 (go ahead and look — I'll wait), but also mention it here because it's a worthy goal to consider in your online reputation management goal-setting.

Building Your Stable Foundation

It would be nice if you could market your brand without giving up any of your privacy, but unfortunately this is just not possible. These days, in order to gain publicity online, you have to determine just where you're willing to let go of your privacy and then maintain that standard consistently in all your online profiles, whether they are public or private. Always remember that there is no guarantee that anything you e-mail, tweet, post, update, or blog online won't become accessible to somebody who really wants to know.

If you're in a position where you need to e-mail sensitive information, I strongly suggest hiring a professional to install and test e-mail encryption software onto all your e-mail–related devices.

Securing your personal privacy

Not so long ago, you could share private information online in certain forums without fear of having it shared across multiple platforms. Times have changed! Thanks to social media, you really can't be sure that your more personal status updates aren't going to get leaked to search engines and spread around the web.

My advice is to only post things you wouldn't mind seeing on a billboard later!

Why is this important to establish now, before you even get a team started? Without a plan, it's easy to make mistakes. For instance, how safe do you feel about what you shared on the web five years ago? It's okay to feel a little sick right now. When I joined Facebook less than a year after Mark Zuckerberg created it at Harvard, my friends and I made snarky comments and shared dorky pictures. This content was harmless and only somewhat embarrassing, but a couple of things still make me shudder: my weak passwords (something I help you to solve forever in Chapter 7) and the information about my kids I innocently shared. When strange people began following my kids on Facebook, I realized what I'd done. Thankfully, my kids rejected the friendship invitations and soon left Facebook altogether in order to socialize in a more protected environment.

I later learned how to customize my Facebook settings so that people can't see who I'm friends with, thus cutting down on "friend trolling" for my friends. People can still see what other people are saying on my profile, however, and can choose to send them a friend invitation at that point. My initial naivety taught me a valuable lesson:

If you have a Facebook profile created for professional purposes, don't use it to Friend your kids (unless they're grown) or any naïve family members, because they may accept friend requests from innocent-looking people looking to exploit them for information about you. Social-engineering experts can be casual and friendly even as they gather information from your different social profiles in an effort to make better educated guesses about your security questions and passwords.

If you want to stay in touch with family and old friends, I suggest creating a more private profile, in hopes that it won't be discovered.

Delete all old e-mail and forum accounts where you are no longer active, so that you have control over what information is available about you online.

You pay for the fun, games, and connectivity on social networks by giving away a little (or a lot) of your privacy. And no governmental organization or private agency can protect you from yourself once you've shared. Here are some tips to keep you safe, sound, and able to manage your online reputation smoothly:

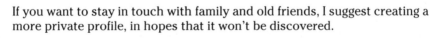

✔ **Use a bulletproof password** on every social networking site, domain registration, e-mail, and even on your computer login if you use it outside the privacy of your home. (See my foolproof guide for creating passwords in the section called "Creating super-safe passwords," later in this chapter.)

Set a short bulletproof password on your smartphone, if you have one, especially if you use online banking, blogging, and social network applications. A phone thief doesn't have inspiring moral values. If your phone gets snatched, a crook may have a lot of fun stealing your cash or posting insulting pictures on your sites before you even know what's happened.

Consider using a "find my phone" service. That way, if you do lose your device, would-be reputation assassins can receive a lovely "the cops know right where to find you!" message as you remotely disable your phone. I'd love a phone app that takes a picture of thieves' faces as they receive the heart-warming news that they are about to be busted for stealing. But that's just me.

✔ **Be wary of the kinds of applications you authorize on your cellphones and your computers.** Many applications seek as much information as you'll divulge; they aren't afraid to ask. Decide ahead of time what you're willing to share — and stick with it.

✔ **Unless you have a really good reason to enable geo-location tagging, don't.** There are too many instances of people suffering from theft or violent crimes because they shared too much about their locations. If you must tag your location, do so after you've left. Even this can be risky, however. I try to limit it to conferences where I'm speaking to promote the event.

As always, if you don't feel comfortable sharing information on the Internet, don't put it anywhere online in the first place. Keep in mind, though, that few people need total web anonymity, and sharing a bit of our authentic selves is part of the price we pay for relating with people online.

Removing a listing from Yahoo! White Pages

While checking out my own settings for this book, I went onto Yahoo! white pages and discovered that any stranger could look up my name, age *(gasp!)*, and address, and even locate my home on a Google map. Because I work from home most of the time, this is a really scary discovery. I'll wager that you aren't wild about having your confidential information online either!

So, with all the love in my heart, I'm giving you this tutorial on how to remove your precious name from the Yahoo! White Pages. It takes a business day for the changes to appear, but the wait is well worth it!

This guide takes less than a minute. All you have to do is follow these steps. Ready? Set? Go!!!

1. **Go to** www.WhitePages.com.

2. **Look up your name (maiden or former married names included).**

   Stop being horrified. You're about to fix this problem.

3. **Go to** www.yahoo.intelius.com/optout.php, **fill in the brief form, and click Remove Me.**

Congratulations!!! You are now much safer. I feel a lot better about your well-being.

There seems to be an endless number of search-for-pay sites that will aggregate personal information for a price. Take a look at the most popular ones and ask them to remove your name from their lists (although some of them may not comply). Here's a list of some sites you may want to visit in your quest for personal privacy online:

- ✔ 123people (`www.123people.com`) *Not there*
- ✔ AnyWho (`www.anywho.com`)
- ✔ EmailFinder (`www.emailfinder.com`)
- ✔ InfoSpace (`http://infospaceinc.com`)
- ✔ InfoUSA (`www.infousa.com`)
- ✔ Intelius (`www.intelius.com`)
- ✔ Melissa Data (`www.melissadata.com`)
- ✔ MyLife (`www.mylife.com`)
- ✔ RapLeaf (`www.rapleaf.com`)
- ✔ Spokeo (`www.spokeo.com`)
- ✔ SuperPages (`www.superpages.com`)
- ✔ USA People Search (`www.usa-people-search.com`)
- ✔ ZoomInfo (`www.zoominfo.com`)

I hate to point this out, but there are millions of infected computers conducting illegal attacks on a routine basis. Is yours one of them? Protect yourself by getting your computer thoroughly scanned and keep up with your updates!

Protecting your privacy on Facebook

Google and Facebook are in stiff competition to see which is the most powerful Internet brand. Most of this book covers privacy issues within traditional search engines like Google, Yahoo!, and Bing, but tackling your Facebook Privacy settings is every bit as important.

Facebook wants to be where you live your life online. Whether you want to see the news of the day, to go shopping, or to know people's brand preferences, Facebook wants you to seek all that information there — no Googling required.

It often seems like being on a social network doesn't really "count" as being online, but I promise you that every bit of information you share can become just as widespread (or even more so!) now that Facebook's become an established presence on the World Wide Web.

Right now, you can use more than 170 settings to customize your privacy on Facebook. Over the next 405 chapters, you will be exploring them in depth. Oh, wait — wrong book! Okay, I don't have room to do that here, but I can at least show you how to use the most effective settings. Friends don't let friends post unsafe status updates.

Keep an eye on your settings. Every time Facebook revises its privacy settings, it assumes that you want to share as much as possible with the world. So, even if you're fully confident that you've customized your settings, they may all go out the proverbial window next time Facebook changes things around.

No matter what privacy settings you set on photos you share on Facebook, there's a sharing link at the bottom of the page. Facebook always says that it wants "everything to be social." Your definition of being "social" may be different from sharing everything with the world! Before posting anything there, remember to determine

- ✔ What kind of information is wise for you to share
- ✔ What kind of information is yours to share

Be wary of giving up your information and opinions on all sites. Until 2010, Facebook compiled user information even on non-members through Like button clicks on more than a million other sites. You never know when another networking site will decide this approach is a good idea or if Facebook will try it again by using another approach, like Timeline permissions. (See the nearby sidebar, "Frictionless sharing.")

Some people, particularly solo entrepreneurs or celebrities, are comfortable with sharing their information online and view their Facebook profiles as another way to meet potential clients or fans. This is okay, but be sure you know what you're sharing.

Here are some tips you can use to protect your privacy with Facebook's settings:

- ✔ **Share on Timeline:** Whatever you do, never authorize a site to share information on Facebook. Such sites typically doesn't use the phrase "share on timeline" — they usually word things so it feels like you're just "liking" a post, even though you're actually authorizing them to always share every post you go to. (See the nearby sidebar, "Frictionless sharing," for more information.) Figure 2-1 shows what one of these invitations looks like.

Frictionless sharing

When Facebook introduced Timeline, its gurus soon after held a special press conference where they announced the concept of "frictionless sharing." From now on, when you visit places like the *New York Times* or Pinterest, you will see a cute, harmless little Share on Timeline button. If you click that button, every page you go to and every picture you click on will automatically get posted to Facebook.

That means that all those unpleasant medical conditions you looked up to talk about in the crime novel you're writing could make their way to the Timeline on enabled sites.

My advice, then, is never to click any Share on Timeline buttons at all. If you have already done so by mistake, go to your permissions and change them back to not sharing on Timeline. Meanwhile, half of your friends may be making the same mistake — tell them about it and you could be a real hero!

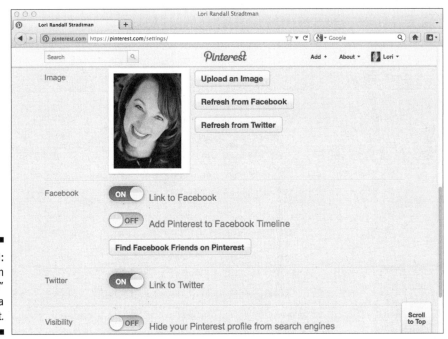

Figure 2-1:
A "Share on Timeline" invitation via Pinterest.

✔ **Public Search:** Go to Privacy Settings in the upper-right corner drop-down menu⇨Public Search and deselect the Enable Public Search option if you don't want search engines to show a preview of your Facebook profile. Even after you deactivate this setting, however, already-cached versions will keep showing your information on search engines for a while until they're cleared out.

✔ **More Privacy Settings:** Go to Privacy Settings in the upper-right corner drop-down menu and then scroll down to "How You Connect" and click on the "Edit settings" link to the right of it (See Figures 2-2 and 2-3.) This is a gold mine of privacy settings where you can prevent whole categories of people from contacting you via Facebook. For example, you can designate that only friends can send you messages, but that everyone can see your "Likes."

✔ **Checking into Places:** I disabled this setting because it felt creepy being in New York   City and having someone I didn't recognize check me into a restaurant with him. If you're more freewheeling and think this is fun, go for it, but as your online reputation management mentor and confidante, I suggest disabling it.

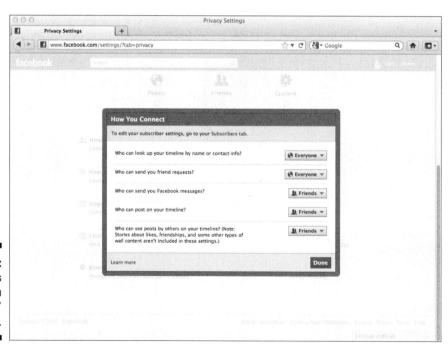

Figure 2-2:
Facebook's
"How You
Connect"
Setting.

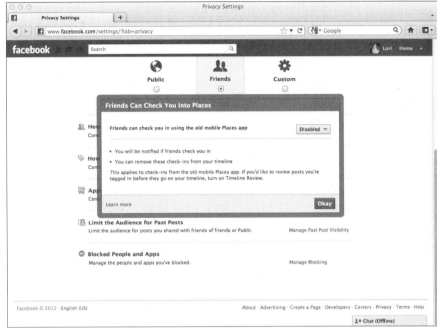

Figure 2-3:
Choosing
your privacy
settings.

Unspamming your profile

Just now I took a break to check my Facebook profile. A distant friend sent me and everyone else on his friend list a "miracle weight loss cure" and bragged about his 23-pound weight loss. I immediately unfriended this particular person and marked the post as spam.

It's easiest to remove spammy posts via the desktop computer because mobile apps can't always keep up with Facebook's ever-changing platform. Now you have my permission to always blame the app and never your knowledge level. Doesn't that feel better?

How to unspam your profile: Go to the offending post, hover over the upper-right corner until the

"edit or remove" options appear, and then take the appropriate action. Sometimes you may just want to remove the "tag" (Facebook asks you if you'd like to "tag" friends in your photos. It means linking your friends to that image so that their friends can see the picture too). This disconnects you from their update and all the replies it may generate, without isolating you from your friend. In my example, after I removed the tag I didn't get notifications every time somebody commented on the "miracle weight loss cure" picture and didn't appear to be endorsing it by having my name under the picture in a link.

✔ **Instant Personalization by third-party applications:** Again, I'm a "just say no" girl when it comes to allowing sites like Pandora or Spotify to notify my friends every time I listen to a song. After all, people may learn that I have corny musical tastes (like Tony Bennett and movie soundtracks) and damage my reputation as a cutting-edge hipster. (Oops, I just gave that one away, didn't I?) To opt out of those Instant Personalization settings, just go to Account⇨Privacy Settings and click the Edit Settings link next to Ads, Apps and Websites. Then click the Edit Settings link next to Instant Personalization, and at the bottom of the resulting box deselect the Enable Instant Personalization on Partner Websites box. (See Figure 2-4.)

✔ **Photos Sharing:** This one is tricky because you can set different sharing options for every picture you post. You can set general settings, but any previously shared pictures will not be protected. I suggest going into your old albums and customizing the sharing options for each one. The safest thing you can do for your online reputation management is to delete any photos you aren't comfortable sharing anymore. People change, relationships change, and jobs change. Acceptable behavior in college isn't always appropriate in the workplace. Now that Facebook is available in most workplaces either officially or via mobile devices, you need to protect your interests. Figure 2-5 shows you the "want to share your album" link at the bottom of the screen.

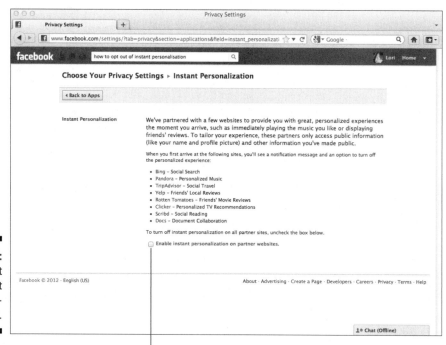

Figure 2-4:
Opting out
of Instant
Personaliz-
ation.

Enable Instant Personalization on Partner Websites checkbox

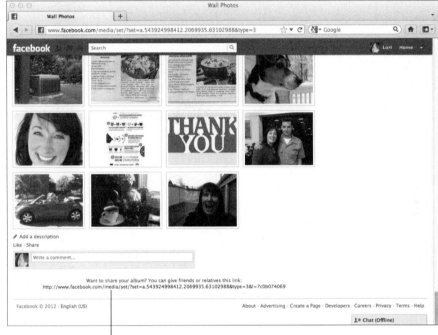

Figure 2-5:
Sharing
photo
albums —
or not.

The "want to share your album" link

Believe it or not, Facebook's default settings are always "public." This means that not only does Facebook's search engine share what you're saying and doing with others on Facebook, it also shares that information with regular search engines like Google, Bing, and Yahoo!. What happens on Facebook stays . . . online!

✔ **Info accessible through your friends:** I find the wording here very interesting! Technically speaking, this information goes to your friends, but if they share it, it does indeed become information that goes "*through your friends*"! There's a lot more than meets the eye to these settings. Even though you may have tight privacy settings, some of your friends may share your information without realizing that you want to keep it private. That's the problem with posting sensitive material online. It can get messy in a hurry! Figure 2-6 shows different categories you should consider customizing. For example, I don't want anybody knowing if I'm online or what my religious and political beliefs are. You may feel more protective over your photos and videos.

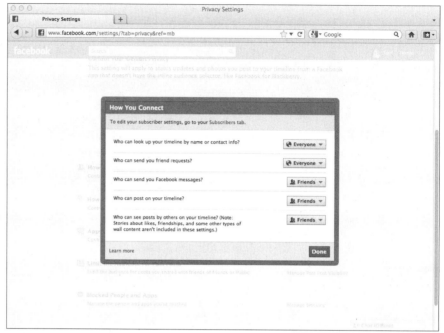

Figure 2-6:
Customizing
your info
accessible
through
your friends.

Protecting your privacy on Google+

Google has been around for what seems like forever. You may have an account with it via gmail or Google docs, but for the purposes of this section, I want to introduce you to the privacy settings on Google + and explain how they differ from Facebook's. Thankfully, Google + was released into the wild, er, made available to the public in August 2011, so the developers got to examine other social networks, such as Facebook, to look for ways to do things better. Privacy is one such area that Google+ makes things simpler than Facebook.

When you create a Google+ profile, you have the option of adding anybody who has a Google+ profile to one or all of your circles. A *circle* is how you organize your friends, family, colleagues, etc. on Google+. Some important things to know about circles are

✔ Nobody knows what the names of your circles are. You could name one "hot prospects" or "people who bug me" and nobody would see.

✔ Nobody knows who else is in your circle with them.

Facebook's privacy settings

In November 2011, the Federal Trade Commission ruled that Facebook has "unfair and deceptive" practices regarding privacy and user data. Even after getting brought before Congress in May 2010, Facebook continued to change privacy defaults from private settings to public without notifying users. The folks at Facebook did this by making new, widespread changes and "forgetting" to tell users who thought they were protected that they needed to change their settings . . . again. Facebook had also shared personal data with advertisers and user data with outside application developers. Remember, if a site appears to be giving you a free ride, look again. You're paying for it with your information. Beware and share as little as possible. Some people even enter fake information (such as birthdays), but I can't endorse that here because it's against Facebook's rules of use.

All you have to do to add somebody to one of your circles is to find her profile in the search field at the top of your profile and then click on the red Add to Circles button at the top of her profile. You will be able to select which circle you want to add her to or create a new circle just for the occasion.

On Google+, circles are the main way that you share information with the world and see what others are posting via Google+. The biggest difference between circles and Facebook friends is that the information you share with friends on Facebook isn't private by default. For example, if I'm friends with you on Facebook, the default setting is that I can see all of your posts and you can see all of mine unless either of us customizes that post to say otherwise. On Google+, however, if I circle you I can share information with you, but you may not have circled me back, which means that I don't automatically get to see your updates and/or information. Privacy has everything to do with how you set up your circles. Consider the following

- ✔ Information is not necessarily two-way. You can share personal information with people you have circle, but they may not have circled you back.

- ✔ You can block others' information (such as a co-worker's) without blocking them from seeing your information.

- ✔ You can even unlist the circles you don't want to receive updates from. This is becoming particularly meaningful as Google+ has recently rolled out its "Events" feature, which closely parallels Facebook's "Events" capability. I have been receiving repeated event invitations and need to change one particular circle that generates most of the event invitations. Figure 2-7 shows you how this works.

Assuming you have a few circles set up, I'm going to show you how to customize your privacy with them. Your most important setting is the All My Circles setting that comes up every time you share a post. What if you only want to share a joke with your close friends? You can designate that. You can also create a default bunch of circles that you want to share content with via the newsfeed on a regular basis. Here's how you customize your All My Circles setting:

1. **Go to your Google+ profile page and click on the little gear-looking graphic in the upper right-hand corner.**

   Clicking the gear opens a drop-down menu.

2. **Click Settings.**

3. **Scroll down to the Your Circles Section, just before the Photos section at the bottom, and click the Customize button. (See Figure 2-7.)**

4. **Click on the boxes in front of the group (circle) names you have already designated. These people will always be able to see what you are posting.**

   Consider removing your "colleagues" circle from this list if you're using Google+ strictly for personal use.

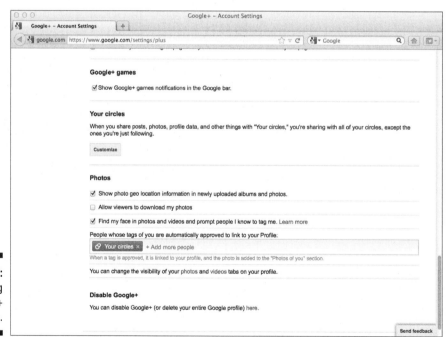

Figure 2-7:
Customizing
Google+
circles.

While you are setting up or refreshing your Google+ privacy settings, I suggest you take a look at your privacy dashboard to control what kinds of people can see your information. Here's how

1. **Go to** www.google.com/settings/privacy.

2. **Log in to your Google+ account. From here you can click on the following categories to customize your profile settings (see Figure 2-8):**

   - Edit visibility on profile

   - Manage circles

   - Edit network visibility

   - Edit photos settings

   - Sign in to Dashboard

   - Go to Privacy Center

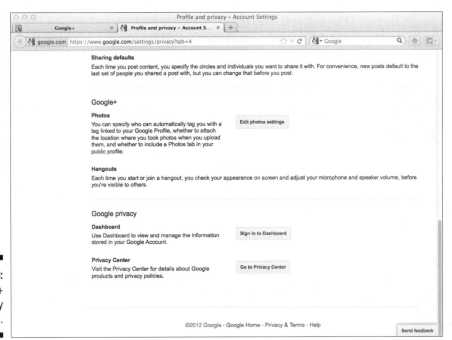

Figure 2-8:
The Google+
privacy
dashboard.

Google Buzz

The Federal Trade Commission discovered that Google had automatically opted users into Google Buzz without their consent and only offered vague instructions for how to opt out of these default settings. Google didn't realize that people view their privacy in terms of context, and it went too far. When building Google Street View, the developers accidentally collected personal information, including entire e-mails, password information, and web addresses. Because of this and other notable online privacy concerns, the Federal Trade Commission mandated that Google and Facebook are subject to privacy audits for the next 20 years.

If you're a Google+ user you'll see posts from people whom you have chosen to add to your circles among the results from regular Google searches.

You can circle anybody on Google+ you want to. That person gets to choose whether he will circle you back, of course, but it's a pretty sweet deal if you're interested in following industry and thought leaders because you can see what they're posting without having to be friends with them.

If you have any questions at all about Google's policy, you can read its full privacy policy all in one place: www.google.com/policies/privacy.

Securing Your Brand's Accounts

People often set up their brand accounts in a perfunctory fashion, not realizing that the little decisions they make along the way can create problems later on. Since your online reputation management strategy must begin with a secure foundation, I suggest reading through the following sections so that you have a good handle on how to set up your brand's accounts more securely. The key is to make sure that *you* have full control over your accounts, not someone who's working for you at the moment. Protect your interests more fully with these tips.

Registering your domain (s)

One of the most important decisions you will make in connection with having control over your online reputation management is really simple and easy to implement! The flip side of that good news is that if you're considering entrusting that information to a third-party vendor, such as a site designer, you need to get that party to transfer those rights and responsibilities right back to your organization. It's a fairly simple process that varies a little bit with each service but is really important to do.

If you haven't registered your intended domain(s) yet, I strongly advise you to review Chapter 6 before you do. There I show you how to use search engine optimization (SEO) keywords more effectively.

Where you register is important. You will always make a better decision when you consider the Internet in terms of the American Wild West. Wear a cowboy hat and pin a silver star to your shirt as you work, and you'll have the right frame of mind. There are outlaws there, and the American legal system is at least 15 years from learning how to negotiate online reputation management. Be savvy and be careful in your choice of domain registrars. I use Register4less, although there are many other reputable registrars. Figure 2-9 shows you how easy it is to search on Register4less's site.

Figure 2-9:
Registering
your
domain at
Register4less.

How NOT to register

Don't let anybody else register your domain(s) for you unless you also trust that person with the keys to your car and your kids' savings account information. I know too many firsthand stories of disgruntled web designers who held site domains "hostage" until they got satisfaction. Whoever registers the domain owns it. Period. Make sure you own yours!

Here are some reputable providers:

- **Register** (www.register.com): Clean, easy-to-use interface. Features monthly service bundles and the domain search information you need right at the top of the page.

- **Register4less** (www.register4less.com): My favorite registrar because of its reputable business practices and ease of use.

- **Name** (www.name.com): Cute, hip interface. Features a "domain nabber," (a feature that claims a domain for you) and some pretty interesting hosting and web-page building tools.

- **Namecheap** (www.namecheap.com): Voted best domain registrar by Lifehacker readers. Offers domain registration with free e-mail, URL forwarding, and privacy protection.

You can always register a domain as private if you're a solo entrepreneur and don't need to disclose that information.

Using a professional e-mail address

These days, people expect to see a brand use an official-looking e-mail address, not something like INamedMyCatAfterABreakfastCereal@yahoo.com. Such an address looks unprofessional, and its function within your organization isn't clear. After all, it's best to have different mailboxes for different kinds of correspondence so you won't waste time tracking down important messages in a catchall e-mail inbox. Here are some tips to get the most out of your e-mail account:

- **Don't use your personal e-mail address.** I suggest creating your own, like AwesomeYou@AwesomeYou.com. You can also create a domain with Google's tools and have it look like AwesomeYou@AwesomeYou.com. Don't let me catch you using MyDog'sName@gmail.com. People probably won't take your brand seriously online.

- **Don't get too colorful:** When I went back to college, I thought it was cool to have nontraditional as my e-mail address — after all, I was something of a nontraditional student. Although I had kids in middle and high school, I had gone back to school and was sharing classrooms with 20-year-olds. I was clearly different. "Nontraditional" may have been accurate, but it wasn't the most flattering term I could have used. After college, when it was time to create my resume, a trusted advisor counseled me to lose the address because it just didn't look professional. Sage advice!

✔ **Don't give everyone the same address:** Reserve your professional and personal e-mail addresses for people you trust. Direct everything else (product inquiries, newsletters) to a more anonymous e-mail account.

Framing your positive publicity

You will never find a better way to turbo boost your brand online than via social media. It's probably the most common reason people want to master their online reputation management, and it makes a very worthy goal to add to your strategy if you have the extra time and resources. I tell you everything you need to get started with a winning strategy in Chapter 9.

When one well-known speaker (a frequent Morton's customer) tweeted that he'd love nothing better than a Morton's steak when he got off the plane, he found a steamy, fragrant steak with all the trimmings waiting for him in the airport just after he arrived at baggage claim. Now that's customer service!

This hasn't happened to me just yet, but I have experienced phenomenal customer service via Twitter, such as the time I tweeted about visiting New York City for a speaking engagement. Somebody from my favorite hotel there sent me a direct message offering me a press discount and a fancy room with a gorgeous view. You can bet I feel really special just remembering that event, and I now refer people to that hotel every chance I get.

I have friends whose computer problems were solved through amazing customer service from Dell via Twitter. (I tell you a lot more about Dell's super sophisticated setup in Chapter 3.)

I guess the big story is to use Twitter for customer service!

Taking control of your password security

It's easy to dismiss password security. In a casual moment, it's easy to think that a goofy or simple password suffices and that nothing bad can come from setting the name of your favorite football team as your Facebook password.

Lots of people do this. Two of the most common passwords used online today:

✔ **ncc1701:** The ship number for the Starship Enterprise (You'd think geeks would know better!)

✔ **8675309:** The number mentioned in the 1982 Tommy Tutone song. The song supposedly caused an epidemic of people dialing 867-5309 and asking for "Jenny."

Having a weak password is like using a screen door to prevent break-ins. For any number of unsavory reasons, dishonest people all over the world spend lots of time creating bots that roam the web and look for weak passwords. Odds are high that you or a friend have had your Facebook profile hacked. Maybe you got creepy messages from him. (Never click on these, by the way. They vary, but they're never good for you. Avoid them and inform your friend that she's been hacked.)

If this happens to you, Facebook has a recovery process you can use to attempt to get control back over your good name, er, profile, but your best defense is to have a first-class, bulletproof password. And in this section, I show you a fast, easy, thoroughly awesome way to always have a great password. It's probably the most important thing you can do to preserve your reputation online.

Here's the Top Ten Hall of Shame for commonly hacked passwords. If you're using one of these, particularly for your bank account, I insist that you stop reading (after I show you how to create super-safe passwords, of course) and change your password to something that should help you to sleep better at night:

✔ password

✔ 123456

✔ 12345678

✔ qwerty

✔ abc123

✔ monkey

✔ 1234567

✔ letmein

✔ trustno1

✔ dragon

Creating super-safe passwords

There are two issues to remember about creating the very best passwords:

- ✔ They must be easy for you to remember.
- ✔ They must protect you from hackers.

Here's how you do it:

1. **Brainstorm for a minute on a sentence or phrase that has some special meaning to you.**

   (However, try not to choose one that's really popular right now.) For example:

   - A favorite song lyric
   - A line of poetry
   - A movie quote (my favorite)

   Let's use "All we are is dust in the wind" as an example.

2. **Convert your phrase into an acronym.**

   We're using "All we are is dust in the wind," so the acronym is "awaidinw." It's just the first letter of each word.

3. **Substitute at least one letter with a number.**

   With "awaidinw," it may look like this:

   - awa1d1nw (the letter i is replaced with the number 1)

4. **Substitute at least one letter with an upper-case letter.**

   Our password in progress could look like this:

   - awa1d1nW (the last letter, w, gets capitalized)

5. **Substitute at least one letter with a symbol.**

   Our password in progress could look like this:

   - @wa1d1nW (the first letter, a, is replaced with @)

Congratulations! You've just created a password that's 1.34 tresvigintillion more times, or 1.34 trillion trillion trillion trillion trillion trillion times stronger than your chance of winning the lottery.

Please don't use this particular one! Now that I've described, created, and published this password, it is no longer a strong choice. Come up with your own!

Odds are good you're going to be very happy with your new passwords:

According to the National Weather Service, the odds of being struck by lightning in your lifetime:

1 in 10,000

According to the power ball lottery site, your odds of winning are:

1 in 175,223,510

According to simple math, if you create a 7-character password out of characters from the 96 printable characters in the ASCII character set, the odds of someone guessing it is:

1 in 1,347,137,238,494,276,600,000,000,000,000,00
0,000,000,000,000,000,000,000,000,000,000,000,00
0,000,000,000,000

or specifically . . .

1 in 1,347,137,238,494,276,547,832,006,567,721,87
2,890,819,326,613,454,654,477,690,085,519,113,57
4,118,965,817,601

Feel better now? I do!

Storing your passwords safely and conveniently

After you create the world's best password, no matter how easy to remember it may be, you should record it somewhere, just to be safe. However, what's the safest way to store password information? The first step in creating a password storage system that's going to make your life easier and more secure is to consider the following:

✔ Who needs to be able to get her hands on these passwords?

✔ Where do these passwords need to be accessed most often?

- Desktop at office
- Desktop at home
- Laptop
- Mobile device

If you're a solo entrepreneur and you only work from your desktop at home, you may be able to get away with a dedicated, locked Rolodex, but even that can cause irritating problems if you start using a smartphone or tablet device to check in with your adoring fans online and discover you need to re-enter your password.

If you're working with a team, everybody needs a unique login so that you all can track who is saying what, and when they say it. It keeps your communication records squeaky clean. I love clarity, don't you? (For more on building your team, see Chapter 3.)

Here are two proven password storage options:

✔ **Good: Store your passwords in "the cloud."** Create a spreadsheet with your login information and encrypt it. This function is built in to Excel and some other spreadsheet programs. Setting it up on a PC depends on the version you're using, but a good place to start is to

1. Start Excel and open the workbook or spreadsheet you want to encrypt.

2. Open the File menu, select Info from the tab on the left. Click Protect Workbook and then Encrypt with Password.

3. Enter your password and then re-enter it.

   Use a different password for your spreadsheet encryption than the one that you use for your computer. It's the first password that somebody will try to get in to your password document.

4. Write down your password and save it somewhere else that's secure.

   Your passwords are now encrypted and ready to go. If you store your passwords file online via a service like Dropbox, it will be available on all devices when you need your passwords on the run. (See Figure 2-10.) Please don't name your file "passwords," however! Name it something meaningful to you, not something obvious to somebody snooping around.

   You will get much more secure encryption when you use the 2003 or newer version of Excel.

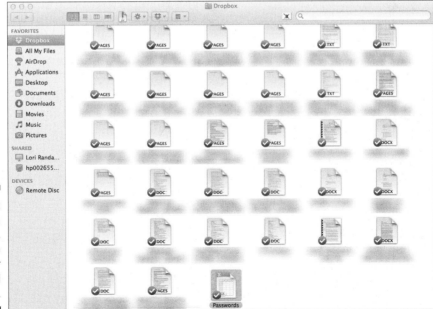

Figure 2-10:
Drop in on
Dropbox,
a free
service for
password
storage.

REMEMBER

Open your document with the same application you use to create it. For example, if you use MS Excel to encrypt, you want to use an MS Excel mobile version to de-encrypt it.

✔ **Better: Sign in via Google, Facebook, or Twitter as an "Identity Service Provider."** Don't trust some small site like SocialNetworkingforCrossStitchers.net to adequately protect your password information. Many small social networks enable you to sign in using your login from more popular sites such as Google or Facebook. (See Figure 2-11.) Use this option whenever it's available. These developers work 24/7 to keep your login information secure.

Switching your super passwords

If hackers and dishonest people would only take a vacation, you and I would not have to switch our passwords periodically. But until somebody figures out how to talk them all into taking up another avocation, I want you to assume that somebody is trying to get into your accounts and that it's only a matter of time before they do by one means or another.

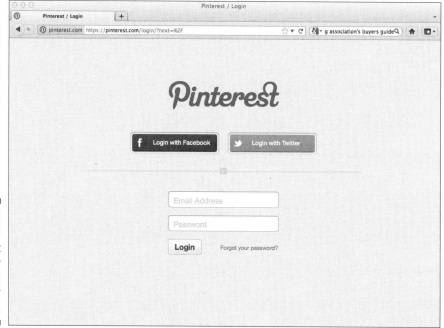

Figure 2-11:
The Pinterest Identity Service Provider login.

One of those ways is by hacking their way into getting lists of e-mails and passwords. In 2012 more than 6.5 million LinkedIn accounts were compromised and had to change their passwords. I have one of those accounts and experienced lovely peace of mind because I do the following

1. Create super-safe passwords.

2. Use a unique one for each major profile and account.

3. Replace with fresh super-safe passwords periodically.

Change your password on your other devices and update your storage at the same time to stay organized.

Sticky-note security

A not-to-be-named network security expert contracting for a system of mental-health facilities discovered that absolutely all employees there kept their account names and password information on a sticky note underneath the keyboard at their cubicles. Any patient or visitor could have logged on to the system and copied privileged patient or credit-card numbers.

Industry reports estimate that even IT professionals admit to storing their passwords on a sticky note left somewhere on their desk or under their keyboard.

Dishonest people are well aware of this practice as well and take advantage of it. If you're a sticky-note user, I suggest you stick to a new password storage habit!

Part II
Organizing Your Teams

The 5th Wave   By Rich Tennant

©RICHTENNANT

"So, you want to work for the best browser company in the world? Well, let me get you a job application. Let's see...where are they? Shoot! I can never find anything around here!"

In this part . . .

In Part II, I take you through the steps of organizing your online reputation monitoring teams. In Chapter 3, I give you considerations that will help you decide whether you want to fly solo or whether pulling together a team is better for your strategy. I even show you how to pull together fully integrated teams for organizations of every size. In Chapter 4, I go beyond the everyday planning stage and dive into creating senior-level crisis management teams. Your team can make the difference between nimbly averting an online crisis and broadcasting one on the news.

Chapter 3

Creating Your Everyday Team

*I*n Chapter 2, you determine the online reputation management goals that may be a good fit for your organization. Now you need to build an everyday social media team around those goals so you can focus your energies in the right places. A *social media team* is an organized, trained group of people who work together to monitor and respond to online conversations on major social networks and blogs.

Social media isn't all fun and games. When it can boost your online visibility in a remarkably short period of time, and for a fraction of the cost of traditional media, it can also help you make a lot of money!

In this chapter, I give you several different ways to pull together your own everyday online reputation management team. In Chapter 4, I show you how to create a special crisis team so that you'll be able to function at your best in the event of an online emergency. If you're a solo entrepreneur like me, you probably won't need an everyday team or a crisis team. I suggest you page through this chapter and Chapter 4, then, to pick up any important points that relate to you, move on to Chapter 5, where I introduce some online tools that can make your life easier.

Organizing Your Team

If you are a solo entrepreneur or an owner of a small business with just a few employees, you can either designate one person to take charge of your online reputation management, or split up the job among a few members of your organization. Benefits of having only one person manage your reputation include

- ✔ Your brand will have a consistent voice.
- ✔ Odds are better that online relationships can be cultivated and deepened because the same two people will be conversing every time.
- ✔ If you decide to take the company in a new direction, you only have to inform one person.

Liabilities of the one-person approach include

- ✔ Employee burnout — especially if this person continues to have all his original responsibilities or if he just isn't that into socializing online.
- ✔ Lackluster communications, as the one-person approach is prone to stagnation.

If you're part of a medium- or large-sized company, I suggest you create a team with at least three members, so they can each have time off periodically. At this point you may be wondering what social media teams typically do while they're representing companies online. Every organization is different and has its own unique way of integrating this function, but common responsibilities include

- ✔ Monitoring what people are saying about you and your brand online via social networks and blogs. I tell you a lot more about how to do this in Chapters 5 and 7.
- ✔ Customer service.
- ✔ Educating people about your brand.
- ✔ Creating excitement for your brand.
- ✔ Keeping up with industry trends.
- ✔ Checking out what the competition is doing, how they're pricing their products and services, and what people are saying about them.
- ✔ Listening for new product and service ideas.

Normally, your social media team will be run by somebody who reports to (or at least communicates regularly with) sales, customer service, and product development departments within an organization. It's good to consider which departments have a stake in your online strategy as you decide how to integrate this team into your company's communication structure.

Creating an Easy-to-Follow System for Your Team

I'm a huge fan of the KISS principle (Keep it Simply Sensational). As you read through in order to decide how you want to organize your regular team, please think in terms of efficiency. In this section, I show you how to pull together a system that will help you use social networking to build a stronger and more resilient brand online.

Much of online reputation management can be done simply and without using up all your time and resources. After all, you have a business to run, don't you? And you can save even more time by focusing your attention to listening and responding online for brief periods of time, scheduled periodically throughout the day.

Multitasking works just about as well in online reputation management as it does in the rest of life. If you're part of a small team and need to check in to your social accounts a few times a day, I suggest you invest in an ordinary kitchen timer (or a kitschy one like the one I use) and set it for 15 minutes at a time. This way you monitor, ask juicy questions or make dazzling statements, share useful posts, respond to people, and then get back to work. Frequency of interaction is more important than duration of your stay on that network.

Examining common challenges

As you organize your social media team and recruit new members, please keep in mind that it's realistic to expect some training and adjustment time. This stuff looks simple but can be quite involved. The online environment and the tools it takes to navigate it are evolving constantly. Make regular training and Q&A sessions for your team a priority. According to the Forrester Consulting survey of 2011, 200 U.S.-based companies shared the following about their listening and digital engagement initiatives:

- 42% struggled with having an adequate budget
- 34% expressed difficulty managing programs across multiple technologies
- 30% cited availability of talent as a concern
- 20% struggled with the "learning curve associated with new technology such as social media tools"
- 17% expressed concern over privacy issues

Committing to your objectives

Here's where the Chapter 2 goals I admonish you to define come in. The main goals make great objectives for your team. Write down your top three goals as clearly as possible and post them so that the people you report to and the people you're leading can understand at a glance what the ultimate goals are.

Everybody working with you will enjoy having such easy-to-understand direction. It saves you an enormous amount of time and energy as you move forward and will be a huge asset if a crisis should arise. Your team members should function like a well-trained soccer team, with each member playing her role and knowing how to work together effectively.

If you're leading the online reputation management charge for a smaller organization or even if you're a solo entrepreneur like me, you still ought to consider formalizing your objectives so you can have a clear and consistent presence online. People really respond to that, especially when you're emotionally invested and positive.

In Chapter 9, I show you how to use these objectives to effectively communicate your brand online. Having a well-designed online reputation management system is one of the most powerful things you can do to build your business!

Creating your social media policy before you hire

In Chapter 4, I share specific issues for you to consider as you create your employee online reputation policy, because it should pass through your executive, human resources, legal, and public relations professionals before you make it official to prevent avoidable problems down the road.

This simple act can save you time later if an employee violates the rules and does something harmful to your brand. It gives you recourse to take action without fear of legal entanglements, for one thing, and even helps to prevent violations from ever taking place.

Think of it as preventive medicine. It may taste a little funny at first, but you'll be very glad you took care of it!

Preventing a costly rookie mistake

Newcomers to online reputation management often use their personal profiles to proselytize for the brand or create a Facebook profile in the name of the brand. They think that all profiles are the same, so what difference does it make where the information comes from. This is one of the most basic mistakes you can make.

Unfortunately, Facebook can and does delete profiles being used as a brand and does so without any warning. You just suddenly lose your page and all the followers on it.

Don't customize the Facebook profile for your brand. Establish your team on a firm Facebook foundation by creating your brand page at `www.facebook.com/pages/create.php`.

Now that Timeline has been extended to pages, Facebook is also cracking down on advertisements posted there. How exactly it defines "advertisements" is the million-dollar question, and it's yet to be answered. It's wise to market softly and provide a lot of entertaining or informative content that points back to your site, where you're free to "advertise" all you want!

Choosing what kind of team members you want

Now that you have your goals set in order of importance, it's time to recruit the right kind of team to deliver on them.

I list all the different social media team animals in the zoo so that you can have an idea of what they do, though job descriptions and responsibilities vary wildly. My best advice is to evaluate people closely and to get concrete examples of the kind of work that they do on a routine basis.

I suggest you begin by recruiting people who are experienced with social media monitoring tools and who can

- ✔ Accurately interpret reports
- ✔ Discern trends
- ✔ Communicate how to use momentum from trends to further your goal
- ✔ Enjoy keeping up with the latest monitoring tools and techniques
- ✔ Always keep an eye out for return on investment (ROI) with social media activity
- ✔ Effectively create and communicate strategy
- ✔ Exude enthusiasm about your brand

Sometimes your best brand evangelists are customers whom you can recruit for your team. You'd be surprised how much more effective a genuinely excited person can be versus somebody who's just socializing online for the money. People spot the difference very quickly. Hire for genuine excitement about your brand. The rest, as they say, will come.

I can't say enough good about truly humanizing your brand! Do this by getting people online used to seeing your real representative's picture instead of a logo. Studies show that only 37 percent of people are willing to be polite to a brand logo online, whereas people are 67 percent more likely to be more polite when they see a human face connected with the brand representative.

There seem to be as many job descriptions for social media roles as there are Twitter accounts, but if you just focus on covering these skill sets, you'll do well, no matter what sorts of positions you decide to create in recruiting your team. A rose by any other name is still a rose! These are your most crucial roles.

Who should not be on your team?

Online reputation management is a new area for most organizations, and most people have a few misconceptions about the skill sets involved. Don't draft the following types of people just because it may seem like the logical thing to do. It may not be logical at all!

- ✔ Somebody from the IT department, based on the fact that he probably won't be intimidated by learning the tools. You need somebody with a passion to socially share your brand and further your particular goals.

- ✔ A junior executive, based on the perception that she's young and "with it," so she ought to be able to take this on as well as anybody else. You need somebody who truly understands how to build and influence community online, which just isn't taught in traditional MBA programs.

- ✔ A self-proclaimed "social media guru" with no testimonials. Being online a lot doesn't translate into understanding marketing principles or being able to evangelize your particular brand.

Deciding who runs your team

It's crucial to hire inspiring, effective, social media team leaders. Ideally, they are

✔ Diplomatic people with strong "people skills"

✔ People who can recognize trends through data and analytics

✔ People who are terrific at saying a lot with a few words

✔ People who are genuinely enthusiastic about your brand

✔ People who are able to spot the right kinds of content to share from fans and competitors

✔ People who understand your particular online social ecosystem

✔ People who are sensitive to other people's race, sexual orientation, and religion

✔ People who keep quiet about their political views

✔ People who are empathetic to the feelings of people online who are sincerely reaching out to the brand for either customer service or information

✔ People who stay levelheaded under pressure

✔ People who write well

✔ People who are able to consistently inspire others online to take action

As you pull together your social media team, it's probably a good idea to name it something that other people can recognize quickly. Since this is still a very new area, I'm sharing the following list of possibilities for your consideration. Respondents in the Forrester Consulting survey of 200 U.S.-based companies named these as their top-five departments:

✔ Social Media/Web 2.0 Team

✔ Marketing and/or Public Relations

✔ Web-Interactive Marketing

✔ Product Marketing

✔ Marketing Operations

Authorizing your employees to engage during a crisis

I go into this topic in greater detail in Chapters 14 and 15, but right now it's important to contemplate the pros and cons of allowing your employees to engage during a crisis. Some considerations include

✔ **Your typical employees:** If your organization overflows with outgoing, levelheaded people who enjoy social networking, this may be a really good idea, after they have been apprised of your social media policy for employees and the crisis communications message of the moment. It's essential for everyone to be on the same proverbial page so that your message can go out as smoothly as possible.

✔ **Your inter-departmental communication:** If your organization can communicate quickly and effectively throughout departments, authorizing employees to engage during a crisis may be a great relief.

✔ **The nature of the situation:** You need to protect your employees if an issue turns ugly by not asking them to involve their personal profiles and social accounts. Use your best judgment and err on the side of caution.

Identifying brand ambassadors

It's always great to have friends when you are experiencing pressure online. Your best friends can be people who already know and love your brand who will stick up for you to their audiences. These kinds of people are often called *brand ambassadors.* (I cover this in greater detail in Chapters 14 and 15.) For now, consider cultivating relationships with your brand ambassadors by researching the following:

✔ Who are your most passionate fans online?

✔ How large are their audiences?

Ask your team to use research the answers to these questions. When you've found your ambassadors, brainstorm ways to deepen your relationships with them.

Outsourcing your team

Sometimes it's more convenient and cost-effective to hire someone outside your organization to perform a specific function. This section explains some of the best choices available.

Using virtual assistants (VAs)

Virtual assistants are people who work remotely and can communicate with e-mail, phone, Skype, or instant messaging (IM). Hiring VAs has lots of perks, such as

✔ They save you time by creating reports, creating templates for repetitive tasks, and performing general assistant work.

✔ You don't have to provide office space or supplies for them.

✔ They're paid as a vendor, so you can write the expense off on your organization's taxes.

✔ They can organize your team's schedule/efforts for you.

✔ Many can serve as a simple site administrator and keep your organization's blog up to date.

The best way for you to find a qualified, reputable VA is via personal recommendations from trusted colleagues based on the assistant's stellar qualifications and record. Second to this, you can find terrific ones online here:

✔ **Twitter:** Just tweet out your desire for referrals from personal connections and you will start to hear back soon.

✔ **Craigslist:** This may be a viable option if you want to meet someone face-to-face before deciding if he's the right VA for you. Discover your local Craigslist at `www.craigslist.org/about/sites`.

✔ **VA networking:** Find them where they live online! This is where VAs collaborate on the most efficient ways to do things. Come to think of it, I need to browse there to pick up on a few ideas myself! You should consider doing the same. Here are a couple informative sites where you can submit a request for proposal from a virtual assistant and learn more

  • International Virtual Assistants Association (`www.ivaa.org`)

  • Virtual Assistant Networking Association (`www.vanetworking.com/clients`)

✔ **Resource Nation:** Streamlines the process for you by matching you with pre-screened, qualified VAs. It provides this as a complimentary service. You can find it at `www.resourcenation.com`.

✔ **Tasks EveryDay:** This site, which has been featured on CNN and the New York Post's website, is based on a monthly fee but is truly spectacular if you want 24-hour live access to a VA. It even provides local phone numbers for the people you're working with. This is one example of how life can really be a lot easier in this new, worldwide economy. Check it out at `www.taskseveryday.com`.

✔ **AssistU:** May be more cost-effective because this site is where many VAs start their training. Learn more at `www.assistu.com`.

Hiring a social media (or "digital") agency

Many people believe that social media teams belong under the direct supervision and direction of a marketing department or firm. Some people think that public relations firms should hold the key to your social media team's leadership. Either way, there are lots of benefits to hiring out because it can save you the time, effort, and resources involved in hiring, training, and supervising new recruits.

The downside is that many of these agencies have sprung up overnight. Just because they have awesome graphics and bold copywriters on their blogs doesn't mean that they necessarily have the savvy and strength to contribute to your brand's goals in a meaningful way. Beware of baloney!

Here are the best ways to find a social media marketing agency or public relations firm for your online reputation management needs:

- Seek personal recommendations from a trusted friend who thinks the agency is great based on actual results
- Use a qualified social media directory, such as
    - Investinsocial.com's Social Media Directory (see Figure 3-1)
    - Facebook's list of Preferred Developer Consultants (see Figure 3-2)
    - Word of Mouth Marketing Association's *Buyers Guide* (see Figure 3-3)

Once you find a potentially good candidate, always research the firm by

- Following up on brands it claims it helped to promote
- Following up on at least three references

Beware of providers who use sketchy qualifiers like these:

- **Acting like a know-it-all:** No one knows it all. It's usually a smoke screen intended to cover one obvious limitation or another.
- **Saying they will completely manage your social media presence online:** How can an uninformed third party possibly communicate details about what's going on with your organization? You definitely will need to be involved, but you don't have to read every tweet.
- **Saying that they have a large, experienced team:** Anybody can say that. Get specific information about the people who will be working on your campaign and follow up on it. You may be surprised to learn that they're just sorority girls back from spring break working on their internship until a real, paying job comes along.

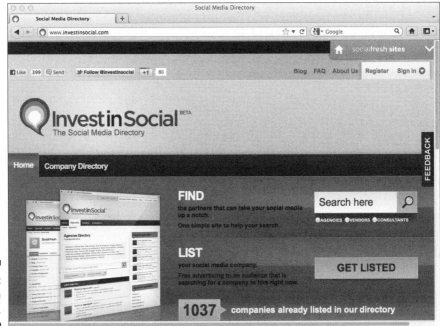

Figure 3-1:
Investin
social.com.

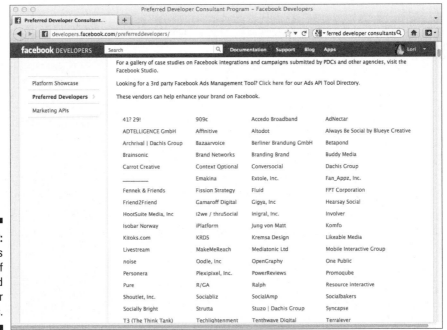

Figure 3-2:
Facebook's
list of
Preferred
Developer
Consultants.

Figure 3-3:
Word of
Mouth
Marketing
Association's
Buyers Guide.

Creating an easy-to-follow framework

Putting together your team is a great investment that will pay off via a healthy reputation online, especially when you create an easy-to-follow framework. By *framework* I simply mean the way you choose to organize your team's time spent engaging online. I offer some tips below for creating your easy-to-follow plan. Please keep in mind that this can be customized to help other departments (like product development and sales) with their goals as needed. Begin by

- ✓ **Training your team on how to use the social media monitoring tools that you choose:** I tell you much more about which tools are available in Chapter 5 and show you how to set up the most popular ones in Chapter 7.

- ✓ **Deciding and communicating what your goals are:** I give you some sample engagement goals at the beginning of this Chapter.

Once you have trained your team on how to use the tools and given them the direction you want them to follow, I suggest giving them the following easy-to-use framework for organizing their time and efforts online. Please keep in mind that small companies may only need to check online three times a day, whereas a large company needs people to constantly maintain and engage with people. Regardless, this is a simple framework to follow:

1. **Listen to what people are saying about you, your brand, your industry, and your competitors via your monitoring platforms and direct searches via Google or the social network you're looking at.**

2. **Respond to questions and comments.**

   In Chapter 4 I tell you how to pull together a senior-level crisis team, which involves a PR professional. It's sometimes useful to ask this person to create a glossary of useful answers to tricky questions for you. Make sure they're 120 characters long or less so you can tweet them easily.

3. **Engage with people about your brand, industry, and so on. Share company blog posts and respond to commenters on the blog if that's within the scope of your everyday social media team's responsibilities. This can also include**

   - General engagement

   - Educating people about your brand and/or industry

   - Market research — asking people for what they already like/dislike and what they would love to see from your company

   - Customer service

4. **If things get a little heated, invite someone to communicate with you via e-mail (or some other private backchannel) instead.**

5. **Resolve only the issues you can and allow senseless issues to rest.**

6. **Cultivate and deepen influential online relationships.**

7. **Repeat Steps 1–6 as needed.**

8. **Report and share this information with other team members and departments as appropriate.**

Maintaining a schedule for online engagement

Online reputation management issues happen on weekends too! You must protect your organization's interests by maintaining a consistent schedule where weeknight and weekend shifts are covered. A check-in every hour would suffice for most brands, with backup team members available to call in case a crisis arises.

Dell's command center success story

Picture a futuristic blue room with soft, indirect lighting, and huge, high-definition monitors covering the wall in front of you. You're sitting at a long table, joined by others as you all continuously monitor conversations involving your brand's name on all the major social media networks as they emerge, and some lesser-known networks too. Twitter alone transmits tens of thousands of tweets invoking your brand name.

This is Dell's Command Center, which the company created in 2010. Here, blogs are monitored. SEO (search-engine optimization) is tweaked. Content is developed. Conversations are maintained and documented. Heck, the energy is so focused, the President of the United States may be visiting at any moment.

Dell discovered that it really didn't feel like the company had a handle on what people were saying about it and wanted to do something definitive about it. Since Dell manufactures computers and monitors, creating this center probably wasn't as much of an expenditure as it would have been for some other organizations, but as a public-relations boost, it's been a huge success.

Social media meltdowns are an escalating trend (no pun intended). Repeating somebody else's grudge had become a quick way to get attention online and boost one's own ratings. Your best bet is to have your everyday team respond quickly and effectively in order to avert an online meltdown. Responding wisely takes all the fun out of having a good rant, so people move on. I tell you more about how to do this in Chapters 4, 14, and 15.

Creating your own social media command center

Probably you won't need to consider creating a crisis command center. Such centers are necessary only if you represent a huge brand or if you're in the midst of an enormous social media firestorm. This takes every aspect of your online reputation management in-house and gives you a geographic place for crisis team members to meet and make the best decisions possible about how to move forward.

To me, the concept feels a lot like what a NASA control room might look like or even a war room buried deep under the Pentagon. I'm not sure how many brands need this level of online reputation management, but it's clear that they're listening intently. And especially in online reputation management, listening is love. I tell you much more about this in Part III.

Recruiting Your Team

Most organizations find themselves scrambling to pull together an online reputation management team from already stretched resources. A common mistake is to assign responsibilities to people who really aren't very good at them, even when there may be a perfectly good candidate left ignored in a completely different department. If your IT person can't stand writing compelling blog content and socializing via social media, then by all means recruit someone from a different department to do the job. Instead, just let the IT person do what he does best — maintaining your software, performing analytics, and keeping an eye on emerging technologies and approaches that will make your organization run more smoothly.

Who knows? Your assistant could be the best content writer in the organization. Your people will love you for paying attention to what they actually enjoy doing, and you'll get much more consistently rewarding outcomes.

It's interesting to note that there are groups within organizations online, such as Social Empire (`www.socialempire.com`), who are dedicated to gaming social networks in order to raise everybody's influence scores. Services such as Klout (`www.klout.com`) measure influence based on a user's ability to drive action online, both by publishing content and engaging with others online. Recruit your team members based on demonstrated merit, rather than their "influence score" at the moment.

Consider the following positions within the team:

- **Social strategist:** Looks at how different regions of online activity can be better integrated to further your brand's goals. I like to refer to this person as a "cat herder." It can be murder on the allergies, but somebody's got to do it.

- **Monitoring specialist:** Really listens to what people are saying online and knows how to cue into the most important conversations about your brand and steer them into the direction of your goals. See how important goals are?

- **Community and support staff:** Pays close attention to the issues that people post online. Such dedicated attention nets a gold mine of market research that can (and should) be shared with your organization's other departments. These staffers spread content created by the content strategist and may report to a community manager, which I cover in more detail later in this chapter.

- **Content strategist:** Creates content to be shared online, whether written, video, or audio, and serves as a face to the brand. Brings in guest bloggers with great communications skills and large audiences, and supports your brand's goals so that everything is integrated and working together like a well-oiled machine.

Handling a #McDisaster

Brandjacking is a growing issue in online reputation management. To illustrate, in January 2012, McDonald's social media team rolled out a Twitter campaign using #McDStories in hopes of stimulating personal stories about the farmers who grow produce for the world-famous chain restaurant. Instead, harsh critics effectively brandjacked the McDStories hashtag. They posted disturbing employee hygiene stories, frightening obesity via fast-food statistics, and food-poisoning tales. You need to hire the kind of people who can diplomatically deal with these kinds of situations in a hurry.

The following list offers characteristics of people with a high ability to engage with people online. These characteristics may influence your decision to hire, but none of them should be deal-breakers. Someone's genuine ability to relate and influence should always be more important than her numbers:

- **High Klout score:** Oftentimes, people with a lot of time on their hands can generate a very high influence score for a period of time. I have a friend who's a technical genius when it comes to developing strategies to "game" social media networks. He's shy, introverted, and (by his own admission) not a natural networker. He's able to boost super high influence scores without relating to much of anybody! It's fair to note, though, that some truly influential people online do enjoy high scores simply because people love and share their content all across the recorded networks. You can learn more about Klout at www.klout.com.

- **High number of friends on Facebook:** This number may seem obviously important. However, does a high number of friends on Facebook really demonstrate a person's ability to authentically build community around a brand? I'm not so sure.

- **High number of fans on a Facebook page:** This is a better indicator, especially lately, because it's become a lot harder to get "Likes" online. Since Facebook's initial public offering, it's become a fixture rather than a novelty so the excitement's wearing off a little.

- **High number of fans on Twitter:** Early adopters on Twitter got followed for just about anything and not for posting fascinating, funny commentary. These days, gaining fans is harder, and there are plenty of truly artful and entertaining people on there who post quality information.

There are many groups on Twitter like #teamfollowback who automatically follow back anybody who follows them. It's a great way to build your numbers when you post this in your profile description because bots (fake, robotic accounts) search for this identifier. The downside is that you end up with a mechanized list of zombies following you instead of actual people who may relate with you and help you to share your brand's message. This is one more reason why hiring somebody on the basis of a huge Twitter following may be misleading.

✔ **More than 500 connections on LinkedIn:** LinkedIn is a little more difficult to game, but lots of people have dedicated themselves to figuring it out and teaching others how to use it to look like they have a stronger influence online than they really do. The best things you can do to gauge true talent via LinkedIn are to

- Review how thoroughly individuals' profiles are filled out
- Check out their recommendations (both given and received)
- Look to see what groups they're involved in
- Examine those groups to assess the quality of their interaction
- Are they spamming?
- Are they asking thoughtful questions?
- Are they genuinely seeking to learn, rather than to influence?

There are many fan swaps circulating around Facebook and LinkedIn groups. It's a great way to create your initial "vanity" URL for a Facebook page, but engaging in many of those swaps can damage your credibility. Be wise about whom you engage with online, or it will cause people to feel like you're inviting them to post spammy stuff on your page.

✔ **High Pinclout score or more than 500 followers on Pinterest:** Even though it's hugely popular right now, Pinterest simply may not be relevant to your brand. Somebody with a huge interest following may be the world's most influential cat fur felter, but not somebody who's going to be able to translate that niche appeal into being able to evangelize your organization's brand. (See Figure 3-4.)

Pinterest is more fun and games than I can describe. When I'm stressed, I post pins and create boards because it feels like I'm publishing a women's magazine full of slick, gorgeous photos. Still, even though new people follow me every day, I'm not sure it has any bearing on my overall brand influence. If you really want to integrate Pinterest into your strategy, your homework is to figure out how to make your brand highly visual in a way that gets people excited about sharing. Get your marketing team going with meme development or something really visually catchy.

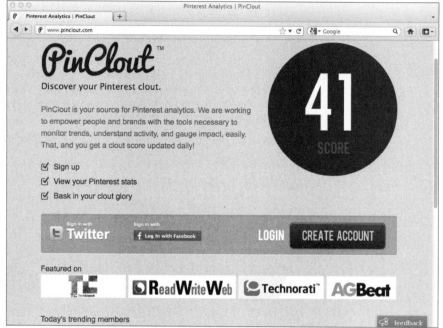

Figure 3-4:
Screenshot
of my
current
Pinclout
score.

Looking to In-house Geeks for Support

Your built-in IT department (if you have one) can be a wonderful resource for your online reputation management strategy. It's best to channel the energies of your online conversationalists into online activity rather than wrestling with network engineering. Here are seven things your local techie can contribute to the effort:

- ✔ Installing updates
- ✔ Keeping hardware in order
- ✔ Keeping software in order
- ✔ Individual help on aggregators/tools with team members
- ✔ Training on new and existing tools
- ✔ Customization of open source tools
- ✔ Integration with existing internal network

The most important thing your IT department can contribute is to devise a troubleshooting ticketing system for your team so that every complaint gets resolved with a clear history for anybody else to see. I show you more options for this in Chapter 5, where I introduce you to all the most popular online tools.

Connecting with savvy, energetic PR interns

Believe it or not, most of the time when social media management agencies brag about having an extensive team of seasoned social media professionals they're usually exaggerating about the abilities of their college interns.

I'm a big fan of hiring interns because they're comfortable and familiar with social media networks, having grown up with them, and will probably be able to pick up your own system pretty quickly. The trick is to use them for monitoring and making conversation within clear guidelines. Savvy, energetic interns can

✔ Save you time

✔ Save you money

✔ Give responsible college students a chance to try their wings (that equals good karma!)

✔ Give you a boost with the audiences they already have

✔ Stimulate good conversation most of the time

Hiring professional community managers

As a brand manager, you may decide you need a qualified, professional community manager who can brainstorm with you and then share your vision for where you want to go with your brand. A *community manager* is an online brand representative who engages with people personally via social networks and blogs. He functions as a brand evangelist, peacekeeper, and market research analyst, since he becomes the heart of the brand online. Here are some guidelines you can use to better understand what he contributes to an online community:

✔ He's really excited about your brand.

✔ He adds value to the conversation.

> ✔ He knows how to graciously enforce house rules.
>
> ✔ He recognizes people who add to the discussion.
>
> ✔ He keeps his finger on the pulse of the mood in your community.
>
> ✔ He understands the art of online engagement.

Investigating their profiles thoroughly

Nothing's more important than knowing you're hiring the very best people to represent your brand and influence what actions people take with it online. You want to be sure that the people you're trusting are able to handle the unexpected with speed, savvy, and presence of mind.

When you evaluate people as possible team members, ask yourself: How's his or her emotional energy? If the individual generally is snarky or sarcastic, even if really funny, approach with caution. Such people may not be the best voice for your brand during a crisis. It may be like throwing gas on a fire.

Some ideas for checking out their communication skills:

> ✔ Look for how they are already communicating online
>
> ✔ Listen for the tone they use most of the time
>
> ✔ Look for people who exhibit levelheaded responses in hot situations
>
> ✔ Check out how positive their status updates tend to be

Researching your job candidates

It's always useful to follow up on a candidate's references. However, since references can just be people who want to help out a friend, the information you get may not be totally objective or accurate. I suggest going beyond references to research your potential job candidates.

These days, the Internet is quickly becoming an online resume of people who have trusted you at some point in time, in different capacities. You can find out quite a lot about your potential employees by searching for them via Google, Facebook, Twitter, LinkedIn, and YouTube. Be sure you cross-reference your research with photos and background info, where possible, so that you can be sure you're looking at the right person!

With this in mind, check out how this person relates with people online and ask yourself the following questions

✔ Does this person appear like she consistently exercises sound judgment?

✔ Does this person appear to hang out with trustworthy people?

✔ How does this person appear to handle pressure?

✔ Is this person genuinely friendly?

✔ How current are her profiles?

Motivating Your Team

Social media teams are particularly prone to burnout, especially during exciting online events or during stressful, such as when one of your monitoring tools just changed how it works. Keep in mind that you need to take every opportunity to reinforce a sense of camaraderie and purpose within the team. That's why goals are important. These people aren't just babysitting a brand online. They're contributing to something larger than themselves that improves your world in some way.

Defining guidelines for behavior

You may want to reach out to the PR department for more help in communicating what kinds of messages are okay (and not so okay) in keeping with your brand. I tell you more about working with your PR department (if you have one) in Chapter 4. If you are part of a smaller organization, please consider the following:

✔ People have a tendency to say and do things online that they would never say or do in person. Your team needs to be aware of this, and understand that rude language, harsh remarks, angry criticisms, or even threats usually aren't personal and shouldn't be taken that way.

✔ Some social media hangouts, blogs, and forums foster a "keeping it real" sort of tone that can quickly degrade into just being rude in the name of "authenticity." Don't be snowed or intimidated. If it looks like a duck, walks like a duck, and quacks like a duck, you may just be dealing with somebody who's abusing her relative anonymity online to be abusive.

Have no fear. I show you strategies to deal with people who are being rude in Chapters 14 and 15.

Reinforcing a culture of trust

Fostering a culture based on earning and maintaining trust among your social media team members makes your work much easier. Listening to people over a variety of social networks, non-stop via monitoring platforms, and then responding to their seemingly endless questions and comments can be pretty draining. A team that believes you are trustworthy and that they can depend on each other is much better able to deal with situations as they arise. As you create the environment they will be working in, ask yourself the following questions to see if you're on the right track:

- ✔ **Are your team members set up to feel like winners or losers at the end of the day?** Setting clear, achievable goals (such as customer satisfaction expressed) helps with this and gives you a frame of reference for evaluating their performance.

- ✔ **Can your team members express their doubts and concerns without fear of reprisal?** If not, collaborate on an appropriate way for them to be able to do this comfortably.

- ✔ **Do your members fear failure or are they confident that if they don't have the right response that there's willing backup?**

Training your team

In today's constantly evolving, continuously growing world of online interaction, you can never have too much training for your team.

It's essential for you to provide them with opportunities for ongoing technical training. Many companies provide instruction free of charge, so there's no reason not to embrace the process. Do your best to keep your team on top of

- ✔ **Aggregators:** Aggregator applications learn what people are saying about you, your brand, and your industry online because they pull together streams of updates from major social networks into one service. I tell you more about these in Chapters 5 and 7.

- ✔ **The latest Facebook tips:** Facebook changes almost constantly. Sometimes those changes will dramatically affect engagement and your organization's goal setting. Keeping your people informed is crucial to their sense of well-being and success.

- ✔ **Trending topics on Twitter that affect your brand:** It's a great idea to teach your team how to check out trends and use the attention being given to that topic to educate your potential (and existing) customers about your brand (see Chapter 5 for more detail).

✔ **YouTube:** There is an entirely different art and science to working with YouTube because its search algorithms are very different from Google's. For example, you can educate your team on how to search YouTube more effectively and fill in video descriptions more effectively.

✔ **Memes:** Memes are basically private jokes passed around for all to see on the Internet. They are often funny, and used judiciously can be useful in promoting awareness for your brand.

Keeping your team fresh and savvy with ongoing social media training pays off big-time for you and your brand. Here are some things you can do:

✔ Check up on their activity periodically

✔ Find things to sincerely praise

✔ Suggest clear alternative tactics for weak spots

✔ Stay positive so you build loyalty for when it really counts, such as during a crisis when people need to pitch in some overtime to meet the need:

- Keeping it pleasantly objective

- Retaining their enthusiastic support

- Focusing on what should be done, versus making it a personality issue

Toyota turns lemons into lemonade

During a social media meltdown concerning a recall, Toyota took charge of its messaging on all available social media services, including staging a live broadcast interview of Toyota's CEO and President Jim Lentz on Digg. Digg is an online community that had more than 40 million people at the time of the interview. The interview lasted for almost half an hour, and Lentz addressed the top-ten questions that people were asking about the recall. This is a brilliant example of a huge company really taking the time and energy to connect with its customers and the public in a transparent, responsible way. Toyota acted quickly, decisively, and positively, turning a lemon (if you'll forgive the pun) into lemonade.

Chapter 4

Recruiting Professionals for Your Crisis Team

- -

- -

*O*nline reputation management crises are always forged in the fiery furnace of public opinion. It seems only natural for me to think of strategizing and training your specialized teams by using a firefighting metaphor. Besides, it's fun!

Just as with professional firefighters, online reputation management departments train their everyday team members on regular practices, rescues, emergency care, and disaster preparedness. They also maintain specialized teams for complicated or unusual disasters so that when worst-case scenarios become realities, these teams are ready to take action.

Please take a moment to consider your organization's size and needs. My online reputation management system (see Chapter 5 for more detail) applies to everyone from a small business to a Fortune 100 company — everyone, in other words. If you're a

✔ Large-sized business with several departments and executives, you need to

- Train your everyday team on the crisis management steps that I share in this chapter, as well as Chapters 14 and 15.

- Identify backup team members in case of an online emergency. These members are folks who may normally work in other departments but who have been trained to function in emergencies alongside your everyday social media team. Some organizations even empower *all* their employees to respond, but I suggest this only in cases where your organization's morale is high and your communication is super effective.

- Recruit senior-level professionals for the executive team. I tell you more about who should be involved and why later in this chapter.

✔ Medium-sized business, you should

- Identify qualified backup team members in the event of an escalating online situation.

- Decide who functions as the senior-level decision maker(s).

- Go through the steps I describe later in this chapter to be as prepared as possible for an online reputation issue.

✔ Small business, examine carefully all the steps in this chapter. Make sure you follow the logic used for each step, so that you can prepare yourself, according to your own scale, in the event of an online emergency.

You just have to find the right adjustments for your situation. If you're a celebrity starring in a hot TV series or movie right now, you probably just need a backup team of professionals to manage things for you. If you're overseeing online reputation management for a large organization, you should consider adding every layer of protection I give in this chapter. If you're a small business owner, you should read through this chapter so that you can understand the steps.

In this chapter, I show you how to create your specialized teams by recruiting other industry professionals into your crisis team. They won't be there every day to monitor social media activity and they won't be the face of your brand, but they will be those special people who craft your grand crisis strategy so that if something does happen you'll be ready to take action right away.

Your crisis team needs to be made up of senior-level people who can collaborate effectively on major issues. Depending on the size of your organization, it may be a good idea to plan ahead by identifying a backup team of trained employees or outside help from an agency that you can bring in to reinforce your regular social media team, if need be.

Keep in mind that reviewing the steps in this chapter is like going through a fire drill. You gain confidence as you discover and strengthen as many weak spots as possible during a relatively tranquil time and mentally go through the process of successfully putting out a social media fire.

Creating Your Crisis Response Team

Imagine, if right in the middle of an emergency, you could suddenly have your best-qualified, most experienced advisors from a broad spectrum of departments weighing in on the issue and supporting you from each of their perspectives. That's what a great crisis team of senior-level professionals can do for you well in advance of any issues that may crop up online.

I suggest recruiting your team from these different departments because each area of expertise has a perspective that can be brought to bear on must hot issues online. Getting them to collaborate and problem-solve worst-case scenario strategies takes some time, especially in the beginning, but it shouldn't require much of a time commitment from them once they have collaborated and formed some initial worst-case scenario action plans. It's really smart to have them meet periodically, just to stay current on industry trends and to address any new developments before they become intense.

For best results, you should have at least one representative from each of these professional areas:

- ✔ Public relations
- ✔ Legal
- ✔ Human resources
- ✔ Executive

I suggest getting the most experienced people available to work with you to craft your organization's crisis response system. Let them know it won't cost them much time or effort, but you must have a plan and some possible scenarios in place before a situation heats up or else everybody works a lot harder later to contain the damage and clean up afterward.

Crisis management is largely about prevention. Few things are harder to do than suffer through an online reputation management crisis that could have been minimized or averted up front with the right crisis response system. Your crisis response team needs to craft an overall strategy that the every day team will be able to follow, as well as to be on hand should a situation escalate to a place where new decisions have to be made quickly. It's also good to have back up social media team members trained so that you have more coverage in the event of an emergency.

In case you're a political candidate or a celebrity

If at all possible, keep an experienced defamation litigator on retainer instead of turning to a PR firm for responding to accusations and damaging information that's being published. The general perception is that quotes from a public relations firm generally are not much different from political spin statements.

You must be able to respond from a standpoint of credibility. Going the legal route for accusations and damaging information being published has more teeth because there's the threat of legal action if someone is violating the law.

Weighing in with public relations professionals

One of the coolest things about public relations professionals is that they maintain their own audiences online and tend to foster relationships with influential friends in the media. They're great people to get to know better as you master your online reputation management.

They can help you to craft a plan for what to do via traditional media to address a situation that has gotten so hot online that it's been picked up by mainstream media. Odds are good that they also have a long-term perspective on your company's branding and message that you need to consider when crafting your crisis response options. They could also be aware of a long-standing issue that raises it's head from time to time and have strategies figured out for dealing with that issue that may make sense for your online communications.

Oftentimes, PR professionals have relationships with traditional media and reporters. During a crisis, it's important to notify them as soon as possible.

Once you recruit your PR person, take advantage of his expertise and ask him to create a glossary of probable complaints and response ideas that can be customized (rather than cut and pasted). I know this may sound like call center scripting, but your team will thank you for providing them with these goodies should they draw a blank in the middle of a situation.

Getting legal advice

If you own a small business, it's probably beyond the scope of your budget to hire an in-house attorney, unless you have a one in the family who is generous with her time! As such, I suggest you have a look through these suggestions and keep these ideas in mind as you formulate your worst-case scenarios and what you would do if you needed legal help in the event of a crisis. If possible, it would be great to meet with one and talk about some worst-case scenarios that you have thought through. You can at least identify qualified, reputable lawyers that can help you in the event of an emergency and make sure their contact information is on hand.

If you're part of a medium- or large-sized organization, you may be in a position to afford legal advice about your brand's overall crisis response strategy as well as about any specific responses you make as situations arise. The larger your company is, the more likely it is (and important) that you can get legal counsel on all aspects of your crisis response strategy.

When it comes to legal counsel for your online reputation management, you should always

- ✔ Include legal representation in your crisis team
- ✔ Have a general plan in place in anticipation of an event happening or an accusation being made
- ✔ Have the beginnings of an orderly and efficient response

If you don't already have in-house counsel or a firm on retainer, you should decide now whom you will call when there's a potential legal situation and make emergency contact arrangements. In times of crisis, you don't want to have to wait until your lawyer comes back from her honeymoon in Barbados.

Engage with lawyers now to make sure you're meeting your legal obligations in terms of compliance.

The bottom line is that the legal profession is really behind the times when it comes to deciding on issues that come up as a result of online communication. It's probably going to be 15 years before any kind of monetary or time limits are set and can be enforced. Technology is going to continue to expand and develop, so there's really no telling where this is going to stop — but you can bet it won't be any time soon.

You should know what a lawyer can and can't do for you if somebody says something ugly about you or your brand online. Slander and libel laws used to be able to protect people from attacks like these, but times have changed. The truth is . . . these days, lawyers can't do much about such attacks — at least not before it's way too late. The wheels of the law move slowly. By the time your lawyer has been consulted, has researched the matter, and has had time to create a case, it's often too late. Your good name has already been dragged through the mud, and tried in the fiery court of public opinion. Before you assume your online slander/libel problems will all be painlessly taken care of by your lawyers, here's some food for thought:

✔ Libel/slander is terribly difficult to prove.

✔ The time frame for a ruling typically ranges from 1 to 6 months.

✔ You're at the mercy of the court's schedule.

✔ Your legal efforts may cost a lot of time and money and result in a judgment against somebody with little or nothing to lose.

Never threaten with legal action unless you're fully prepared to follow through. It costs you credibility.

Getting help from human resources

Now that social media is available to everyone with an Internet connection, online comments can make your employees a gold mine of support or a source of endless consternation. One of the most important things you can do for your online reputation management is to get help from your human resources department in crafting an employee policy.

In terms of your crisis team, having a senior staff member from your human resources gives you an informed perspective when online issues involve former or current employees. Your team member will know current regulations and potential human resources liabilities surrounding issues that nobody else on your team understands. They may be very familiar with the type of situations that is presented and have a standard way of responding to similar issues.

When your team formulates nightmare scenarios, be sure to include some from current or former employees, as well as situations that are intentional and accidental. It's amazing how many online reputation issues have escalated via an employee "drunk tweeting" on the wrong account on a Saturday night!

Working with your executive team for guidance

Many times an organization's executive team views social media as an unwelcome intruder into its formerly organized, understandable professional life. In most cases, however, having an overall crisis-response strategy in place will save a tremendous amount of time and trouble. Only during an escalating situation will online crisis events suddenly and completely disrupt your work flow.

Why being a limited public figure matters

If you're a blogger or are online as yourself instead of an anonymous brand logo, you should know that in legal terms you're a "limited public figure." This is the legal status shared by U.S. presidents, Hollywood actors, and other famous people. This may make you feel a bit like a swanky celebrity, but be warned because this means your legal rights to fair and decent press treatment just evaporated quite a bit. To be specific, people who are limited public figures have a really small chance at making a defamation claim that can stick. In most circumstances lies or slanderous distortions of the truth about a limited public figure aren't legally actionable, and even when such cases are actionable they are very difficult and expensive to prove. To be forewarned is to be forearmed! This is all the more reason to

✔ Monitor for early issue detection

✔ Act quickly by responding

✔ Be open and honest, not seen as evasive in times of crises

✔ Fix any problems

✔ Report back that the problems were addressed

✔ Repeat as needed

The most important thing you can do is to embrace the process and use it to your best advantage, because the double-edged sword of social media networking potentially can bring enormous profits to your door in record time if you use the medium wisely and give it the respect it deserves.

It's critical that you have an information hub for your online reputation management team so that you can effectively present a unified message.

Your executive team needs to collaborate on

✔ Creating your employee social media policy

✔ Organizing your company to best deal with crisis

✔ Determining whom your company will inform in the event of a large-scale crisis. Some important examples include

- Stockholders
- Customers
- Newspapers
- Government officials
- Employees

✔ Brainstorming for worst-case scenarios

✔ Formulating policies for periodic employee training

Keeping an executive spokesperson accessible during crisis

Sometimes a crisis happens that an organization learns about from its own people, such as the BP oil spill. When something like that occurs it's useful to keep an executive spokesperson on standby for media interviews, statements, and being featured on company videos, in order to address the situation head on. Having a designated executive spokesperson on your crisis team, streamlines the decision-making process. In BP's case, it wouldn't have made any less oil spill, but it may well have helped to contain the spill of public resentment toward BP that arose from the impression that BP didn't care. Being responsive during a crisis helps everyone involved.

Other times, an organization may face an unpredictable, escalating online crisis that's being orchestrated by others who have a grudge against it that isn't directly related to a current event. Having a designated executive spokesperson can make your communication much more effective, should you choose to give live interviews or record a video to share online.

Decide right now who will be your media spokesperson in case you are asked for blog and mainstream interviews.

If you do get asked for interviews by bloggers or media, carefully consider whether you should give any exclusives. Depending on your particular situation, offering an exclusive could give rise to speculation that you're getting the "kid glove" treatment from a friend instead of participating in unbiased, objective journalism.

Evaluating Impact and Credibility

When a reputation attack occurs, always consider the source. Often the most awful–sounding gossip, rumors, or accusations about you or your brand come from sources who simply aren't credible. Most people understand this and are well aware that such rumors may very well be the ravings of a deranged lunatic. However, you can't always count on this.

The biggest issue you need to consider is how influential this source is. If you're really dealing with a deranged lunatic, odds are good that he is probably just talking out loud to himself online, and his words should not affect your credibility. If your source is someone with influence, on the other hand — someone with plenty of followers or readers — then you'll have to take matters more seriously.

The easier it is to disseminate information to an increasingly large audience, the greater the threat to your reputation.

When you encounter a situation that's serious enough to take action, consider first demanding a retraction or correction. If the attack is unfounded, your chances are good for getting what you want.

How can you tell how influential attackers are? In Chapters 14 and 15 I go into greater detail on how to determine whether a threat is credible or not, but the following are the first things you should look at in order to more accurately assess an attacker's influence online:

- ✔ **Size of his Twitter following.** Remember, though, that this value can't always be taken seriously. Sometimes it constitutes a number of fake (bot) accounts.

- ✔ **Size of his Facebook following:** Look at his actual profile to see how active it is. Is anybody actually listening to or conversing with him?

- ✔ **Whether or not he has a blog or a site that people actually visit.** Look for comments and shares, though this can be misleading. For example, every time I experiment with commenting systems or sharing plug-ins on my WordPress blog, some comments and shares inevitably evaporate.

- ✔ **Search video sharing sites, such as YouTube for his**
  - • Publishing frequency
  - • Number of views
  - • Comments

Perform a general Google search for the person's name. Maybe he's using his real name. Try to get an idea of who you are communicating with and what his interest may be in your organization.

Bringing in the geeks

It isn't always easy to evaluate an online threat. However, rest assured you aren't alone. You can always rely on a number of professional services that exist to identify the people saying defamatory things about you online. These services can also accumulate and clean up remarks, false information, and accusations that have been made against you and your organization online. Oh, and by the way, I use the term "geeks" with great admiration.

The top-two, most popular, online reputation management services are Reputation.com (see Figure 4-1) and ReputationHawk.com (see Figure 4-2). These services offer a free consultation and initial scan, as well as some search engine optimization (SEO) services. (For more on SEO, see Chapter 6.)

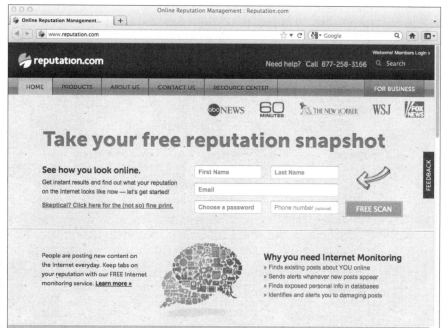

About anonymity

Just because somebody's using an anonymous profile, it isn't wise to make judgments about her impact and credibility based on that fact alone. Unfortunately, if someone's posting anonymous comments, it's impossible to assess her influence online. It's a good idea to respond with the assumption that she may have a lot of influential friends online. Using this extra level of caution never hurts and can pay off later by defusing an escalating crisis.

I want to be clear that there are lots of innocent reasons why somebody may elect to create an anonymous profile, including some of the following:

- ✔ They believe this protects them from having to be accountable for what they say and do online, as is most often the case with trolls. (See the section, "Troll-spotting for fun and profit," later in this chapter.)

- ✔ Most people in general tend to show a little different part of their personality on different social networks and blogs. It's normal, for example, for people to make up names for sharing on forums where they share more personal information.

- ✔ Some people have been victims of online identity theft and fraud and they're extra cautious about all their interactions online, lest it happen again.

Troll-spotting for fun and profit

There's a term for those who behave unpleasantly online. Such people are known as *trolls.* Trolls typically are bored people seeking to provoke controversy in order to gain attention for themselves.

Unpleasant behavior isn't just for trolls. Sometimes perfectly ordinary people can slip into troll-like behavior online, especially when certain hot topics arise. The difference is that trolls tend to be unpleasant all the time.

It's important to be able to identify when you're dealing with trolls because they almost always lack credibility and influence. Wasting valuable energy on these kinds of interactions is useless because it only dignifies the response and gives it more credibility. When it comes to trolls, it's almost always true that ignoring them is your strongest stance.

Trolls typically use these emotional tactics to manipulate situations online:

- ✔ Flattery
- ✔ Appeals to sympathy
- ✔ Rage
- ✔ Being insulting (usually accompanied by bad grammar and spelling)

Trolls often use logical fallacies to get what they want out of an organization or to at least get some attention out of brand representatives. Here are just a few of the most popular logical fallacies used by trolls:

- ✔ **Ad hominem attacks:** Personal attacks in which the troll makes value judgments about one's characteristics or beliefs. ("Everybody knows you're a liar and a cheat!")

- ✔ **Arguments to ignorance:** Insisting something's true because it hasn't been proven false ("UFOs must exist because you can't prove they don't!")

- ✔ **Appeals to pity:** Exploiting one's sense of pity or guilt. ("Think of all the poor, hungry kitties in the animal shelters!) If you see a consistent pattern of using appeals to pity or guilt, your attacker may be a wolf in sheep's clothing. The attacker adopts a weak persona to gain support within an online community or forum. When he determines that he has enough popular support to drop the sheepskin, he does so and attacks the person hosting the community and can often disenfranchise him from his own group! In this instance

  - Handle with caution. Invite this person to discuss any heated issues outside the forum, on private ground, such as e-mail, Facebook messages, or via Twitter direct messages.

  - Post a "house rules" kind of message on your forums or community, so that everyone has already been advised that only polite, productive conversation, will be tolerated. It's okay to disagree, but needs to be expressed rationally.

  - Exercise your right to quietly remove a trouble maker if after several attempts to "right the wrong" or explain something privately haven't changed the commenter's tone.

- ✔ **Arguments ad nauseam:** Saying the same thing over and over again.

- ✔ **Sweeping generalizations:** (All Belgians are ugly.)

Again, ignoring them is your best strategy if they have very little genuine influence or credibility online. If you have any doubts, check their references to see if they really are.

Anything you write in an e-mail, private message, or direct message on Twitter can and will be used against you by an angry troll. Maintain your cool and only write things you would share on a Times Square billboard.

In-house social networkers

You may be wondering if people in your organization are really using social media to communicate about their jobs. The 2011 National Business Ethics Survey, (download full report at `www.ethics.org/nbes/files/FinalNBES-web.pdf`) notes the following trends:

✔ Misconduct witnessed by U.S. workers is now at historic lows, while reporting of misconduct is now at near highs.

✔ Retaliation against employee whistleblowers rose sharply. I suggest you reinforce existing human resource department guidelines for dealing with employee grievances in your social media policy for employees.

✔ Active social networkers typically report far more negative experiences in their workplaces.

✔ On a positive note, the study indicated that you may be able to work with your active social networkers to say positive things about their company and coworkers, instead of posting negative things.

Creating Your Employee Online Reputation Policy

Some companies still believe they can get away with having an ad hoc sort of social media policy for their employees where they're pretty laid back and only institute rules after there's been a crisis resulting from an unfortunate recent event. These days, however, online conflagrations can escalate to dangerous levels within a couple of hours if gone unchecked and cause quite a stir within an organization, to say the least.

There are too many case studies out there already about major losses incurred by actual employees from the organizations that suffered the embarrassing social media frenzy. Here are a few examples of activity that unfortunately happen all the time and need a clear guideline before your organization's online reputation management gets out of hand because of "friendly fire."

✔ Rude commenting on the company's profile by accident

✔ Griping about management online

✔ Gossiping about coworkers online

✔ Taking unauthorized office pictures and sharing them online

✔ Posting negative rants (by disgruntled employees who still have access to company profiles)

✔ Taking disturbing or foolish videos while at work and posting them online

Because many people in a given work population socialize online, you should get your crisis team together and create an employee online reputation policy that provides guidelines for behavior. This policy should

✔ Be realistic

✔ Be flexible

✔ Be able to accommodate new technologies or social network trends

✔ Not invade anybody's individual privacy

✔ Not compromise your organization's privacy

✔ Give positive examples of what's acceptable

It's important to be consistently decisive. Include some clearly stated actions that your organization will always take when confronted by employees breaking the social media policy. This ought to include

✔ Issuing a warning to offenders. This should be written, dated, and signed by the offender, acknowledging that she has been informed/warned.

✔ Dismissing employees who don't comply.

Modeling your process after others

Organizations often prefer to model their own behavior on that of their peers. Creating an employee online policy is no different. If your team would be more comfortable working this way, here are a few examples they can use:

✔ **Social Media Governance:** Database (see Figure 4-3) including more than 195 companies, includes

  • Nonprofits

  • Government agencies

✔ **Dave Fleet:** Database of policies to inspire and inform you

✔ **Compliance Building:** Database of policies to inspire and inform you

✔ **Toolkit Cafe:** Sells a social media policies toolkit that can streamline your process

It's interesting to note that many of these companies have a couple of different policies covering a range of online reputation management topics. For example, in Figure 4-3, About.com offers both a Template: Blogging and Social Media Policy and a Template: Internet and Email policy. You may find that you're more comfortable devising separate strategies for your organization, depending on its size.

When your employee social media policy is so complex it resembles the tax code, it's time to simplify. (See Figure 4-4.) My best advice is to keep referring back to the timeless KISS principle. Adding too much complication makes things hard for everybody to understand and follow.

Always be positive and proactive. People always respond better to positive direction instead of a list of don'ts. (See Figure 4-5.)

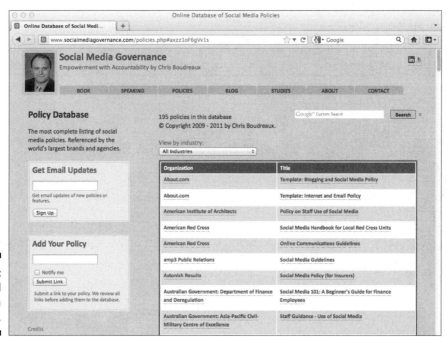

Figure 4-3:
Social
Media
Governance.

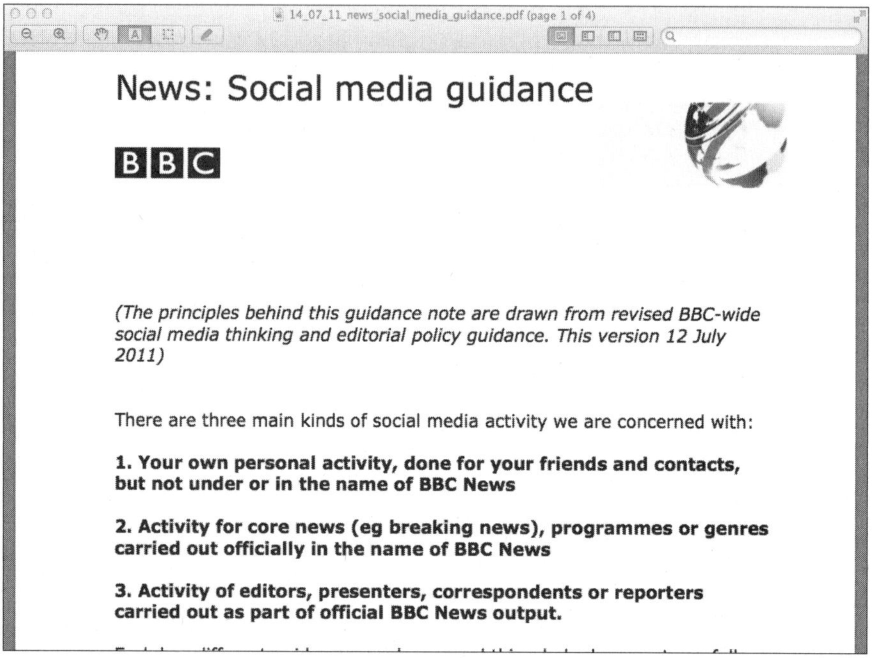

14_07_11_news_social_media_guidance.pdf (page 1 of 4)

News: Social media guidance

BBC

(The principles behind this guidance note are drawn from revised BBC-wide social media thinking and editorial policy guidance. This version 12 July 2011)

There are three main kinds of social media activity we are concerned with:

1. Your own personal activity, done for your friends and contacts, but not under or in the name of BBC News

2. Activity for core news (eg breaking news), programmes or genres carried out officially in the name of BBC News

3. Activity of editors, presenters, correspondents or reporters carried out as part of official BBC News output.

Figure 4-4: BBC's simplified social media guidance policy.

Putting a name on your policy

As you research and start developing your own approach to writing an employee social media policy for your organization, you'll see all kinds of names that refer to basically the same thing, with some refinements. There is no codified system for naming your particular organization's social media policy, though you can search for examples by using the following terms:

- Online social media principles
- Social media guidance
- Staff/volunteer presence on social networking sites
- Facebook policy
- Online community guidelines
- Using social media internally
- Using social media to communicate with the public
- Internal postings policy
- Social media staff guidelines

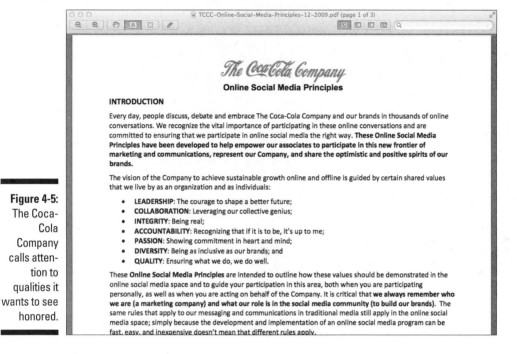

Figure 4-5:
The Coca-
Cola
Company
calls atten-
tion to
qualities it
wants to see
honored.

Implementing your new policy

Changes often take time to implement. Make sure that when you present your new policy to employees, you do so in a way that gives them time to read, digest, and adjust without feeling cornered or threatened. After all, your main focus is to avoid trouble, not to create resentments.

You will have the easiest time introducing this policy to your newly hired employees, who haven't developed any routines or habits that will need to be broken. However, give existing employees at least 30 days to get used to the new policy, and be there to answer any questions. Be willing to refine your policy as good questions are asked that show where a point here or there may not be as clear as it looked when you were writing it at night while sipping something relaxing. Everybody gets to learn through this process together.

You even may have compelling internal issues brought to light and be able to act on them proactively, which is always preferable to waiting until they hit crisis mode.

Creating Your Crisis Response System

What should you do when a crisis occurs? Just as with anything else, having everything organized ahead of time saves an enormous amount of effort later. Establish who on your executive team will respond during a given time frame. Make sure somebody is always on call just in case a quick crisis response decision or video needs to be made. I tell you more about this in Chapter 15, but now is a good time to get your schedules coordinated.

Here are some scheduling considerations that will cover all your bases in the unlikely event that you will actually be called upon to create a video response on the spot. Only you know what kind of scheduling system will integrate within your organization but be sure to address these time intervals in the crisis response on-call rotation that you create. If a social media meltdown starts to brew off hours or over the weekend, you can have peace of mind knowing that you have a strategy in place for dealing with the issue effectively.

✔ During the workweek (creating your "on-call" schedule)

✔ After hours (why it's important)

✔ During weekends: More issues escalate over the weekends because

• People tend to have more time to share on social networks

• Companies tend to have less coverage over the weekends

When crisis strikes online, whether it involves only one person or it's the latest firestorm of public opinion, silence most certainly is not golden! People often perceive silence as a tacit admission of guilt. Be sure your everyday social media teams understand that they always need to respond as quickly as possible, even if it's only to say "we're looking into it and will let you know more as soon as possible."

It's always best to handle complaints with honesty, so you aren't seen as dodging criticism. Even when customers are angry, always remain level-headed and address their problems as honestly and directly as possible.

Use facts to squelch rumor.

Don't depend on the legal system to maintain your online reputation management. Your chances of success in a lawsuit are probably slim to none because the decks are stacked against you. Use the system you create here and keep refining it as trends change.

Crisis response breaks down into the following steps. Almost every case study I look at tells the same story. This is what the winners do:

1. **Detect issues early via effective monitoring. (See Chapter 5 for more on monitoring).**

2. **Respond quickly.**

3. **Acknowledge any problems on your part quickly.**

4. **Follow up the moment you get more information.**

5. **If the press is involved, be sure you get to have a say in the story, even if it's just a quote.**

   People will perceive you much more positively if you demonstrate that you're taking responsibility for your brand's actions and that you're being transparent.

The people who lose millions of dollars and months of sleep are those who take too long to respond.

Don't be afraid to make mistakes. You can always refine as you go. Online reputation management combines both art and science. As long as you're doing something about it, you're better off than waiting until you feel like you understand everything perfectly.

Document every detail of a crisis resolution as soon as you learn about it and keep records of all communications from related parties.

I'm not sure why, but it's often true that simply being prepared keeps lots of bad things from ever happening. I call it being "loaded for bear." Your brand will be perceived as having it together and not an easy target.

With online reputation management, failure to plan is planning to fail!

Brainstorming: "What's the worst that could happen?"

By now, you're probably thinking that online reputation management isn't all fun and games. Not so!

I want to introduce you to the "what's the worst that could happen?" game. Here's how you play:

- ✔ Round up all your public relations, human resources, legal, and executive crisis response team members.

- ✔ Take them all out for a meal, preferably dinner with drinks.

✔ Get them brainstorming about possible worst-case scenarios. Appetizing, right?

✔ Serve more drinks.

✔ Really start concocting worst-case scenarios that actually could happen.

This next step is where it gets really interesting and when it's time to start serving coffee. Get everybody to look at it from her own professional perspective. You need everyone to

✔ Analyze what possible outcomes need to be avoided.

✔ Share informed suggestions for how this can be done.

✔ Make educated guesses about crisis keywords to tell monitoring teams to watch so that you can have advance notification.

✔ Consider where the silver lining may be to every rain cloud that's being discussed. I'm a firm believer in looking for this in every instance and taking advantage of the momentum of public opinion to move your goals forward.

You will get the best results with this heavy subject by pulling people out of their usual elements and into someplace refreshing and light. I promise it works! You want people to be able to brainstorm freely, and concoct scenarios that just could happen (even though you hope they don't!).

A "good enough" fast response is better than a "perfect" response.

Creating a response video

You may discover one weekend that a member of your executive team needs to record a video with a smartphone so your team can quickly distribute it to all networks. Videos are a great way to add to your more traditional kinds of responses, such as press releases, media interviews, tweets, and Facebook status updates. People are much more likely to share videos, and there's something personal about seeing and hearing the authenticity in someone's demeanor that carries more weight than a faceless statement.

It's often more effective to record something quick and casual instead of flying in a Hollywood team and going the professional route. Just get it done. Casual works, but please avoid filming

✔ **In front of a burning building.**

✔ **In front of something controversial.**

- ✔ **In the presence of a noisy background.**
- ✔ **Wearing red or dark colors.** The colors you wear actually trigger emotional cues. Wearing light colors portrays innocence and likeability. I tell you more about response strategies in Chapter 15, where I go more in-depth about managing social media emergencies.

Be prepared to offer help in whatever way your organization can to make the situation better.

Responding when there's nothing to say

In a crisis, information is in great demand, but it's almost always scarce. When formal announcements are given, people tend to hang on every word. Choose your words carefully. Try not to use words like *always, never, definitely, for sure,* and so on, which are usually exaggerations and are easily contradicted. Here are some safe alternatives until you can follow through with a clear and direct statement:

- ✔ I don't know, but I hope to be able to tell you more soon
- ✔ We're doing ____ and hope to announce something soon
- ✔ Normally
- ✔ May
- ✔ Often
- ✔ Typically
- ✔ In most cases
- ✔ It's possible that
- ✔ It's planned for
- ✔ Usually
- ✔ It's likely
- ✔ It's scheduled for
- ✔ Looks like
- ✔ Prefer to

During a crisis, limit your statements to the immediate problem.

Checking out the competition

It's a smart idea to research within your industry for clues as to what crisis problems tend to develop online. This proactive strategy will you get a jump on what issues may be heading your way, plus you'll have case studies to analyze so that you can learn from what others have already done — successfully or unsuccessfully, as the case may be (pun intended).

Deciding on an effective response time interval

You need to be realistic here, but I can't emphasize enough how glad you will be that you acted quickly to a rising social media crisis. It's the number-one reason why online reputation management plans fail or succeed. Stack the deck in your favor by agreeing in advance on what's appropriate.

If you're serious about making sure your organization's prepared for any crisis online, I highly suggest holding fire drills to put your teams to the test. Hey, it works for the fire department!

Part III
Listening Is Love

In this part . . .

In Part III, I share the basis for all harmonious communication: Listening Is Love. In online reputation management terms, this effectively breaks down into listening closely to what people are saying about you and your brand online. In Chapter 5, I introduce you to the wide world of online monitoring tools, plus I share some special goodies that just might come in handy for your particular situation. Chapter 6 addresses a time-honored favorite: researching search engine optimization (SEO) keywords. Here I serve up delicious geeky goodness in the form of tutorials that show you how to determine your own SEO keywords. With Chapter 7, I give you step-by-step instructions for setting up the basic listening tools that every brand needs for a good listening foundation.

Chapter 5

Choosing Your Best Monitoring Tools

*I*n this chapter, I get to play doctor. The patient, of course, is your online reputation — after all, monitoring mentions of your brand and name online is essential to the health of your reputation, which is essential to the health of your brand. Stick with me for a moment, please, because I have a narrative that's going to help you think about social media analytics and monitoring systems in a brand-new way.

So for this chapter, I'm your doctor. I show you the best tools for taking care of yourself online no matter what size or shape you're in. As with any health-related treatment, this technology evolves daily. Here, though, I do what I can to give you the most accurate, up-to-date information possible about monitoring platforms. By choosing the right monitoring tools, you'll be able to best assess how you're doing and decide what to do about the problems you find. Just bear in mind that the tools themselves will change, and the online landscape may change, but the basic principles that I outline here will remain the same.

Monitoring Matters

Pretend for a moment that I am a doctor and you are coming to see me because you want to be in top physical condition. If all I did was weigh you and give you a 5-minute checkup, you wouldn't trust me, would you? Isn't it unlikely that I could accurately assess your condition after such a brief exam?

It's the same with assessing the health of your reputation online. You need to either hire a professional with targeted results and glowing client recommendations or use the right tools to gauge your present condition and future progress. Plus, you need to know how to use those tools accurately.

Gauging your condition and using these tools is known as *monitoring*, and it's a big part of online reputation management.

Covering over unfair reviews

You can search for your name on Google or Bing and get an idea about what people are saying about you or your brand online at any given time, but it isn't absolutely accurate. Trusting a Google search to tell you what's being said about you online is about as effective as looking at a newspaper headline and feeling like you already know all the details to the story. The larger the reputation you're managing the more closely you need to monitor what's going on. Search engines have their proverbial hands full with trying to sort out information that's relevant and top quality. They simply miss a lot of information.

This is terrific news if you're trying to bury your one unfair review in the search engine rankings by publishing lots of blog content and positive reviews. Many online reputation management services focus on this aspect.

However, online reputation management is about much more than covering up negative reviews. Responsible brand managers address negative reviews and try to make things right. Sometimes a negative review can be turned into a positive one by the commenter, based on the kind of personal attention and service he received.

This is how you convert people with credible complaints into some of your most passionate supporters online. It's one of the ways that you establish your reputation as a person or organization that operates with integrity and the right kind of pride. Covering things up will make a Google search look better, and sometimes that's what needs to happen when there's been an unfair review or somebody has targeted you for no rational reason. It happens. The online reputation management system I share with you will not only cover up negative reviews, but it will boost your business and be your lifesaving insurance policy in the event of a crisis online.

Your strongest online reputation management involves creating meaningful, appealing, and bite-size content that helps people. This is the kind of stuff that wins you fans and devoted followers who will defend you to anyone and share your best stuff with all their own audiences.

Monitoring misconceptions

While this is no cookbook with step-by-step recipes for monitoring your brand, I have a scalable system for learning and understanding what people are saying about you, your brand, and your industry online. Just being able to learn what people are thinking and saying about your industry before your competitors get a handle on it is a major advantage.

Introducing the system

The world has expanded and yet become very cozy all at the same time, thanks to social networks and blogging becoming mainstream. Your fans, clients, future employers, and friends all expect to see you online. They want to be able to Google your name, your business, and to get an accurate picture about what you're up to and how other people regard you. This stuff is serious. Jobs are won and lost according to how you look online.

Sure, you can cover up bad reviews and artificially create positive ones for short-term gain, but it takes much more than this to cultivate a positive reputation online. By using this strategy you can have a strong, stable, long-lasting reputation online — one that even your grandma would be proud to see. And you never know when grandma may be Googling you.

Here's the basic system:

1. **Run your online business with the same kind of customer service and the same degree of integrity you would apply to a bricks-and-mortar shop on Main Street.**

   Whether you're online or not, when you do good things for people those people will support you. Your customers and supporters are your most passionate allies.

2. **Listen for what people are already saying about you, your organization, and your industry online.**

   Look deeper: You can't catch everything in a simple Google search. Look on social networks and blogs, as well as Google. Make sure you

   • Use the best tools. I show you my favorites later in this chapter, and show you how to set them up in Chapter 7.

   • Monitor for the SEO keywords that I show you how to determine in Chapter 6.

   • Apply the right-sized solution. Once you've decided what size solution works best for your needs, set it into action yourself or create an everyday team to handle this for you. I show you how in Chapter 3.

3. **Craft your crisis communication strategy.**

   If your organization is large, create a crisis team involving executives and representatives from the legal, marketing, and human resources departments. Brainstorm worst-case scenarios and solutions. Decide who's going to be involved and how they are to be contacted. If you run your business by yourself or with a small group of people, at least go through some online nightmare scenarios so you can problem solve. Sometimes you see inefficiencies that you can fix without ever experiencing an issue in the first place. It's great to take this perspective now and then in order to avoid trouble and strengthen your organization's reputation online. (I show you how to determine how involved your strategy needs to be in Chapter 2 and explain crisis teams in Chapter 4.)

4. **Research your SEO keywords.**

   These keywords are the seeds to getting noticed online. Plant these seeds into your content, water them with consistent care, and they germinate into positive, reputation building credibility online in your industry. I show you how in Chapter 6.

5. **Reach out as a friend.**

   Make sure you reach out to

   - *Influencers in your industry online.* It may not be feasible for you to become close friends, but if you demonstrate that you've got something worthwhile to add to the conversation they're engaged in, you each may discover you have more in common than your industry.

   - *Focused interest groups that relate to your interests or your organization's function.* I show you how to explore them in Chapter 11.

   - *Your influential customers, clients, fans, or donors. I* explain more in Chapter 14.

   - *Your existing and potential customers, clients, fans, or donors, no matter how influential they are online.*

6. **Publish engaging content that helps or at the very least entertains people in connection with you and your industry.**

   Weave in your SEO keywords that I show you how to determine in Chapter 6. I share greater detail about how you can do this via

   - *Engaging easily:* In Chapter 8 I show you how to balance buzz with meaning in order to create morsels of information that are too tasty for your followers not to share it with their audiences.

   - *Writing your way to the top:* Check out Chapter 12 for more.

   - *Looking at visuals to spread your message:* Check out Chapter 13 for tips.

7. **Respond to people effectively.**

   Be sure to

   - Avert escalating crisis situations (see Chapter 15).

   - Handle crisis communication (see Chapter 16).

   - Learn from your mistakes and apply productive critique wisely (see Chapter 17).

8. **Promote goodwill online.**

   You need to do this every day, but doing this during and after an online crisis is particularly meaningful. (See Chapter 17.)

 Your online reputation management strategy depends on listening to what people are actually saying about you and your brand — and then responding. Pay attention to people who are talking about your brand and the sites where those people tend to share information online.

Integrating your goals

You can discover and investigate many awesome developments and emerging trends within your industry online, which in turn, you can use to increase your brand's success. Monitoring your industry trends is a great way to be more informed, but I suggest tracking specific terms that relate to the goals you identify for your social media strategy and then communicate to your entire organization. (I tell you a lot more about how to do this in Chapter 3.)

Many social media agencies are just randomly "minding the shop" because they haven't been given specific goals that can be measured. If you don't have a focus for your online strategy, and just use your online reputation management strategy to keep up with customer service, you're probably wasting a lot of valuable opportunities to emerge as an informed and decisive thought leader within your industry.

Making a splash online is lots of fun, but it's a lot more rewarding when you integrate it with a focused online reputation strategy that's going to take you where you want to go. When you're considering what kind of goals you want to set, ask yourself

- ✔ How is this helping potential clients?
- ✔ How is this helping my brand to grow?

 It's perfectly okay to experiment with your goals until you find traction. The key is to keep playing with it until you hit the right note.

Introducing the Tools

You can't monitor your online reputation without the right tools. A great number of tools are available, and in the following sections I cover a number of favorites. Different tools are appropriate for different organizations, of course, so here I break them down according to cost. For example, when I reference "smaller" tools, I'm mostly referring to tools that are a good fit for small businesses because of the price point and range of services. Larger, more comprehensive (and expensive) tools dig deeper into the data stream and slice up more closely defined areas of information into more detailed reports cost more. The most cost-effective tools are the easiest to learn and manage on your own. More advanced platforms offer greater customer service and training benefits. So no matter whether you're responsible for a small business or a Fortune 100 company, you should be able to get started quickly.

Everybody can benefit from using the free and more cost-effective tools, but the larger an organization gets, the more it can benefit from tools that dig more deeply into the massive pool of information and share information that the simpler tools miss. If this is you, check out the larger scale tools I share further into this Chapter. I show you how to set up the simple tools in Chapter 7.

I suggest using three tools in tandem with each tool measuring something different. You will get a much clearer picture when you can look from three viewpoints.

A number of propriety services are also available. Ideally, a proprietary monitoring service is custom made to fit an organization's specific hardware and software needs. It's like getting a suit expertly tailored to fit your body perfectly. This tailor is your best source for information on how the suit is made and can keep up with alterations as needed. Because of this, I can't cover proprietary platforms, but please keep in mind that this is a very new area, and it's much more complicated to get quality results than meets the eye.

If you hire a professional to develop a proprietary, in-house system, I suggest checking her references closely and making sure that she develops something that integrates into your existing systems as seamlessly as possible. Ask her about what kind of results she has delivered for others and what kind of training and maintenance she will agree to.

Keep in mind that new tools spring up overnight, and even the most reputable tools will continue to add to their features over time. Some of the tools I describe here may be different by the time you look at them.

Using small-business tools

This section is ideal for entrepreneurs. The following tools have limited capabilities and involve a lot of manual research, but it's hard to beat the price. In

Chapter 7, I go into much greater detail about the tools on this list and show you how to set up these accounts for yourself:

- ✔ Google Alerts are e-mails sent to you when Google finds new results — such as web pages, newspaper articles, or blogs — that match the search terms you set. You can find them at `www.google.com/alerts`. This service is free.

- ✔ Google Trends is a free service that explores how often topics have been searched via Google over time. You can find it at `www.google.com/trends`. Figure 5-1 shows you how easy it is to get started. Enter up to five topics and see

  - How frequently they have been searched via Google

  - How frequently they have appeared in Google News stories

- ✔ Which geographic regions have searched for them the most

- ✔ **Social Mention** is a free service that provides daily e-mail alerts like Google Alerts does, but it searches social media. Receive daily e-mail alerts to see the latest real-time buzz about you, your blog, brand, product, or company.

Figure 5-1:
Google
Trends.

✓ **HootSuite is a service that you can either access for free or upgrade to its Pro version for $5.99 a month, depending on which features and capabilities you need.** HootSuite has surprisingly robust analytics and is well designed for individual or team use. Its popular dashboard enables you or your team to monitor conversations and track the success of campaigns. The free, ad-supported version can be used for up to five social profiles. You can check it out at www.hootsuite.com.

✓ **TweetDeck is a free service offered by Twitter that you can find at** www.tweetdeck.com. (See Figure 5-2.) It's constantly evolving, packed with features, and is also easy to use. Like HootSuite, TweetDeck offers

- *Columns,* which organize streams of information, such as your mentions on Twitter, comments on Facebook, and saved Twitter searches.

- *Scheduling of updates*, which give you around-the-clock flexibility. For example, you can sit down a month before a special event and schedule notifications over Twitter and Facebook.

- *Filtering capabilities,* which give you the power to save specific searches about anything you may find useful.

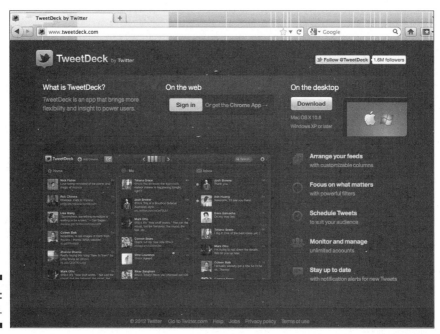

Figure 5-2:
TweetDeck.

- **Trackur (simple plan):** $18 to $377 per month, depending on features and capabilities. This is the simplest version of Trackur, and it includes

  - *Saved searches,* which give you the power to save specific searches about anything you may find useful, whether it's your name, your organization's name, your industry, or even a competitor.

  - *RSS/e-mail alerts,* which send you the kind of information you designate either via RSS (Really Simple Syndication, a family of web feed formats used to publish frequently updated works, such as blogs) or by e-mail.

  - *Sentiment tagging,* which refers to the way people seem to be emotionally responding to the term. This doesn't work perfectly because the way people express themselves tends to vary by geographic region. A kid in Boston may call last night's concert "wicked" and mean it as a compliment, but a sentiment tracker may gauge it as a negative comment. There is still a lot of room for this technology to grow, though it is still really useful to get a handle on a general trend. (For more on sentiment tagging, see the section, "Getting sentimental," later in this chapter.) I discuss the more advanced version of Trackur in the next section.

  - *CSV export,* which enables you to transfer data into Spreadsheet applications like Excel.

  - *Coverage of Twitter, Facebook, and Google+.*

  - *Influence metrics,* which give you information about the kind of online influence that your commenter enjoys.

Using medium-sized businesses tools

At present, the cost of these tools ranges from about $400 to $1,000 a month, but this is subject to change as features change:

- **Meltwater Buzz:** This tool offers social media monitoring, direct social engagement, and social customer relationship management (CRM). Provides deep insight into communications happening across the social web. You can find it at `http://buzz.meltwater.com`. (See Figure 5-3.)

- **Radian6 (basic plan):** This is a more simplified version of the Radian6 tool described in the next section, but it's still robust and highly competitive with the other platforms in this category. You can find more information about both Radian6 plans at `www.radian6.com`.

Figure 5-3:
Meltwater
Buzz.

✔ **Trackur (advanced plan):** This plan includes RSS/e-mail alerts; senti-ment tagging; CSV export; coverage of Twitter, Facebook, and Google+; influence metrics; analytical insights into the information you see; the capability to group results by profile; and branding number of other features for companies offering branded social media services. You can check it out at www.trackur.com.

✔ **Lithium:** Lithium is a social CRM and social listening tool. Lithium's social media monitoring platform is fairly simple to set up, shows results in real time, and finds the best content via social media. You can check it out at www.lithium.com where you can sign up for a free trial and get customized pricing information.

✔ **MutualMind:** Ranked as a top-tier, social media monitoring application, MutualMind packs lots of features, including coverage of consumer trends and sentiment. Pricing packages start at $500 a month, and you can find out more at www.mutualmind.com/plans-and-pricing. (See Figure 5-4.)

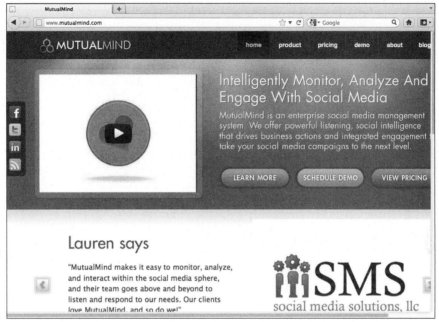

Figure 5-4:
Mutual-
Mind.

Reviewing tools for large-sized businesses

Here's the big end of the scale. The major difference between the tools I have already discussed and these high-end tools is that with these tools you can ask much more specific questions and search significantly larger pools of information. Each one of these high-end tools is distinct, but each of them provides information about search engine results and about

- Blogs, such as LiveJournal, TypePad, Tumblr, and WordPress.com
- Message boards and forums
- Microblogs, such as Twitter and Plurk
- Video-sharing sites, such as YouTube and Vimeo
- Photo-sharing sites, such as Flickr, Pinterest, and Picasa
- Wikis (sites that allow anybody to change or update definitions)
- Social networks, such as Facebook, LinkedIn, and Ning
- Classified-ad sites, such as Craigslist
- Review sites, such as ePinions and Angie's List

Whether or not to make the jump to using these higher-end monitoring tools can be a big decision. They aren't for everyone. Unless you're running social media for a large-scale brand or organization, you can probably get the job done without making this kind of monthly investment. Monthly usage rates for these tools range from about $900 to $3,500 a month, but this is also subject to changes in the technology and pricing structures.

Even though each of these tools searches the kinds of information I list above, they do it via a different method, so you may find one that works much better for you than another. They also change the way they do things frequently, which really changes their effectiveness in certain areas. If you need the best system money can buy, I encourage you to hire a professional who can help you to navigate this process by using three tools in tandem so that you can get a better overall picture.

- **Radian6 (advanced plan):** Radian6 is an integrated platform that gives you near real-time access to social insights like the ones that follow. It's also scalable within an organization, so you can designate which department responds to certain comments. You can learn much more and sign up for a free trial at www.radian6.com (See Figure 5-5.) This platform offers

  - *Demographics,* which give you as much age and gender information as your commenters share on their social profiles.

  - *Geolocation,* which helps you to isolate how different geographic regions are responding via social media to a commercial you are airing, for example.

  - *Influence,* which tells you about the audience sizes people enjoy online.

  - *In-depth sentiment,* which takes a deeper, more exact plunge into online activity that tells how people are feeling about your search terms (in this case, your brand).

  - *Topic categorization,* which gives you the ability to organize conversations by topic.

- **Sysomos:** Sysomos provides tools that measure, monitor, and engage within the social media landscape. As with the other tools in this section Sysomos provides instant access to all social media conversations from blogs, social networks, and microblogging services to forums, video sites, and media sources. You can learn more and sign up for a free trial at www.sysomos.com.

Figure 5-5:
Radian6.

✔ **Alterian SM2:** This is another business intelligence tool that provides a comparable level of visibility into social media channels and lets you tap in to what customers are saying about you and your product. You can check it out and opt in for a free trial at www.alterian.com/social media/products/sm2.

✔ **NetBase:** This is an enterprise-level social intelligence platform. It offers a way to operationalize social media by instantly capturing billions of social media conversations from millions of sites globally. It offers sentiment analysis and clean, normalized data that has been filtered to remove irrelevant content. (www.netbase.com)

✔ **Visible:** Visible (www.visibletechnologies.com) is a social media monitoring and analytics platform. It analyzes social media conversations to better understand consumer preferences, market dynamics, competitive strengths and weaknesses, and other information critical to the company's reputation and brands. (See Figure 5-6.)

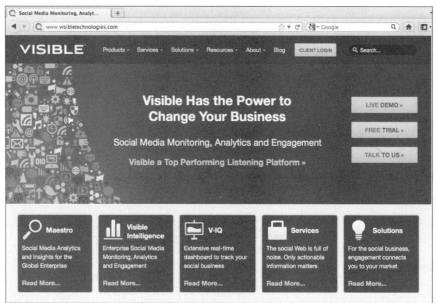

Figure 5-6:
Visible.

Getting sentimental

Some of the tools I mention earlier offer what's known as *sentiment analysis.* This basically means you can program the tool to determine whether commenters are expressing positive or negative feelings. This can be pretty terrific, but it has some definite limitations, such as difficulty discerning ironic comments, sarcasm, or regional differences in speech, such as "bless her heart," which, down south where I live, is not a compliment.

For example, if a New Englander comments that a concert was *wicked sick,* she loved it. Few people in the Southeast, however, would use the word "wicked" to describe something they liked. Sentiment analysis tools are useful, but they haven't quite caught up with some of these regional differences.

One of the most effective, yet cost-effective (meaning: It's free!) resources you can use to check sentiment involves a little bit of time and effort, but it gives you direct access to what people are actually saying about

- You
- Your brand
- Your industry
- Customer service opportunities
- How well your advertising campaigns are doing
- How well your crowdsourcing campaigns are doing

Crowdsourcing means asking online audiences for an answer or to help solve a problem. Many heads are better than one, of course, but crowdsourcing also drives up the number of comments you are likely to receive via social media or blogging.

This tool is Twitter Search (`www.twitter.com/search`). Twitter Search is simple to use. Just enter your search term, and the result shows up, complete with time stamp. (See Figure 5-7.)

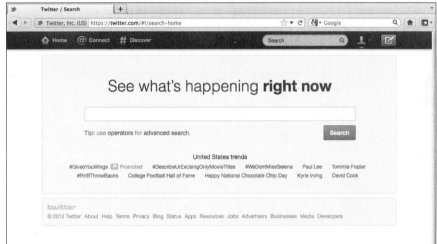

Figure 5-7:
Twitter
Search.

Here, I've searched using the term *chicken wings*. (I chose the term because chicken wings are my younger son's favorite food.) (See Figure 5-8.) From the results, I can track

✔ People who tweet about chicken wings

✔ Top videos of chicken wings

✔ Top images of chicken wings, for when you want to know what the most popular images have been over time

✔ The very latest tweets mentioning chicken wings. This is a great way to see how people are feeling about a given topic and exactly what they're saying about it right now

Twitter Search is particularly cool because you can take a virtual snapshot of how people are feeling about something. A Twitter search for "chicken wings" will result in a list of tweets describing places where people eat wings, how much they love them, how to prepare them, and so on. A Google search, on the other hand, would give you the major chain restaurants that happen to sell chicken wings. Regular people's comments on the matter rank very low in Google's search algorithms.

Crowdsourcing for the little guy

Most people assume that crowdsourcing is only for really big brands with really big budgets. This is not necessarily so. It's basically asking your followers to share with you, and then you listen respectfully to what they share, pick out the best ideas, and reward them generously.

Many people use this to create "Top Ten" blog posts. Consider this one rainy day when you're looking for something meaningful, bite sized, and interesting to share.

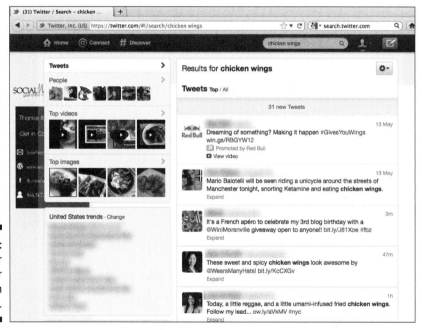

Figure 5-8:
Twitter
Search for
chicken
wings.

Chapter 6

Researching Your SEO Keywords

. . . .

In This Chapter

▶ Discovering what SEO keywords are and why they're important

▶ Building a solid foundation SEO foundation for your site

▶ Researching your SEO keywords

▶ Incorporating SEO keywords into your online reputation management

. . . .

***M**aybe you've never heard of SEO (search engine optimization). Maybe you think that "keywords" are a form of alien communication in a bestselling science-fiction novel. Don't worry! You're in good company.*

In this chapter, I introduce you to SEO and help you to understand why you need it. I show you why you must have the most effective SEO keywords possible to communicate your brand online, and I explain how to research them. Keywords may not seem like much, but they can help you get more traffic, and therefore more clients, and they can keep you looking good online. Even better, you can achieve this just by taking a couple of hours (or less) to research your SEO keywords and start implementing them.

According to BIA/Kelsey Group, a whopping 97 percent of online consumers research products and services online before buying.

Defining Social SEO

Search engine optimization (SEO) is the process of improving the visibility of a website or web page in search engines' regular search results. In plain English, it means using keywords, content, and links to get your organization or name to appear closer to the top of the page when somebody Googles your name or keywords. I tell you a lot more about that and share tips with you in Chapter 6. It's essential to your online reputation management, so please give it your best shot. I promise it's easy to learn and start using in less than an hour.

Social SEO, on the other hand, is a brand-new term that is sometimes referred to as *social media optimization.* Now that social media has become mainstream, relevant and credible news and information often break on social networks like Facebook and Twitter. This term is a new designation that's emerging among seasoned SEO veterans, in recognition of the shift that social media is bringing to the search algorithms

Social SEO is sometimes referred to as "social media optimization." Because relevant and credible news and information breaks in social networks, Google and the search engines now value "temporal relevance" — meaning that fresh and new information, must be more important. Therefore old content has significantly lost search value. Old websites used to rank in search engines because of old practices around keywords, content, links, and other factors. Currently that is still true, but it's not enough. Content needs to also be continually changing, growing, and engaging. For any two otherwise equal posts, the post with more tweets or comments will rank over the other. Credibility is measured on the same factors as before but now the social networks are also taken into consideration.

News becomes more social

These days, I get as much of my news about current events via social media as I do from more traditional means like TV news or newspapers. Word travels faster than ever: They don't call the Internet the information superhighway for nothing.

Huge news that broke on social media

I am convinced that more and more news stories will break on social media. Think about it. News stations are actively recruiting their audiences for fresh stories and footage. This gives average citizens a chance to participate in the flow of information, but it's also a very clear sign of the social times that we live in. The following are seven huge news items that broke on social media:

✔ The royal wedding announcement for Kate Middleton and Prince William broke on Twitter

✔ Whitney Houston's death was first shared on Twitter

✔ Osama bin Laden's death was first learned via Twitter

✔ Hillary Clinton's decision to not serve on Obama's cabinet again broke on Twitter

✔ Egyptian uprising broke on Facebook

✔ Bahrain protesters killed first became known via YouTube

✔ Hudson River plane crash story broke on Twitter

Since relevant and credible news now breaks on social networks, Google and other search engines have come to value what they call "temporal relevance." If information is fresh and new, they reckon, it must be more important.

This is significant because it means that old content has diminished in value. Old websites used to rank highly in search engines because of the way search results were calculated — the old algorithms stressed keywords, content, links, and other factors. This is still true today, but it is not enough. Nowadays, you need to be timely, as I mentioned, but you also need to rank on social networks.

If two otherwise equivalent posts were evaluated by a search engine, and one has more tweets or comments . . . that post will rank more highly than the other. Credibility is measured on the same factors as before, but now the social networks are also taken into consideration. If you want the best standing possible, then, your online presence needs to also be continually changing, growing, and engaging.

Keeping it fresh

The Google Panda algorithm update shook up the Internet world with huge changes to Google's process of assigning weight and value to individual factors when evaluating websites and social media content. A social profile can have just as much value as the website it links to. To be successful, an organization must cultivate a holistic relationship between your social profiles, websites, content, and engagement. You need a strategy that combines modern site architecture, targeted content, and activity-based considerations.

Targeting your content

In this chapter I show you how to identify which SEO keywords are going to work the best for getting your messages seen online. It's important to use them in some of the following places, without making it seem like you're loading a blog post full of the same four terms over and over again in hopes of getting search engines to rank it higher. Folks tried that a long time ago, and Google always gets wise to these kinds of tricks.

One little trick that gets caught (and penalized!) is to host a page that has SEO keywords written in the background color, over and over again. It looks invisible to people, but the search engines pick it up. Frankly, it's a lot less trouble to just write valuable posts that happen to have your keyword phrase in them

 ✔ At the top of the post, preferably the first sentence or paragraph.

 ✔ In the title, if it makes sense to one of your fans reading it.

✔ In both the top and the title, if you can make it sound natural. Your readers are much more apt to share something that is enjoyable to read and useful, and that's more powerful than the off chance that this post will rank a little higher because you used your SEO keywords everywhere possible.

Thinking like a Panda

Since Google's Panda update that I tell you about in the section above, it's very wise for you to focus on more than blog posts, white papers, and articles in order to make your name more visible online. Social media activity is getting a lot more attention, so you can get a real edge over your less social media savvy competition by considering the following

✔ Cultivating more comments on your blog posts. It's often surprisingly effective to just ask people to share their own experiences with the topic

✔ Posting Facebook updates that link to your blog posts

✔ Tweeting catchy intros that link to your blog posts

✔ Guest posting on other sites that will link back to your site via an "About the Author" section where you are featured

✔ Optimizing your YouTube video descriptions so that they link back to your site

✔ Linking to your site via your Pinterest profile and individual "pins" that link back to your site

✔ Linking to your site on your LinkedIn profile and share your posts there

✔ Customizing your Google+ profile to include a link to your site and share your posts there with an appealing introduction

✔ Linking to your site and posting status updates on other social media profiles, such as

- Quora

- Foursquare

- Tumblr

- Podcasts

One of the smartest things you can do to boost your social search engine optimization (SEO) is to hire a qualified expert (with specific, glowing references) to optimize the linking of all your social networks and then review your settings periodically as the online landscape changes.

> ## Social media design
>
> When I first started Social Media Design in 2009, I combined two of my loves: blogging on a WordPress platform and engaging in social platforms. Within a few months, the term social media design became very popular, and my site became number 1 in the rankings out of as many as 1 billion other listings.
>
> I made a lot of mistakes along the way, but I attribute my rapid rise to the top in the rankings for such a popular term to consistent blogging, social media engagement, and paying attention to linking. It's proof that social SEO is worth the time and attention it takes to learn the basics.

Improving Your SEO and Why It's Important

Search engine optimization (SEO) is the art and science of helping people to find your website more easily via search engines like Google. This is important for taking charge of your online reputation management because making your site the most prominent source for information about you gives you a huge advantage in defining your reputation online.

You have a reputation to establish and maintain. There's no better way to establish yourself than to have a vibrant, well-maintained site where people can find you easily.

If you want effective online reputation management, there's no better way than having lots of traffic coming to your site to show who you are, what you do, and whom you do it for. And the best way to do that is to make your website *optimized*.

Joke: "Where's the best place to hide a dead body?" Answer: "On page 3 of Google's search results." The only way to be influential is to be found via search engines!

There are a number of search engines out there, so SEO can seem a little overwhelming. I have good news, however: You really need to pay attention to only two search engines, Google and Bing.

If you can win Google and Bing's affections, you're set in the world of search engines because all the other major search engines in the Western world get their information from these two big kids on the block:

- ✔ Yahoo! gets its information from Bing
- ✔ Comcast, AOL, and EarthLink get their information from Google

Defining SEO keywords

People love to find a site that matches what they thought they were getting when they entered their keywords into the search window. Google does too, and if your site gives people what they want, Google will reward your site with higher rankings.

Rankings are another way to say "search results." You want to be as close to number one for your subject area as possible in order to influence public opinion about your organization more effectively. By properly researching SEO keywords, you can reach that goal.

An SEO *keyword* is a word or phrase of up to five words that people can use to search for you or your organization online. It's the thing that you put into your Google search window when you're looking for an answer to a question or a service. By setting the correct keywords for your site, you can ensure the right audience comes to you.

Some people run a business for years without ever defining their keywords. Maybe you've been in the flower delivery business for years without knowing that your shop isn't showing up in web searches for floral delivery at all!

Here are some reasons why it's worth taking a couple of hours to refine your keywords:

- ✔ **Keywords help you understand what your market is looking for.** Sometimes people are using different terms to search for your kind of business than you might expect.
- ✔ **Keywords drive more traffic to your site.** Since you're interested in managing your online reputation well, it's always good for people to come to you first when deciding how they're going to evaluate you online.

Some goodies that can show up when you do your keyword analysis are

- ✔ You learn fabulous new keywords that never occurred to you to use
- ✔ You can save yourself some trouble by weeding out keywords that aren't being used much anymore

Keywords are as essential to your online reputation management as correct breathing is to exercise. Just as a color scheme can define the decor of your home, your SEO keywords can determine your entire online reputation management strategy.

You need to represent your organization with clear, easy-to-understand branding, and keywords are the bedrock of getting your site found and understood. When correctly used, your fresh keywords show up in your site's architecture, copywriting, posts, and status updates.

SEO keywords help you establish and manage your online reputation, and they're also useful for boosting sales, increasing donations, and generating positive name recognition! When you use SEO keywords, you will see positive results across the board.

It's helpful to think of ways other people may perceive what you offer and approach it from their points of view. For example, if you sell a pain reliever, it's helpful to think about what kinds of pains that your product relieves. People often search for answers online by asking questions. Try to anticipate those questions via your keywords. Sometimes it's easy to assume that everybody knows as much as you do about your field, and you may underestimate how clear you need to make your SEO keywords. Think about how casual web surfers may search for your company.

When your marketing infrastructure runs on current keywords, you're a communications powerhouse! People who understand and love your brand will even be willing to share your messages with their own audiences. This is a major benefit when you're looking to extinguish online forest fires relating to your brand. It's also a lot of fun when you produce a great video or have an uplifting story to tell. People love sharing positive stories with their audiences. It lifts everybody up and creates warm and fuzzy feelings for your brand that are better than any amount of advertising. Positive stories have heart!

Staying up-to-date with search engines

To stay at the top of your field, you need to stay at the top of a search engine's results. However, only one thing stays the same with search engines: change. Google, the granddaddy of all search engines, is always changing. Google continually refines its search engine algorithms so that people can't easily "game the system" by using keywords that don't really contribute to the discussion.

Failing to optimize your SEO keywords is like leaving money on the table.

SEO is a continuously moving target. Even the most experienced, respected experts review their keywords and monitoring tools periodically to stay current.

Organizations at the top of their game hire SEO professionals who constantly investigate and adapt their strategies to Google and Bing's ever-changing, top-secret refinements to their search algorithms. Occasionally, search engines will announce a change in the way their search algorithms work to make sure truly useful sites come up first in their search rankings, but experts debate what these changes mean and how they impact the current thinking and best practices in SEO.

You can keep a jump ahead of most of your competition by starting with a solid keyword analysis and then reviewing it periodically. These are your best approaches

- **Hiring a reputable SEO professional:** Make sure you investigate any candidates. Check referrals and get solid before/after data to make sure your candidate really knows what she's doing.

- **Doing it yourself with some free and/or paid tools online:** Later in this chapter, I show you step-by-step instructions for using Google's AdWords tool, as well as introduce you to some reputable fee-based services.

- **Assigning it to an in-house team:** Make sure your team members have the tools they need — either the tools I share here or something equally comprehensive and well documented. Ideally, your team will comprise a dynamic duo of tech and marketing so they can fuse smart SEO with your branding.

One of the most important things you can do once you identify your best SEO keywords is to make sure that everybody in your organization learns about them and keeps them in mind. You can even publish an interoffice list of keywords that gets refreshed periodically so that everyone on the team is (literally) on the same page.

You'll be delighted with the results if you make sure your content creators, social media team, and crisis team are on the same page as your IT department. Having one clear vision to guide your organization is highly effective when it's been accurately researched, as yours is about to be.

Building a Solid SEO Foundation for Your Site

Google looks at more than 100 factors when it assesses your site. What factors? Well, Google won't tell. No one knows the formula, and even confirmed experts debate about how best to approach SEO. Never fear: Your online reputation management mentor Lori is here to get you acquainted with this fascinating, useful puzzle piece to every online strategy.

It's a cliché by now to say that websites need to be created so that they appeal to search engines as well as actual *gasp* people! As with most clichés, there's a lot of truth to that. I agree: Cater to real people. Give them a compelling site that's useful, interesting, and maybe even entertaining while remaining relevant to their interests. Search engines are looking for quality search results for their advertisers, so you will always be in good taste when you design for people, no matter how often the search algorithms change.

Looking at your architecture

Believe it or not, one of the factors search engines evaluate is how well your site is put together. They look at keywords, which are those things you enter into the search window, and they also look at metatags, which are informative descriptions meant for search engine "eyes" only. A discussion of metatags is beyond the scope of this book, but you should bring up the subject with your web designer, IT staff, or SEO professional. Working with metatags doesn't have to be difficult: You can use plug-ins, such as WordPress's All in One SEO, which can help you to customize your own site with little fuss.

In addition to metatags, here are the three best things you can do to improve your site's architecture for SEO.

✔ **Get less graphic:** Graphics are the heart and soul of many websites. Everything is communicated by using an eye-grabbing banner or graphic with cool information cleverly arranged. Graphics are fun and people love them, but they are often invisible to search engines. People just draw a blank and wonder what else they're going to see that will give them a clue to what your site is really all about.

Eliminate excess graphics where you can and substitute text. Additionally, make sure you use keywords in your headers because headers signal that something important is being said and has a higher value than words buried in the middle of a blog post.

✔ **Tone down the flash:** Adobe Flash animations are also invisible to search engines. Flashy sites (pun intended) leave search engines guessing about what's going on at your site. Also, in 2010, Apple stopped supporting Flash for the company's extensive mobile product line, so the steadily growing population of Apple users won't be able to view Flash animations. Because of the turf war between Adobe and Apple, many modern sites aren't using Flash at all. My advice is to skip Flash and stick to awesome text content, artfully delivered with spot-on keywords.

✔ **Make sure your look communicates your brand:** Sometimes businesses try to save pennies by handing over web design responsibilities to an ambitious teenager, to an employee who normally does something unrelated, like accounting, or to a budget web designer just out of school.

There's nothing wrong with saving a few bucks on web design, but this kind of savings can be penny wise and dollar foolish when it comes to establishing and maintaining your reputation online. Even the best SEO keywords in the world won't do you any good if your site is tacky, old-fashioned, or way behind the times.

You may need to redesign your website before you get the kind of results you deserve. Just be sure to end up with a site that's both SEO friendly and people friendly.

Getting people to link to your site

People who are savvy about SEO may have already asked you to "backlink" to their sites. You may be asking yourself what they mean, how this is done, and why you should do it. Here's why:

- ✔ A *backlink* simply means that somewhere on your site you've linked to their site. It goes "back" to them.

- ✔ Backlinks show Google how popular you are.

- ✔ You get even better rankings from Google if somebody backlinks to your site with anchor text that uses your keywords. *Anchor text* refers to the highlighted words in the link. For example, if you want to write a nice blog post about this book (hint, hint!), you can add the words "Online Reputation Management" to your page and link them to my site at `www.social-media-design.com`. The anchor text in this example is "Online Reputation Management."

Don't play any backlink games to try and fool Google, however. It always finds out what people are doing to "game" their algorithms. I suggest just doing things the reputable way by only linking to sites you actually want people to know about. You're growing your good reputation, after all!

Content

Content is key to creating a strong name online. It also directly contributes to your viable SEO strategy. I give you many specific content creation strategies in Chapters 11 through 13, but for the purpose of your overall SEO strategy, please keep in mind the following tips:

- ✔ Be engaging — the more interaction you inspire, the better.

- ✔ Use the keywords that you will identify while working through this chapter.

- ✔ Keep your content up-to-date.

A few years ago some people decided to jam every post with tons of their keywords. Google wasn't amused and updated its algorithms to actually make those sites rank lower. You only need to use your keywords a few times in your blog posts. Just sprinkle in a few relevant keywords and move on.

Assessing Your Competition

It's easy to get missed if your site looks like a faceless person in the crowd with nothing to distinguish yours from the rest of the brands online. You have to stand out in order to be noticed. I tell you more about branding in Chapter 9, but for right now, be thinking about your service and product offerings and how they're genuinely different from what most of your competitors are doing. If you and your clients agree about what makes you different, then your keyword research strategy is clear.

Sometimes the best resource for figuring out where you want to go is to take a look at what your competition is doing. If you're a solo-entrepreneur, this is an especially good opportunity for you to truly assess what it is you want to provide and to emphasize how you are different.

So charge ahead and look at your competitors' sites. Appropriate great ideas and work with them until they're genuinely your own. Once you figure out whether you want to be doing these same things, analyze what your competition is doing from the perspective of a prospective client. Ask yourself: Does this make sense? Is it complicated or confusing? What's going on here? How can you do yours better?

By all means, take notes on what keywords you keep seeing in titles, headings, and other prominent places. Because most small business owners don't perform a keyword search until they hear enough about it years later, you may find that there isn't really a distinguishable pattern. This works to your advantage until your competitors figure it out and revamp their own strategies. Meanwhile, cheers!!

Again, analyze how what they're doing is working (or doesn't appear to be working) for them and take notes for your own site and strategy. In all fairness, they may have the best product or service ever — but if their sites aren't polished and easy to navigate, they may be suffering from some negative online reputation mojo. I don't want this for anybody. However, because you bought this book (thank you very much!), I owe you straight answers that will propel you along as you become your own online reputation management expert.

Even high-tech companies can neglect their SEO. If hardcore geeks can get distracted from the basics of building a solid reputation online, you can bet your competitors aren't keeping up.

Paying attention to framing

I'm all about framing and don't apologize. Framing is the secret to getting pretty much anything you want in any situation. If you're a parent, you know how clever youngsters can be at framing an excuse, argument, or plea. When your heart melts or you're at least distracted by cleverness, your kids can get what they want—

that later bedtime or a decadent snack. Online communication works the same way.

Your competitor may be framing brilliantly a concept you've been having trouble with. Learn a lesson and adapt your strategy. You can easily reflect the spirit and intent of this better-framed approach without imitating them.

Researching Your SEO Keywords

After all this suspense you're doubtless ready to dive in to your keywords with reckless, overjoyed abandon. It is actually one of the smartest things you'll ever do for your entire online strategy. It's the geeky glue that holds it all together. Let's begin!

Understanding indexing

Indexing is just a scary word for how Google and Bing are keeping track of your site. To evaluate your site, their search engines "crawl" your site periodically, take snapshots of your site, and index them. It's interesting to see what's in there and what isn't. If you're a design addict like me, pay close attention to these results, if only to see how you are being represented to the world via search engine results. You may be surprised.

Your main concern should be to find out what entries Google and Bing are storing in connection with your site. When you know what sites show up, you can take action to eliminate sites you don't like and to promote the sites that work for you.

How can you see what Google or Bing lists about your site? Just follow these steps:

1. **Go to** `Google.com` **or** `Bing.com`.

2. **In the search textbox, enter the term** *site:* **and then the exact URL of the site you want to evaluate.**

   If your site is `myfreakingawesomesite.com`, then your search should be for: *site:myfreakingawesomesite.com*. Figures 6-1 and 6-2 show what a search `for site:social-media-design.com` looks like.

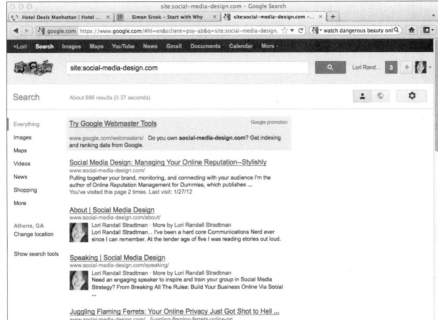

Figure 6-1:
A Google
search for
site:
social-media-
design.com.

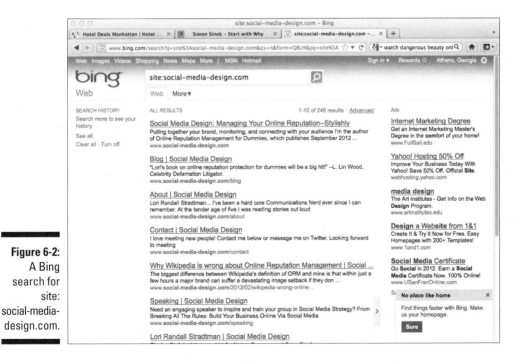

Figure 6-2:
A Bing
search for
site:
social-media-
design.com.

Google will show you a list of the pages it's indexed for your site. I encourage you to take stock of what you see and to set some benchmarks for your online reputation growth. If your site's been around for a couple of years and you have only a handful of indexed pages, then it's time to get started with a redesign. It may be the smartest thing you ever do to establish and maintain a vibrant online reputation.

Here are some important things to look at:

- ✔ **The underlined part:** It's a hyperlink and it comes from a part of your site's HTML called the Title tag.

- ✔ **The text part:** It comes from that description metatag I told you about earlier in this chapter. Casual visitors won't see the metatag — they'll only see the awesome content you create for them.

- ✔ **The URL part:** This may represent a "cached" link. Click on it to see a stored page that Google saved from the last time that it crawled this page. This can be mighty handy if this page on your site got damaged or lost. Your IT pro will back me on this.

All other major search engines in the Western world get their information from Google and Bing, so unless you're interested in a deep exploration, just look at those two search engines and your every SEO wish will come true, sort of. At least you'll be over 97 percent covered.

Beginning your keyword research

As you embark on your keyword research, I suggest starting with the smartest, easiest place on earth, which is your website's analytics report. This report tracks how users get to your site and what they do when they get there. Website analytics are an awfully handy tool for discovering the search terms that brought people to your site in the past. If these terms are relevant, you need to put them at the top of your list of keywords.

Once you've looked through your analytics for relevant search terms that people are already using to find you, it's time to play some guessing games about what search terms people are using that will lead them to relevant information on your site.

I'm making a foolish assumption that you have analytics installed on your website. If you don't, please have your web designer visit www.google.com/analytics to learn more about how to install it on your site.

Playing guessing games

You could almost make a party game at the office with this activity. I may sound silly, but it really is important to be at your creative best while brainstorming for your potential keywords. They're a powerful storyteller for your brand online, and you want to get it right, which can be surprisingly deceptive sometimes.

Here's a good approach:

1. **Create a situation where everybody's as fresh and relaxed as possible and write down a list of ideal words and phrases that you'd like to be searched on that are relevant to what you do.**

2. **If your organization is tied to a geographical area (like a house painting service), then add that region.**

   For example: "Happy Hippie Housepainters of San Francisco." If that's your business name, run with it via your geographical area. This should be your first keyword. Create several, depending on the size and activities of your organization.

3. **List important terms, such as those that describe your organization, services, and products.**

4. **Review these results with each other and see what develops.**

Using the Google AdWords tool

Google's AdWords tool is not only free, but it's also the best tool to use in your quest for the most viable keywords for your brand. (See Figure 6-3.) AdWords should not be the only tool in your proverbial SEO keyword toolbox, but it's the most respected and widely used one. Here are a couple handy features within that toolbox that you can explore:

- ✔ **Keyword Selector Tool:** `https://adwords.google.com/select/KeywordToolExternal`

- ✔ **AdCopy Brainstorm Tool:** `https://adwords.google.com/select/AdTargetingPreviewTool`

Google AdWords is a tool designed to help people with pay-per-click campaigns. While it's a useful tool for researching SEO keywords, it isn't entirely a good fit.

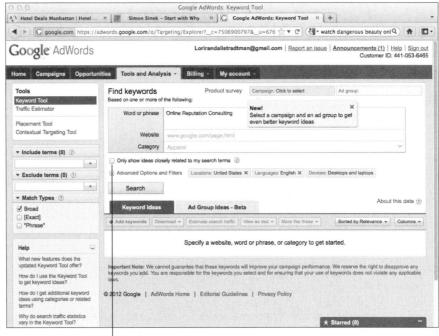

Figure 6-3:
Google
AdWords
tool.

Don't limit your search by clicking this box.

With AdWords, keyword research can be really fun. I like to approach it while I'm feeling fresh and creative because you never know what brainstorms may come up that help you to refine how you want to present yourself to the world online. Google's AdWords tool is marvelously versatile. It can perform in-depth, targeted search analyses and use comparisons for the following kinds of things:

✔ All the wonderful keywords you thought up earlier

✔ Phrases that you feel people will search for when looking for your brand

✔ Website URLs for your competitors to see what terms relate to their sites

If you've never used Google AdWords, never fear. Here's your step-by-step guide to getting started easily.

1. **Go to** `Adwords.Google.com` **and create your free account.**

   You don't have to enter any kind of payment information, but it does work to your advantage to be logged in. Google gives you more information if you log in (refer to Figure 6-3).

2. **Click on the Tools and Analysis tab.**

   A small drop-down arrow appears on the right side of this tab.

3. **Scroll down. On the menu on the left, choose Keyword Tool.**

If you want, you can dig a little deeper by taking advantage of a few built-in settings. For example, a search for *online reputation consulting* would produce results featuring only terms that include the words "online reputation con-sulting," such as

✔ "Best online reputation consulting"

✔ "Online reputation consulting for dummies"

✔ "Online reputation consulting in the United States"

This can be rather limiting. I suggest that you ask Google to show you a wider range of terms. Make sure the Only Show Ideas Closely Related to My Search Terms is not selected. (Refer to Figure 6-3.)

Using AdWords advanced options

When you go a little deeper down this proverbial rabbit hole and adjust your Advanced Options and Filters, you are likely to yield even more information, such as: Which kinds of devices are being used to search for your keyword? You could find out that most people looking for an "online reputation consul-tant" are searching via "all mobile devices" instead of "desktop and laptop devices."

All you need to do to access these goodies is to click on the small blue box just to the left of this option. Figure 6-4 shows you exactly what this looks like. I've also set the number 500 over in the right-hand side box in the "filter ideas" section. This means that I'd prefer to only see what kinds of terms got searched within my location (in this case, the United States) at least 500 times. I suggest you refine your search with a number because it saves you time and trouble. And that's what I'm here for, isn't it?

Figure 6-5 shows you what my results are for "online reputation consulting." Interestingly there were no results! But remember, I specify that I don't want results of fewer than 500 searches a month in the United States. This informa-tion will vary from time to time, based on what people are thinking and doing online. That said, I suggest you refresh your keywords at least once a year, if not more often, if you're involved in fields that move fast, like technology or communication.

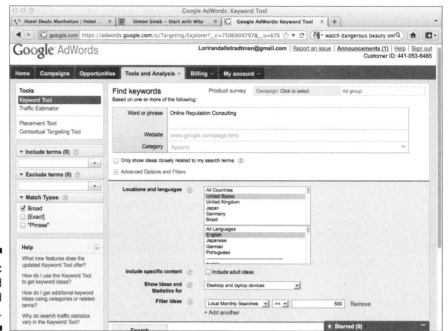

Figure 6-4:
Advanced
options and
filters.

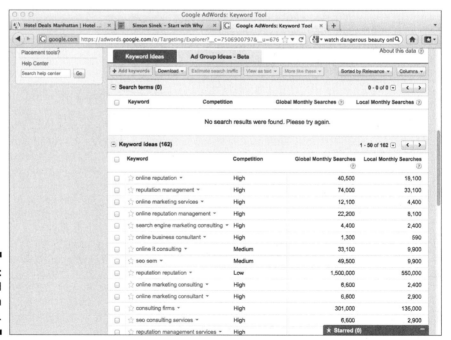

Figure 6-5:
Keyword
search
results.

From this point, there are many ways you can refine your settings and rear-range how your search information is displayed. For example, you can click on Global Monthly Searches to have your results ordered in terms of the highest number of clicks.

Exploring paid options

If you'd rather use a reputable service to perform your keyword research, the following screenshots show you my best suggestions. Many of them help you to organize your keywords according to projects or an area of expertise, which I find very handy:

- **Wordtracker:** Wordtracker is a service that helps you to find the key-words relevant to your brand that aren't being used by your competitors. It gives you a better chance of getting found via search engines. You can check it out at www.wordtracker.com. (See Figure 6-6.) It offers

  - A free seven-day trial on the entire site, though you have to enter your credit card information, phone number, and e-mail address

  - Keyword research

  - Link-building tool

  - A "Strategizer" tool that helps you to find keywords that only a few competitors are using

Figure 6-6:
Wordtracker keyword research tool.

✔ **KeywordSpy:** KeywordSpy (www.keywordspy.com) shows you the keywords your competitors are using. (See Figure 6-7.) It offers

- A lifetime free trial, only your e-mail address is required

- Fairly limited access via the free trial, with different priced options
if you subscribe

- Keyword research

- Link-building tool

- Tools for finding profitable keyword+ ad copy combinations

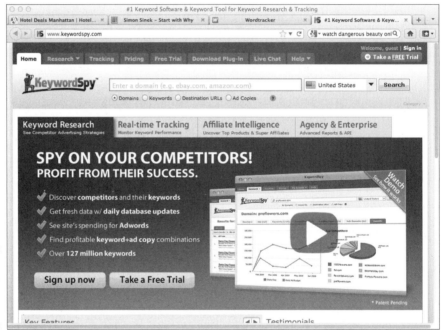

Figure 6-7:
KeywordSpy
research
tool.

✔ **Keyword Discovery (a/k/a Trellian.com, Above.com, PrioritySubmit,
or NeedMoreHits):** Keyword Discovery (www.keyworddiscovery.com)
offers tools that optimize and promote your web pages, to increase your
website traffic and search engine visibility. (See Figure 6-8.) It offers many
things, but these are probably going to be the most useful ones for you:

- A limited free trial, it requires your e-mail address and phone
number

- Fairly limited access via the free trial, with different priced options
if you subscribe

- Keyword research
- Spelling mistake research
- Seasonal search trends
- eBay and shopping keywords database

SEO keywords are a rich topic and can bring a wealth of power to your online reputation management strategy. Use them wisely. Update them every three to six months, depending on your industry. Make sure everybody in your organization has access to them and uses them often.

Now your efforts can be integrated, powerful, and congruent with your organization's internal communication. Aren't you glad you did your research?

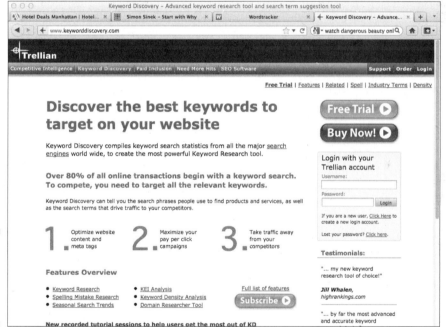

Figure 6-8: Keyword Discovery research tool.

Incorporating Your Keywords

Now that you have fresh, juicy keywords that effectively communicate your brand, it's time to incorporate them into all your messaging online so you can have a coherent, congruent, kicking strategy that's proactive, positive, and ready to communicate your message to the world quickly. I tell you more about creating great messages in Chapter 10, but the following are terrific ways to begin incorporating your keywords right away:

- ✔ **Twitter:** Start by organizing your Twitter messaging so that you address each of your top five keywords with occasional tweets. Give people a taste of what your brand's about. This will drive traffic to your site and work in reverse when it's time for you to push out a message that you'd like for people who understand and love your brand to share.

- ✔ **Facebook:** Revise your Facebook page information to include your new keywords and make sure that your page is now categorized accurately. When I started Social Media Design, I was more involved in creating websites. Now I hire people to do this for me, and I focus more on helping entrepreneurs to thrive online via effective strategy and encouragement. People searching for "Design" are going to find something a little different than WordPress tips and Facebook page design trends. It's important to periodically review your settings so that people searching for your services can find you easily.

- ✔ **LinkedIn:** Create or revise a business page that uses your freshly researched keywords. People using LinkedIn will be able to search those terms and discover you. Ask your employees/partners to link to this page via their profiles so that you can build links, which also boosts your status in the search engine rankings.

- ✔ **YouTube:** Try to use keywords in all your titles and descriptions. YouTube uses entirely different search algorithms from Google and Bing, but these approaches are consistent throughout all the mediums. If I want to create an easily searched video on "online reputation management," I'll create a description something like "Lori Randall Stradtman shows you how to manage your reputation online." This way, people can search for either my name or the subject matter, and my video is likely to show up in their search. YouTube also features a handy keyword area where you can insert your keywords that relate to each particular video.

- ✔ **Blogging:** I cover a lot of ground about your site architecture in this chapter, but just take it a step at a time or hire a pro and tell her exactly what you want before you begin so that you both understand your SEO objectives up front. Life is so much sweeter when our designers understand exactly what we want! Being realistic really speeds along the communication too.

Things you may want to do immediately, in order of importance:

- ✔ Revise the text on your home page.
- ✔ Rework the text on the rest of your pages.
- ✔ Remove unnecessary Flash presentations.

✔ Reconsider the use of graphics to communicate your keywords.

✔ Recognize that you need to use keywords in your post titles as much as possible from now on.

✔ Relax, you're doing great! I'm done using alliteration (for now).

Look closely at every page on your site. Focus on using content with key phrases.

Taking Advantage of Trends

Trends aren't just for music or the stock market. Suppose you're a fancy florist in a large city. Suppose also that a starlet wore a dress made from red carnations to the Academy Awards ceremony, and suddenly red carnations are a fashion rage. You'd want to get in on this trend, right?

You could just stock more red carnations and put up a catchy red-carnation display in your front window. You'd get more business, sure, but what about the online customers who order from you for local deliveries? Unless you're communicating this red carnation trend online, you're most definitely missing out.

Here's what you do.

1. **Update your site with text that talks about "red carnations" right up there in the title, such as "Flashy Fern's Red Carnation Specials".**

2. **Write blog posts featuring discussions about red carnations. Include captioned pictures.**

3. **Share your blog posts on Twitter and Facebook.**

4. **Create a red-carnation–related promotion.**

   The possibilities here are endless: People who mention your clever red carnation designs on Twitter, Pinterest, or Facebook receive a 20% discount, for example. Or anyone who shares a photograph of her purchase from your shop with her online audience receives a coupon for a discount on her next purchase. Just have fun with it!!

Chapter 7

Setting Up Your Listening Tools

. . . .

. . . .

*T*his is one of my favorite chapters. The setups I describe in this chapter are useful for the vast majority of brands (everyone except maybe a Fortune 100 company), cost almost nothing to operate on a monthly basis (outside of payroll expenses, that is), and take little time to maintain. It's an extraordinary amount of value in just a few pages.

In this chapter I, explore several free and almost-free listening tools that you probably should be using every day, if only for 15 minutes, to monitor your online reputation. The larger your name or organization is, the more often you need to check in — and these tools can save you an enormous amount of time.

I start by showing you how to create your Google Alerts. You can set these up to send information right to your mailbox any time your name, company, or industry is mentioned online. I then cover the basics for getting set up on Google Analytics. It's an involved subject, but even getting a simple setup will give you a lot more information than you ever could have imagined about who is coming to visit your site and what site referred that visitor to you.

You can choose from several different aggregators to track mentions of your brand in real time. My personal aggregator of choice is HootSuite, but if you decide to use TweetDeck, for example, many of the same characteristics and tips apply.

Stay tuned for a quick tutorial on Yahoo! Pipes at the end of this chapter. It's a powerful way to host live updates on your site about you, your brand, your industry, or just the fact that you're fascinated with the idea of gophers living on Mars, like me. It's all available to you.

The moment you set up your listening tools, you will have roughly a 1,000,000 times better handle on how people are talking about you and your brand online, as well as keeping track of the very latest trends in your industry.

Online communication is a two-way street. You need to listen at least as much as you speak.

Creating Your Google Alerts

If you want an easy-to-use, not-so-super-secret weapon for staying on top of what people are saying about you, your brand, and your industry online, then you owe it to yourself to set up a few simple Google Alerts. Google Alerts are e-mails sent to you when Google finds new results (something's been changed or added) to the searches that you've entered and saved. You can get alerts for

- Newspaper articles
- Web pages
- Blog posts
- Brand mentions
- Mentions of your name
- Top mentions of your SEO keywords
- Knowing when somebody links to your blog

In just a few minutes, you can set yourself up with custom updates that will be delivered right to your e-mail box on the schedule that you specify. Odds are good that it will take you only five to ten minutes to finish the entire thing, though there are some pretty amazing tricks you can use to give your search a laserlike precision. I cover those, too, mainly because they are fun and more super-secret.

Getting set up

Getting set up on Google Alerts is a three-step process:

1. **Go to** www.google.com/alerts/create. **Then**

   - Log in if you have a Google account.

   - Consider signing up for a Google account if you don't (https://accounts.google.com/NewAccount)

   You are not required to have a Google account in order to set up Google Alerts, but it isn't a bad idea to get one. After all, Google hosts an amazing array of other great, free tools. (See Figure 7-1.)

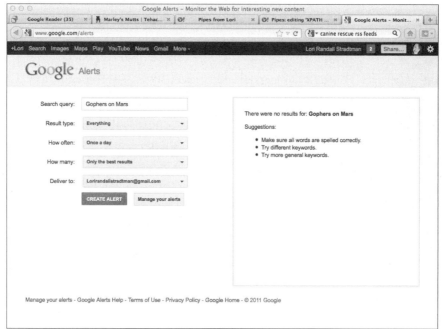

2. **Enter the keywords you want to track, such as** Gophers on Mars, **for example.** The following is a step-by-step guide to help you through the process:

    a. Go to `www.google.com/alerts`.

    b. At the upper left of your window, click Search Query and enter your search term. In this case, I'm using "Gophers on Mars."

    c. If you want, refine your search by type. Click the Result Type drop-down menu and choose to narrow your results to just, say, news sites or blogs.

    d. Choose the search frequency. Click How Often to select your frequency.

    e. Click How Many and choose Only the Best Results (for SEO keywords and industry news), or All Results (for mentions of your name or brand name).

    f. Choose a delivery location. Click Deliver To and select whether you want this alert to go to your e-mail address or to an RSS feed.

    g. Click the Create Alert button, and you're done!

You can create as many Google Alerts as you want. Enter your site's web address as a Google Alert to see who is linking to your site. If you use one last name (say, your husband's) but also have done business under a different last name, create Google Alerts for each name.

Consider how many alerts you'd like to sift through every day. I suggest creating alerts for your name, your brand, your industry, your site, your keywords, and possibly your competition. Get them once a day and only go for the best results and everything but your name and your brand's name. If after a month you feel like you're getting a lot of useless information, go to www.google.com/alerts/manage and make any adjustments necessary.

3. **Organize your alerts.**

Now that you have plenty of alerts coming in, it's time to set up a way to track and organize them. To help manage this new flow of e-mail, try

- Creating a smart mailbox in Apple Mail App or a rule in Microsoft Outlook that will organize these puppies for you.

- Setting up an RSS feed for them so you can read these via an RSS reader. (Go to www.google.com/reader to set up your Google Alerts RSS feed.) Being a Mac user, I like Newsfire, but several other great readers are out there.

Now that you've set up your crucial Google Alerts, consider adding some of these sneaky, er, informative ones:

✔ **Tracking your competition:** No matter what business you're in, you have competitors online. Just for the sake of discussion, if I were your competition, this is how you could set up alerts to track the following. Use the default settings for "result type," "how often," and "how many" for best results. Here's how I'd do it:

- **Mentions of my brand in connection with online reputation management:** "online reputation management" + "Lori Randall Stradtman"

- **White papers that I publish:** "white paper" + "Lori Randall Stradtman"

- **Posts that I share:** "Lori Randall Stradtman" (Just use the result type of "Blogs.")

- **Press releases that I publish:** "Lori Randall Stradtman" (Just use the result type of "News.")

- **My social media profiles and activity (with the exception of my Twitter account and blog):** "Lori Randall Stradtman" -site.twitter. com -site:social-media-design.com

- **Who's mentioning me online:** Lori Randall Stradtman

- **Changes in a competitors site (like mine, for example):** site:social-media-design.com

✔ **Monitoring incoming links:** It's always interesting to know who's linking back to your content. You may be surprised to learn who's interested in your content.

✔ **Intercepting copycats:** If you think you may have a copycat problem (people copying your blog posts and claiming them as their own), write your blog posts to unique phrases like "Gophers living on Mars," odds are good that very few other people will also be using these terms. This gets interesting when you set up a Google Alert for this frequently used (by you) term, and you discover a whole slew of people who are copying and pasting your precious, slaved-over content into their own posts.

Scraping is what seasoned bloggers call copying blog posts and passing them off as one's own.

Sometimes even the nicest people will play dirty without realizing it. Be proactive about protecting your interests online.

Using "super-secret" extras to improve your alerts

Psst. Come here. Yes, that's it. A little closer, if you please. I have a secret to tell you — a secret that gives you laserlike precision on any kind of search you can dream of.

You can use some Google Alerts turbo boosters to make your Google searches more specific and productive. These boosters are called search operators, and searching with them can save you an enormous amount of time and trouble. They may seem a little geeky, but they are worth a little geeky-ness. The following list shows Google's search operator hall of fame and explains how to use each one:

✔ **Searching for an exact word or phrase:** *"search query"*

Use quotes to search for an exact word or set of words in a specific order. Use this only if you're looking for an exact word or phrase; otherwise, you could exclude helpful results by mistake. (See Figure 7-2.)

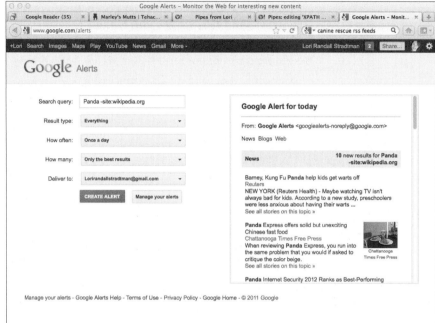

Figure 7-2:
Using
"search
query" on
Google
Alerts.

✔ **Excluding a word:** *-query*

Just type a hyphen (–) before a word in order to exclude all results that include that particular word. For example, if you want to search for the latest news about Google Panda, add a hyphen before the words "animal" or "zoo" so that results exclude updates about, say, Bai Yun's fertility status at the San Diego Zoo.

You can also exclude results from a specific website (for example, enter *pandas -site:wikipedia.org*).

✔ **Including similar words:** *~query*

Typing a tilde (~) immediately in front of a search term gets search results that include synonyms for that term.

✔ **Searching within a site or domain:** *site:query*

Add *site:* (including the colon) and a URL to a search term to search for information that comes only from within that specific website (for example, to search for all mentions of "Olympics" on the *New York Times* website, type **Olympics site:nytimes.com**).

You don't have to use the whole URL. You can search within a specific domain space like .org, .gov, or .edu (for example, *Olympics site:.gov*). You can even search within a specific country by specifying a domain extension like .de or .jp.

✔ **Including a quote fill in the blank:** *" query *query*

Use an asterisk within a query as a placeholder for any unknown or "wildcard" terms. Precede the query with quotation marks (") to find variations of that exact phrase or to remember words in the middle of a phrase (for example, type *a * saved is a * earned* or *" a * in time saves **).

✔ **Searching for either word:** *query* OR *query*

If you want to search for pages that may have just one of several words, include **OR** (capitalized) between the words. Without the **OR**, your results would typically show only pages that match both terms. You can use the pipe (|) symbol between words for the same effect. Here's an example: **olympics location 2014 OR 2018**.

✔ **Searching for a number range:** *number..number*

Separate numbers by two periods (with no spaces) to see results that contain numbers in a given range of things like dates, prices, or measurements. This is an example of what you would type: **camera $50..$100**.

Use only one number with the two periods to indicate an upper maximum or a lower minimum. For example, type **world cup winners ..2000**.

Google's help guide for search operators offers a gold mine of options. Check it out at `http://support.google.com/websearch/bin/answer.py?hl=en&answer=136861`.

Setting Up Your Google Analytics

Google Analytics is a free service offered by Google that generates detailed statistics about your website's visitors. You could spend months getting to know more about Google Analytics, but the most important things you can take advantage of right now are

✔ **Average time on website:** If people are staying on your site for a few minutes, congratulations! You're holding people's interest and educating them about your brand. If not, this gives you a way to track how well your site and content tweaks are resonating with your audiences, in terms of time spent on your website.

✔ **Unique visitors:** Google Analytics tells you how many people come to visit your site every day. "Unique" refers to the fact that if I visit your site 100 times a day, I'll still count as one visitor.

✔ **Keywords:** Tells you which of your SEO keywords (see Chapter 6) are causing people to click over to your site for a visit. When you see a particular keyword attract a lot of attention, it's a good idea to consider focusing your energies there because it's working.

✔ **Traffic sources:** Shows you where your traffic is coming from. Most of my traffic comes from Facebook, for example, so that's useful for me to know that my interaction there is sending traffic to my site. Check out where your traffic is coming from in order to see what's working for you.

Please understand that analytics should represent something meaningful and actionable. Cute graphs are a lot of fun, but it's even more fun when you have a skillful interpretation of what this information means and what to do about it. I suggest you hire a professional or learn how to do this yourself via respected, top-notch tutorials online. They will help you to better

✔ Analyze your site's use dynamics

✔ Suggest adjustments you can make to improve via

- Strategy
- Content

Even though I'm not digging deeply here, I think you will be amazed by the kind of information that you can easily interpret about how your site is doing via Google Analytics.

Although it's possible to create detailed reports via Google Analytics, such as digging deeper into site usage, goals, and e-commerce metrics, you can get a lot of great information without having to dig deep. These simple categories (site usage, goals, and e-commerce metrics) are worth looking at periodically so that you can figure out how your site is doing.

First-blog jitters

I will never forget experiencing Google Analytics in connection with my first blog. I was so proud the first day somebody from another continent visited my site. That person hung out for two whole minutes, looking at two pages. You'd think I had won the lottery I was so overjoyed!

As the weeks rolled past and I got traffic from more than 100 countries, I caught on pretty quickly that this really is a World Wide Web. Even if you're a seasoned blogger, it's a lot of fun to discover the locations of the people who are checking you out.

✔ Tracking what they do while visiting your site, you can glean information such as

✔ Which posts they visit

✔ Which pages they visit

✔ How long they hang out on your site

✔ How many pages they view while on your site

✔ What your bounce rate is (Bounce rate refers to the percentage of users who exit your site after looking at only one page.)

Creating your account

Google offers a wide range of free services. (Google Alerts, for example.) You can sign in to all its services with one Google account, unless you decide to create more accounts, which is an excellent idea if you're separating business and personal concerns. But all your Google services can be organized under one member profile, including Google+.

Setting up your Google Analytics account takes just a few minutes and is well worth your time. You don't need one technical bone in your body in order to get started. All you need is an account with Google. I'll help.

Creating your Google Analytics account

If you don't already have a Google account, use these steps to create an Analytics account with them:

1. **Visit the Google Analytics sign-in page at** `www.google.com/analytics`. **Sign in with your Google account information. If you don't have one, you can create one at** `https://accounts.google.com/NewAccount`.

   Figure 7-3 shows you the sign-in page.

   After you sign in or create a new Google account, you will see the Start Using Google Analytics page.

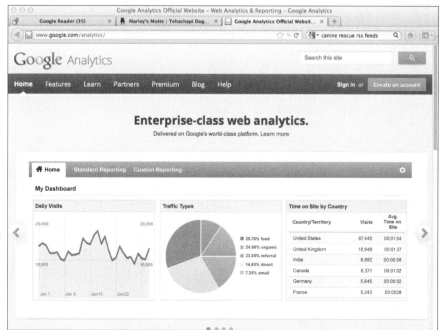

Figure 7-3: Google.com/ analytics sign-up page.

2. **Click Sign In.**

3. **On the resulting sign-in screen, fill in the required fields, read the terms of service (TOS), select the Yes, I Agree to the Above Terms and Conditions check box, and then click Create Account.**

   You are provided with a unique tracking code.

Well done! After you have your unique tracking code, it's time for you to install it into your website. Skip ahead to the "Installing your tracking code" section below.

Check your spam folder if you didn't receive your unique tracking code from Google after a few minutes of creating your account.

Linking your existing Google account

If you already have a Google AdWords account, signing up for Analytics is very easy. Just log in to your AdWords account and sign up for Google Analytics from there, using the preceding steps. These may look and feel a little bit different, but the basics have been there for years and probably aren't going to change anytime soon.

Stay completely safe by backing up your entire site before you add or change anything, including Google Analytics. Even the most innocent change can interfere with your existing setup.

Installing your tracking code

Linking your existing Google Analytics account can be a little tricky if you don't administer your website frequently because you need to install the unique tracking code that you received when you created your Google Analytics account in the preceding section. If you feel a little squeamish about it, ask your web design geek for help.

If you are a WordPress user and feel up to the task, try one of these methods:

- ✔ Copy and paste your tracking code into your theme's `footer.php` just above the </body> tag.

- ✔ Copy and paste the code right into your theme's `functions.php` file. If you need more explanation, you really shouldn't try this at home. Always err on the side of caution with updating and changing your website outside of creating normal posts and updating the copywriting on your pages.

- ✔ Install one of the following WordPress plug-ins and follow the directions carefully.

  - • Google Analytics for WordPress by Joost de Valk (my favorite!)

  - • Google Analyticator by Ronald Heft

Not all WordPress plug-ins play nicely with all WordPress installations. If your site starts looking or acting funny after installing one of these plug-ins, immediately remove it and install your tracking code via another option.

Saying Hello to HootSuite

At the expense of sounding like a dork, I have to say that I absolutely love the social media aggregator called HootSuite (`https://hootsuite.com`). If you're reading this book on an as needed basis, please refer to Chapter 5 for a lot more information on what HootSuite is and what it has to offer. Nobody pays me to say that, and there are a lot of great services, like TweetDeck, that are comparable. As you go through this guide, remember that lots of the same capabilities exist on other aggregators. I just happen to think HootSuite is the easiest to use and the most comprehensive for the price.

Most relatively large companies run their entire social media strategies via something like HootSuite and Google Alerts.

Really large companies, such as Fortune 100 companies, desperately need something a good deal more comprehensive in order to catch and properly analyze all the information being said about them and their industries every day. If you are responsible for running the day-to-day, new-media strategy for you or your brand, you can go really far with these free (or really affordable) tools.

In a nutshell (or should I say owl's nest?), HootSuite offers

- ✔ Unlimited management of social networks and profiles under one interface
- ✔ Scheduling of Facebook posts and Twitter messages
- ✔ Integrated social analytics so you can measure engagement and campaign success
- ✔ Collaboration with team members to enhance social communication and improve efficiencies

Taking a closer look at HootSuite

HootSuite runs from your web browser, mobile device, or tablet. It is pretty much available from wherever you are if you have Internet access. Figure 7-4 shows you what a HootSuite dashboard looks like from the inside. It is made up of different streams of information that you pull together and customize.

Figure 7-4:
HootSuite
dashboard
layout.

The regular version is free, but once you really get into the swing of things or start working with a team, you may want to consider upgrading your account to Pro for $5.99 a month. The Pro version provides the following benefits and more:

- Unlimited social profiles
- One free team number
- Google Analytics integration (now that you've set up your Google Analytics account via the tutorial in the section just before this!)
- Analytics report
- Opting out of advertisements
- Opting out of promoted tweets
- Capability to archive your tweets

HootSuite offers an enterprise option, as well, a scalable solution for businesses to streamline all their social media efforts from one secure dashboard. The HootSuite website doesn't tell how much this exclusive service costs; it is priced by request.

Finally, HootSuite's Pro version offers great functionality for teams of people working on the same brand account. You can invite clients and colleagues alike to participate in your social media management. Assign messages for follow-up and share streams, helping you to increase your efficiency.

I think my favorite part about using HootSuite Pro to manage accounts as a team is that you can share access with team members without compromising your security. The team permission levels and advanced sharing options ensure you remain in control of your valuable social profiles and accounts.

Setting up your dashboard

For the sake of this tutorial, I'm going to assume that you've either chosen the free or the $5.99-a-month version of HootSuite. I use the latter version and am very pleased with it.

Signing up is simple, so I'm launching straight into setting up your dashboard. This is where you will enter all your social profiles that you want to monitor more closely. I begin with Twitter; after you see how it works, you will be able to add your other social networks very easily. It's designed to be extremely user-friendly.

Tabs and streams

One of the nicest things you can do for yourself and streamlining your productivity is to arrange your dashboard. Dashboard is the thing that you see on your very first tab of HootSuite when you log in.

Even though I've been using HootSuite for years, after reviewing all the bells and whistles for this section in the book, I am astonished by how much information you can now view and use via streams. Not many people are talking about it, so these goodies may pass you by unless you take a quick look at what's available to you.

Simply put, a *stream* is a flow of information given in real time that can fit into one of a few general categories, such as Facebook Profile "News Feed — Most Recent," or Twitter "Retweets by me."

You can schedule messages on Facebook via HootSuite, but you get much better exposure to search algorithms if you post directly via Facebook.

Organizing your streams

Organize your streams within HootSuite so that you can have a context for each collection. Here's how:

1. **Create tabs for your personal and business social media accounts.**

   You can customize yours by clicking on the tab and entering your own term.

2. **Group related streams of information under each related tab.**

   For instance, my Social Media Design tab has all the accounts I want to look at every day, organized under that tab heading. It includes

   - Twitter mentions

   - Facebook Page

   - LinkedIn profile

   - Twitter search for the term *Online Reputation*

3. **Create new streams with a search or keywords.**

   For instance, if you want to create a new stream that continuously searches for "online reputation management" tweets you can accomplish this by the following steps:

   a. Click the +Add Stream button at the upper-left corner of the HootSuite dashboard.

   b. The default network is Twitter, so you won't have to click on it, but click on any of the other networks that you have linked to via your HootSuite account.

   c. Click the Keyword tab at the top of the window that appears. (See Figure 7-5.)

   d. Enter *online reputation management* (in this case) and click Add.

Congratulations! You now have a continuously running keyword search for the keyword "online reputation management" on Twitter!

Figure 7-5:
Creating a
keyword
search in
HootSuite.

Shortening links with Ow.ly

A neat feature for sharing links to articles is that HootSuite has a built-in URL shortener called Ow.ly. This gives you some pretty interesting features, such as access to stats (click-throughs, date ranges, regions, and so on), branded URL shortening, and exportable reports that you can opt to receive in either PDF or CSV formats. CSV formats can go into spreadsheet applications like Excel. Ow.ly's tracking campaigns help you to discover how far your tweets go out into the world and who's sharing them for you. These are among your best fans, and it's crucial for you to know who they are and reach out to them on occasion, if only to thank them and find out a little more about who they are and what they do.

You can add a search query in almost the same way, except that you click open the Search tab instead of the Keyword tab, before you enter your search term.

You may want to organize lesser-used, social media networks under a tab called "Other Networks" that you only check in on every week or so.

Deciding on your preferences

The preferences section has some pretty powerful stuff that you should know about. If you are working with the team or manage social media for a company other than your own, I highly recommend that you turn off the new social network selector. Check off all the accounts that you don't want to share messages on accidentally. Reputations have been damaged by tweets that never should have made it out the door.

Another important option is to look at retweeting options. I prefer the old-style retweets because they allow me to edit a tweet or add my take on it before I share. That's what makes things personal or more interesting. Sometimes you just re-tweet something without adding your two cents and that's okay, but I really suggest adding your unique "take" on the tweet and why you feel it's worth sharing.

Attaching goodies

As with Twitter and most other aggregators, HootSuite gives you the option of attaching images and files to your tweets. Its interface is really easy to use. There are different posting options available to you as you click on the message box in order to send a tweet. Please note the icon that looks like a calendar. Clicking this allows you to open your scheduling options.

Dell's command center story

Brands with a comprehensive, truly global reach like Dell have a lot more conversations going on about them and their industries than other businesses. Because of this, it's super important for them to be able to dig down deep into social media, blogging, forums, and more in order to discover just exactly what's being said in real time and to communicate that effectively within their organization so that the right groups of people can be aware of what's going on and take action on that information, as needed.

Dell is a fascinating case story about a brand that didn't just build some cool custom monitoring tools; rather, it built something that its entire organization can use to converse about what's going on elsewhere in the world that affects its brand. People from different departments connect and harmonize. No matter what your budget is for online reputation management, you get a much greater return on investment when you make sure that your company is organized to work in tandem with your social media team by both giving and receiving the latest relevant information seamlessly. Corporate communication has evolved, and the strongest companies are going to change with it.

When you schedule tweets, try to mix things up to keep it interesting. Sending the same message over and over again makes your message feel like spam instead of something important.

Introducing Yahoo! Pipes

I want to introduce you to one final, handy tool that can save you a lot of time and energy as you monitor your reputation online: Yahoo! Pipes. (This is by no means an in-depth tutorial. If you want to dig further, I suggest you try it yourself on Yahoo! or access some of the more popular YouTube tutorials online.)

Yahoo! Pipes is a free service that enables you to aggregate, manipulate, and remix lots of feeds of specific content from all around the web into one handy place. It works in an intuitive way. Instead of feeling dizzy and overwhelmed like you might be if you tried to look up all this stuff every day from different sources, you can have it all delivered right to your e-mail box, RSS reader, or power badge. (I explain these terms later in this section, I promise!)

RSS stands for "really simple syndication." It's a kind of newsfeed that you can send to an RSS reader so you can look through all your RSS feeds in one neat and tidy place. Search online for "RSS readers" if you're interested in using one and want to learn more about your options. Almost all of them are free.

The only drawback to Yahoo! Pipes is that it's different from the way most tools work online. You may take to it easily because it's such a simple, visual tool, but if you're uncomfortable about learning how to work with Yahoo! Pipes I suggest getting your favorite geek to set it up for you if you. I provide step-by-step instructions and screenshots in this section, so you can either take this on yourself or hand it to your favorite geek for reference. The benefits can far outweigh the discomfort, once you create your specialized feeds.

Imagine a turbo-charged, super hero–skilled aggregator on steriods. This is Yahoo! Pipes. While HootSuite offers an easy to use dashboard and is made to work seamlessly with social media teams, Yahoo! Pipes is aggregation software that you can actually program simply by drawing a line (called a pipe) between a couple circles. That's my kind of programming! With Yahoo! Pipes you can create any kind of custom news feed you want. There are many ways you can use it, including

- ✔ You can create an RSS feed and read it from your RSS reader.

- ✔ You can translate news feeds from (and into) different languages.

- ✔ It's automatic and comes to you in a single, tidy information flow.

- ✔ It's powerful and very flexible, so you can customize it to suit your specific needs.

- ✔ It enables you to combine many feeds into one, then sort, filter, and translate it.

- ✔ It enables you to geo-code your favorite feeds and browse the items on an interactive map.

- ✔ It allows you to add power widgets/badges on your website. A power widget (or power badge) is a social media–sharing tool that you can host on your website in order to share all the streams of information that you collated into one news feed.

- ✔ It allows you to grab the output of more than 50 varieties of information publishing "pipes."

- ✔ It's many times more comprehensive than a saved Google Search because it allows you to grab the output of any pipes (of information) such as RSS, so that you can curate content from at least 50 more kinds of sites than Google does. Google searches http (such as FTP sites); it can give you a jump on the latest product details in your industry before even sales websites report the details.

In my case, I'm creating a badge for my website where I can share all kinds of information about my favorite dog breed: the awesomely cute Rat Terrier. Because every Rat Terrier deserves a good home, I've been researching for different sites and Twitter feeds that are worthy of mention. I'm integrating them all into one badge where my site visitors can learn more about the Rat Terrier rescue world in real time. Figure 7-6 shows you the first step in creating a Yahoo! Pipe for "Rat Terrier Rescue."

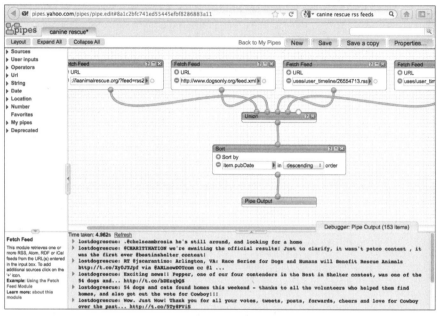

Here's how to get started with your own "Rat Terrier Rescue" pipe. If you really want to create one for something different, say, something that relates to you and your own brand, please substitute with your own juicy RSS feeds. Here's how to create your pipe:

1. **Create a Yahoo! account if you don't have one already.**

2. **Go to** `pipes.yahoo.com` **and click Create Pipe.**

   You see a blank canvas where you can drag modules.

3. **Go to the Library pane on the left-hand side. It's the left-hand column that says "Sources" at that top.**

4. **From there, drag Fetch Feed to the canvas. Copy and paste one of your fascinating RSS feeds into the little window.**

   See Figure 7-7 for what this looks like when all your RSS feeds have been brought in.

5. **Drag the Union Operator over to your canvas.**

6. **Draw connecting pipes from each feed to the top of the Union Operator by clicking on the circle at the bottom of the Fetch Feed box and dragging a pipe to the Union box.**

7. **Drag the Sort Operator over to your canvas.**

8. **Draw a connecting "pipe" from the Union box over to the Sort box by clicking on the circle at the bottom of the Fetch Feed box and dragging a pipe to the Union box.**

9. **Sort by item.pubDate in descending order by clicking the drop-down menu in the Sort box.**

10. **Draw a connection pipe from the Sort box over to the Pipe Output box that Yahoo! automatically put on your canvas.**

11. **Save your work by clicking the Save button in the upper-right corner.**

12. **Give it a meaningful name so that you can remember what you did later.**

13. **Navigate to the top of the page where it says Back to My Pipes.**

14. **Click on your newly created pipe.**

    Figure 7-7 shows a finished newsfeed.

Once you've created a Yahoo! Pipe, you can easily turn it into a badge for your site or any number of different ways to share. It's all shown at the top of your newsfeed page.

You build and edit pipes by moving modules around on the canvas and then "wiring" them together. Don't worry; once you see a picture of this, you'll have a much better understanding of how it works. Figure 7-7 shows you what this looks like.

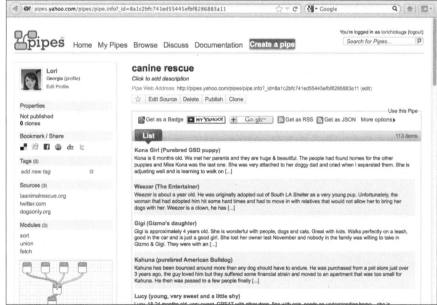

Figure 7-7:
The completed Rat Terrier Rescue Yahoo! Pipe.

Part IV
Establishing Your Reputation

In this part . . .

In Part IV, I take you from listening to what people are saying to deciding how you will respond, and I give you time-tested guidelines for establishing your reputation online. Starting with Chapter 8, I show you how to develop your brand's voice and save you time by showing you how to avoid some common beginner's mistakes. In Chapter 9, I give you ideas for effectively claiming your brand online. Moving on to Chapter 10, I take you deeper into the art and science of creating great messages that get loved and shared online. In Chapter 11, I explain how to tap into focused interest groups that will connect with your industry online in a meaningful (and influential) way. In Chapter 12, you'll draw from your SEO keywords and your online reputation management strategy to write posts and status updates online that get you seen more efficiently. Looks might not be everything, but they may well be online! In Chapter 13, I explore using visuals to spread your message. Chapter 14 rounds out Part IV by telling you how to discover and inspire your best promoters. I share the fine art of discovering and recognizing your own brand-evangelist relationships.

Chapter 8

Engaging Easily via Social Media

· ·

In This Chapter

▶ Developing your brand's voice

▶ Identifying your audiences

▶ Recognizing your audiences of audiences

▶ Empowering your social media team and employees

▶ Customizing your strategy for mobile users

· ·

*B*logging and discussion forums continue to be a big game changer for online communications, but social media networks like Facebook, Twitter, and YouTube put everything into warp speed. When handled with care, this is the most powerful and cost-effective reputation builder available to individuals and organizations today. It's all in how you approach people and how you represent your brand.

Learning how to engage effectively with social media is imperative in maintaining a great online reputation. In order to discover what people are saying about you, your brand, and your industry, you must know how to navigate social media circles. In this chapter I show you how to identify your audiences and communicate with them appropriately via this medium.

Developing Your Brand's Voice

Clearly you want to protect the integrity of your own name online. (Otherwise you wouldn't be reading this!) But is this necessarily a brand issue? In this book, when I speak of "marketing your brand," I'm referring to individuals as well as large corporations. In order for an individual to maintain a reputation online, she first must *gain* that reputation, and the easiest way for her to do that is to think of herself as a brand. A certain degree of marketing know-how is necessary if you want to appear in Google search results or if you want your online presence to include more than just those articles from your college years or your bowling league pictures.

If you are an individual interested in basic online reputation maintenance, then please skip through the parts that are focused more on corporate communications and brand management. You can get all the benefits of online reputation management without nearly as much homework to do!

People look at your brand's voice as a true representation of its heart and soul. Paying attention to what messages people are getting from your brand's voice is essential to successfully building your positive online reputation quickly and powerfully.

After just a few social media interactions, people can usually tell when a company's outside voice doesn't match the inside one. It often raises questions. Organizations with the strongest online reputations and (not coincidentally) success rates use their voices not just for external communications — they integrate those voices into the hearts of the organizations. Such organizations have a thematic consistency, an integrity that resonates from their employees to their customers. If you can achieve this, people will love you for it, and you'll have a stronger online reputation than you ever imagined.

These days, many people are engaging on social media for business purposes. The problem, however, is that so many people don't learn more about the culture on those sites before setting up presences there. They dive in headfirst without really understanding what's okay and what isn't. I congratulate you if you are a social network neophyte who has decided that you're willing to learn how to use them, for the sake of your business. This chapter saves newcomers months and years of trouble that comes from doing what so many people do — treating social media marketing like a used-car sales pitch. This is different. It's a conversation that's sometimes even intimate. It's striking the balance between being a little vulnerable while holding back private information that you've decided isn't appropriate or safe to share.

As you tune in to what your organization's voice is and share it with your psychographic audiences, you will naturally create content that people love and share. And your friends will come to you asking what you do and how you do it so well online!

The more you stay true to your branding message, the more you attract audiences that love it for what it is.

Even if your organization is a well-respected corporate entity, it's important to remember that social media is most definitely not a board meeting. People who make this mistake always end up holding a "bored meeting" where nobody much participates, unless he feels political pressure within the organization to make an appearance.

How can you communicate with social media without boring people to tears? The next few sections offer several ideas.

Spreading good vibrations

Spreading good vibrations is not just for the hippie and surf cultures — feeling good is a universal pleasure! Social networks and online communities evolved because people want to connect with others. We want to feel understood, validated, and, yes, we want the "good vibrations" that come from socializing with genuinely lively, happy people.

It's human nature to want to relate with people who are in a good mood. And nothing puts people in a truly better frame of mind than doing good for others. It turns you into the best version of yourself. Other people notice, and it automatically builds your online reputation. The best way to be liked is to be likable.

Not everybody is an extroverted ball of fire all day long. That's probably a good thing! I love social media and yet I can be downright shy at times. If you sometimes can be shy too, you may be wondering how to "radiantly sparkle" online without seeming fake. My advice is to contribute something good and useful that you really believe helps people. You get bonus points for weaving in a little gleeful whimsy, but it really all depends on who your audience is and what your followers appreciate. You need to radiate the right kind of sparkle for the right kind of people.

Social media team members whom you trust with decision-making authority should radiate true happiness and credibility for your brand.

Standing for something meaningful

When you extend the boundaries of your brand, you can create a powerful vehicle for online reputation management. For example, say you are a dentist looking to attract more clients in your area by building a presence online. You could just share dental hygiene tips (such as brush twice a day) on a website but you'd do better if you approached this from a broader perspective. By associating yourself with a meaningful philosophy, such as "Everybody deserves a healthy smile," your website becomes a force for good. Now your hygiene tips are part of a larger, more comprehensive effort, one that most people can get behind. And from here you can go further by, say, donating a percentage of the profits from every electric toothbrush you sell to a charitable organization specializing in providing dental services to the poor and needy. When you infuse your brand with something truly meaningful, you set yourself apart from everybody else.

Fostering personal connections

The most pleasant, memorable company parties or events promote a genuine feeling of personal connection. With the right personal touch, even if you work in an organization with hundreds or thousands of others, you can feel like a cherished part of something special.

By fostering personal connections, and by using a little imagination, you can breathe life into the most mundane communications. Here are a few tips to get you started:

- **Professionally:** If your organization insists on hiding behind a corporate logo and voice for all communications, I advise you to make the case for a more personal tone, even if nobody knows it's you and not the corporate widget smiling back. On social media sites, "corporate speak" blends in like oil into water.

   White papers accomplish this beautifully. *White papers* are traditionally meant as authoritative guides or explanations. They give you the opportunity to thoughtfully present well-researched ideas or processes that relate to your arena. If you can preserve the integrity of your discussion while infusing it with something that's a hot topic on social media channels, people will share your message with many more audiences. Include some of the tactics from this chapter so that you stay relevant and position your brand as something valuable that people will not want to miss.

- **Personally:** Periodically check the messages sent by you and your team to be sure you're relating to people in a "human" voice. Try to express yourself as though you're speaking to someone in person. Social media isn't a television commercial. Inauthentic voices are routinely ignored online. Managing your online reputation becomes much easier when your tone is consistently "for real."

If you're a solo entrepreneur who's shy about meeting new people online via everyday social media engagement, I suggest you hire a reputable professional or group to do the work for you so you can focus on doing what you do best.

Missing pieces

In order to identify your brand's strengths and weaknesses, sometimes it's helpful to look at yourself from a fresh perspective. In this busy world, it takes a compelling message of integrity to get noticed and attract positive attention online.

With this in mind, ask yourself what the world would be missing if your organization quit breathing. If it isn't vibrant, this is a good time to assess, because an uncommunicative seeming, uncaring organization is ripe for an online firestorm. I want you to be happy and successful, to have a strong organization that never even faces an attack, so pay attention to this section and reassess your goals and current direction. Take steps to continue doing the things that contribute and strengthen areas so that people do feel as though you are listening to them online and care about giving a quality response.

Identifying Your Audiences

Odds are good that you're going to have a series of different audiences online. Some people in your audiences will be those you've connected with face-to-face (such as customers), or they may be people you've met online via a blog or social media and connected with over a shared perspective. These people respond especially well to a personal touch in your messaging, since you have a personal connection. It also holds that they are going to want quality information, of course, but by adding that personal touch you show that you remember them, which is a unique form of appreciation.

On the other hand, some people will be attracted to your presence online because they just like the kinds of information that you share. These people will also appreciate a personal touch, but only after you've taken the time to develop a relationship. I suggest at least checking out their profiles to see what common interests you may have. It's a great way to build a bridge into having a more comfortable rapport.

Make a point to include these newcomers into your online communities because they will share your messages and add to the discussion with their own informed points of view. Information grows and develops with reasonable discourse, so be generous with facts and figures that can cultivate lively and thought-provoking discussion. It's more enjoyable for everyone. Welcoming people who may be more interested in learning fascinating, helpful things about what they love most rather than socializing, can add tremendously to your community by provoking quality discussions.

It's important to recognize that you must cater your communications to your audience. The stories you share with close friends, for example, are probably not appropriate for the About page on your organization's website.

Regardless of who your audience is, assume that they're intelligent, but uninformed. This strategy always works.

Recognizing who your audience is and what kind of followers that audience attracts is crucial in building a great reputation online. As you bear in mind who their people are and what they're likely to want to share with them, you end up creating and sharing really targeted and useful content. Try to put yourself in their shoes.

Every one of your followers is likely to have engaged audiences of her own, whether they're friends or family, business colleagues, or both. With the right post, you can tap in to a lot of social networks.

Making the case for psychographics

Psychographics may sound like pictures drawn by psychos. However, psychographics really are a set of personality or value-related characteristics shared by a group of people — groups of people, in other words, who share the same thinking on a product or subject. Some people refer to these groups as "tribes." When people urge you to "find your tribe" and then "build community," they're talking about psychographics.

Don't confuse psychographics with demographics, which refer to such characteristics as gender and age and income-related groups. Demographics are so last century! Seriously, though, psychographics are surely the future of marketing. With more online communities sprouting up every day, I can't imagine a single psychographic category that doesn't have a passionate community of people discussing it online.

If you're like most organizations these days, you may not have the budget to explore in-depth demographic analysis. But through the miracle of new media, psychographic analysis — spending a couple of hours searching for relevant communities, forums, and groups that are a good fit for your brand — makes a lot of sense.

Think about top magazines that most closely resonate with your brand. They pay lots of money for market research. Take a few tips from them about how to clearly communicate what you're about in a catchy way, and you'll save time and money.

Now that you have all this great information about psychographics and know who your "tribes" are, it's time to get busy searching for online communities, blogs, and discussion forums where these people hang out. Spend some time listening to what people say and how they talk about the subject before you ever begin engaging with them there. Since each group has its own personality and culture, waiting to post until you understand them conveys respect and appreciation.

For example, if you are managing the online reputation for an upscale, boutique yarn company, one of your psychographics is people who love to knit. Armed with information, you can expand your reach by doing any of the following:

✔ Perform Google searches for knitting enthusiasts online by using keywords such as "knitting forums."

✔ Check out the most prominent knitting forums to see what people talk about, what problems they have in connection with yarn, and what they'd love to see in terms of yarn.

✔ Learn the terminology the people in knitting communities use while describing their projects and issues.

✔ Start relating with people on the forum once you have a feel for the place, if it's a good match for your brand. When you engage with these people, always remember to

- Be honest about who you are.

- Respect their community by only adding to the discussion. No sales pitches!

- Use their terminology when talking about knitting, so that you fit in.

- Treat this as a long-term relationship and give it time to blossom. If you don't feel welcome, move on. There are lots of popular forums online with different personalities.

Choosing your social network

In the following chapters I explain how to present visually appealing posts and updates and offer writing tips that help your content draw attention in social media channels. I discuss several social media networks, but I suggest that you focus on, only the three social networks with which your psychographics most closely resonate. For example, if you're a scientist working on solar X-ray measurement, talking about solar flares on Facebook may result in the proverbial chorus of crickets. On Google+, however, more people tend to be interested in science, and you would probably find a bigger audience there. Twitter can also be a great choice, especially if you use a hashtag that looks something like #Xray.

A *hashtag* on Twitter is the "pound" sign followed by a term. You can use these tags to search Twitter for relevant discussions.

Picking the right network for your social media communication is one of the most important choices you will make. Over time you may evolve and adapt, of course, and go through a number of networks before you hit the right one. Here are some popular choices:

✔ **LinkedIn:** Good for professional networking and group discussions. Very friendly toward corporate culture, which makes it a unique social network. Offers content that's fact-driven and less playful than other social media sites. Serious content circulates better here. You can check it out at `www.linkedin.com`.

✔ **Google+:** Runner-up to LinkedIn in terms of corporate friendliness, though there's much more to Google+ than meets the eye. The hangouts feature is particularly powerful and versatile. Hangouts lets you video chat with up to nine people, face-to-face. I plan to host virtual book signing parties via Google+, for example. How much more fun can you have without leaving the computer? It's also home to more men than women and tends to attract a tech-savvy crowd. Have a look at `https://plus.google.com`.

✔ **Blogging:** Interesting platform because you can make it pretty much anything you want for your audiences. It's important to remember that blog readers tend to be more introverted than social network users. Blog content tends to be slower moving and goes deeper. It's the perfect home base for just about any social strategy. Some of the most popular blogs of 2012 include

   • Mashable: `http://mashable.com`

   • Huffington Post: `www.huffingtonpost.com`

   • Lifehacker: `http://lifehacker.com`

✔ **Pinterest:** Feels like the kind of magazines you see at the grocery store check-out line. Shoes, fashion, and craft pictures abound, as well as humor and travel pictures. It oozes estrogen. You can learn more at `http://pinterest.com`.

✔ **Twitter:** Feels like a thriving cocktail party, depending on whom you follow and the time of day. Many audiences embrace Twitter; you can attract whatever groups you want by sharing content that appeals to them. Also updating your profile description with your SEO keywords is smart because people refer to your profile information more often than you may think. You can see what everyone's all-atwitter about at `https://twitter.com`.

✔ **Facebook:** "The Social Network." (One of Facebook's public mantras is "We want to make everything social.") Sometimes Facebook feels like a college dorm. People go there to socialize and share personal information with a group of online friends who resonate with them on some level. It's great for sharing emotional content rather than technical or fact-driven discussions. Learn more at `www.facebook.com`.

Learning from Network Solutions

Network Solutions, a technology consulting company, enjoys great media coverage from top-notch organizations, such as *The Washington Post,* and has garnered prestigious awards and peer recognition — in part because of the company's lighthearted, proactive online reputation management approach.

My friend Shashi Bellamkonda, who crafted the Network Solutions social media strategy, offers these ten approaches that directly contributed to its success:

- ✔ Initiate thought leadership conversations about things customers care about

- ✔ Build online community with good content

- ✔ Extend your brand by contributing to other blogs

- ✔ Get involved in local events

- ✔ Engage in social research by monitoring what people are saying online

- ✔ Host real-time virtual events like Tweet chats and live stream

- ✔ Be transparent during a crisis

- ✔ Maintain an advisory board

- ✔ Reach out to people who send people to spend money with your brand

- ✔ Tell stories via multimedia

Empowering Your Social Media Team and Employees

The most vibrant and healthy social media teams feel empowered to do random acts of kindness for your customers. Savvy companies like Zappos (see the sidebar, "Delivering happiness," nearby) empower their social media team members.

There are many documented stories of people who received flowers or a card during a major life event from a well-run social media team. (Zappos is famous for doing this.)

When you give your team members more control over how they can develop relationships with customers, you'll have happier employees, and most likely happier customers. Give them a variety of tools they can use at their own discretion simply to brighten up somebody's day. They can use these to spread goodwill to customers however it pleases them. Ideas include

- ✔ Free product samples

- ✔ Discounts

- ✔ Advance notification of special events

- ✔ A budget of $100 a month for discretionary spending on clients

- ✔ Beautiful stationery and postage, in case your team member feels moved to write something to brighten a particular client's day

Delivering happiness

At first, online shoe-retailing giant Zappos thought it was in the shoe business. It turns out that it was in the "delivering happiness" business. True, it makes its money from selling shoes online, but the reason it sells so many shoes isn't because it has a flashy logo or because it doesn't have competition — it's because it's good at making people happy. It makes people happy by going way beyond what other shoe retailers do. It commits random acts of feel-good, over-the-top customer service.

Zappos is also famous for going to extremes in making its employees happy, because happy employees make a much better impression on customers. Its founder Tony Hsieh decided to ground the business on the following principle: In order to treat people well, you have to be treated well yourself. He believes in this message so strongly that if an employee wants to quit after the initial employee orientation, Zappos will pay him a thousand dollars.

Since great news travels fast via social media, sites like Facebook and Twitter have been a huge contributor to online reputation success at Zappos. How can you achieve this kind of success? Check out Zappos's "core values":

- Deliver WOW through service
- Embrace and drive change
- Create fun and a little weirdness
- Be adventurous, creative, and open-minded
- Pursue growth and learning
- Build open and honest relationships with communication
- Build a positive team and family spirit
- Do more with less
- Be passionate and determined
- Be humble

Oh! One more thing: Zappos calls its concept "delivering happiness." I agree.

Creating your own successful online community

Your online community should evolve naturally. It's what happens when your organization's voice resonates with your audiences. Still, to get things moving, try these tips:

- ✔ **Ask if people need help (and then help them or direct them to great resources):** For example, if you are a licensed tax preparer, you may ask people to fire away with their questions. Choose some that are more broadly applicable and answer them. Refer them to quality resources for more information, if necessary.

- ✔ **Ask people to help you:** Post a question or a problem and see what happens. You can even ask people in your online community to help you with product development. For example, if you sell fingerless gloves, you may ask your friends in your community whether they think matching scarves or hats that appear to have holes in them are an appealing idea.

 When you give people a platform to share their expertise and perspective, you empower them, which feels really good and builds relationships. It's what distinguishes a true community from a lecture series.

Taking a stand for individual accounts

As you set up your social media teams (see Chapter 3 for the full deal), consider having your members use individualized accounts with their real names. They can still share personal information with those closest to them on social networks. There are definite benefits to keeping it personal, including the following:

- ✔ **Personal accounts get treated better:** Web anonymity makes cruelty easy online. The less anonymous you are, then, the less likely you'll be treated on the web with cruelty. It's harder to be mean to someone whose avatar is a photograph — that is, a real person's face — than to someone with a depersonalized picture, like a logo. Most people respond more warmly to the profile of an authentic-looking person with a realistic profile.

✔ **A human face will emerge from behind your corporate mask:** What better way to win friends and influence people than to humanize your brand?

✔ **You can connect more easily:** It's human nature to want to connect with people rather than things. Even though Fortune 100 companies spend a lot of time and money trying to humanize their brands, the truth is most people will never feel as warm and fuzzy, or allow themselves to be vulnerable, or be as trusting with a faceless corporate entity as they will with a warm, authentic person.

Trying to "speak corporate" in social media is like mixing oil and water. Be personal and really connect.

Earning trust

It's kind of ironic, but simply telling someone to trust you automatically triggers suspicion. It doesn't matter whether you're speaking the truth or not. People want results, not empty promises.

Start building trust by promising small things, like helpful blog posts, and then delivering on those promises. Then surprise your audience by exceeding its expectations — give them bonus materials, such as white papers, how-to videos, or infographics. Or offer a free e-book or a discount on a hot product. You get the idea.

Always make sure you're giving them something meaningful or useful, and with no strings attached. Try these ideas:

✔ Share informational giveaways that are genuinely important to your "tribe."

✔ Explain why the issue you discuss in your informational giveaways is important.

✔ Give some good foundational information for what to do about the issue you explore in your informational giveaway.

People still need to come to you for how to apply these things, so you can earn their trust over time by answering their questions. Remember that you don't have to "give away the farm" with every post or response; you just have to deliver value and maybe point people to a more comprehensive, paid solution that you offer.

Earn bonus points with your audiences by underpromising and overdelivering.

Resolving issues patiently

Patience is most definitely a virtue, but it's a lot easier to cultivate and maintain when you feel like you have some solid backup.

Having an internal FAQ on Google Docs or some other internal network keeps your social media team informed about every important development. When you keep it simple like this, you set your team up to succeed, even with the unhappiest customer.

Your people will be able to

- Respond quickly
- Act decisively
- Think on their feet to brainstorm solutions that fit

Demonstrating human vulnerability

Nobody knows it all, and if she says she does, I start running! It's okay to admit that you need to think something through when you're a business owner, or to draw a blank when being asked an important question. People respect you when you

- Level with them
- Promise to get back with them
- Deliver on that promise within a reasonable time frame

Winning passionate fans

One of the biggest differences between new media and old days is how people expect to communicate with companies. Once upon a time, it was okay to make people wait in line, face a receptionist, or write a letter that never gets answered. Fortunately for consumers, those days are gone.

It only follows that communicating with people via social media should feel as much like a warm, face-to-face encounter as possible. When you give people a cheerful, real person to talk to about their problems, somebody who knows what they're talking about and gets happy at the thought of helping people, you win passionate fans who will defend you and share their great stories about you with their friends.

Customizing Your Strategy for Mobile Users

If you've ever checked your Twitter or Facebook account from your smartphone, you've engaged in mobile computing. From music players that can access the Internet to tablet devices, it seems like everybody is using a mobile device to catch up online rather than sitting by a desktop computer.

Every day, more people switch from using desktops or even laptop computers as their primary computers to using mobile devices. Take advantage of this trend by making sure your content can be easily accessed and shared on mobile devices.

But what difference does it make where people access your information from, as long as they're looking? It makes a big difference, actually! The needs of users on mobile devices are actually quite different for a few key reasons:

- ✔ **Smaller screen:** Smartphones especially have a smaller screen that doesn't lend itself to tiny versions of infographics or lots of text. It becomes tedious to read posts over a couple hundred words unless the subject is very compelling.

- ✔ **Things look different:** Many versions of WordPress now build in a theme for mobile device users, but many sites just look like a miniaturized version of the regular site that was designed to be seen on a much larger screen.

- ✔ **Fewer resources:** Anything Flash-based, like a professionally produced video intro, won't render on an iPhone, iPod, or iPad.

If you're going to engage easily within social networks, you must customize your strategy for mobile users. Work with a web designer to optimize your blog and newsletters. Change the way you write things (see Chapter 12) so that they are mobile friendly.

Technical details about web design are beyond the scope of this book, but these days it's a lot easier to tackle web design than it has ever been. For example, there are even mobile themes for WordPress or mobile versions of existing themes that you can use. My site is built on a platform that looks one way to desktop users and another way to mobile users. I suggest this approach because it embraces the best of both worlds. Make sure your web designer understands designing experiences for mobile users.

Give your site visitors clean and consistent design.

Flashy graphics (pun intended) typically don't translate well on mobile devices. Flash-based animations will not even show up on Apple's mobile devices. They just show up as blank spaces or even worse, a little message saying something like "Apple won't show this." Don't let your readers get distracted by this kind of message or overly flashy graphics that they need a magnifying glass to see on a smartphone. Give them something simple that contributes meaning to what you're writing.

You get bonus points for using funny images to add meaning to your posts. Try to use simple ones that will be easy to see via a mobile device.

Messaging for mobile devices

People use their mobile devices for relaxation at least as much as for getting work done. Walk into any Starbucks on a weekend morning, and you'll see people reading the news, catching up with friends, and checking out what's new in the world via their smartphones or tablet devices. Laptops are becoming so passé!

Here are some tips for messaging for these devices:

✔ **Keep it short and sweet:** You don't always have to scrimp on good posts, but make them the exception instead of the rule and you will hold people's attention over a longer period of time. Many people find it effective to create short posts 75 percent of the time and reserve longer, more involved posts for no more than once a week.

It's powerful when you say a lot with a few words.

✔ **Entertain your visitors:** The more fun and interesting you make your content, the more people will remember you and be interested in hearing more. These days very few people actually go to a website more than a handful of times. The more memorable you are, the better chance you have at getting people to sign up for your e-mail newsletter, RSS feed, or complimentary download. It's the only way to begin developing long-term relationships online.

Chapter 9

Claiming Your Brand Online

· ·

In This Chapter

▶ Discovering what branding is and why it's important

▶ Identifying your target audience

▶ Creating a strong presence via social networks

· ·

Claiming your brand online is a little like what claiming land used to be during the Wild West days of U.S. history. There are few rules and fewer safeguards to your online reputation, and you never know when you're going to find wonderful opportunities or face thieves who will try to take it all away from you in a moment. Just to be clear, when I talk about "claiming your brand," I mean claiming your name or your brand's name on Facebook, Twitter, Google+, LinkedIn, or anywhere else it makes sense for your brand to appear online, including your site's domain name.

If someone else has already claimed the domain name or social media account name that you would like, you will need to get a little creative. I cover more about that later in this chapter. Before you can effectively reach out online to your adoring public — er, *target markets* — you must first identify who they are, where they hang out, and what issues grab their attention.

In this chapter, I show you the best places to claim your brand and some lesser-known places you should establish yourself, in preparation for the day your brand's name becomes a household word. When that happens, be sure to remember your dear friend Lori, who taught you all about establishing your reputation online. I digress.

In this chapter, you also learn about the practical security issues involved with passwords and online account access so you'll have added layers of protection just in case your computer system dies or an employee wins the lottery, leaving you high and dry. This actually happens more often than you may think, because many organizations store all their passwords on (or even under) one computer or with one employee.

With online reputation management, an ounce of prevention is worth a pound of virtual cure. You will learn how to protect yourself from important security issues as we navigate the road to building your successful reputation online.

Establishing Your Brand Online

It may not seem like it, but if you're trying to establish your brand online right now, you are absolutely in the right place at the right time. It may seem that the rest of the world has beaten you there, but nothing could be further from the truth. In terms of legal considerations, social media analytics, and even in terms of culture, new media (social media networks, blogging, press reports, content marketing, and so on) is still in its infancy.

Facebook has become mainstream. You may have already discovered that your parents or even grandparents are socializing with their friends or doing business on Facebook. However, Facebook is only one small part of the picture. There's a lot more to managing your online reputation than making sure you've removed goofy pictures from your Facebook page or discouraging distant friends from posting questionable comments on your Wall.

Everything you need to know about moderating your Facebook content is in Chapter 11. Help is on the way if your New Year's Eva gala was a popular event online and your friends are still posting the pictures to prove it!

Don't just focus on Facebook. You want to distribute your brand as widely as possible. Positioning your brand in more than a couple of places online provides the following benefits:

- ✔ **Makes it easier for people to find you or your business online:** Social networks have a built-in search engine to help you find your friends while you're there. (See Figure 9-1.) Positioning your brand on such networks helps people associate your brand with friends and loved ones and contributes to a positive sense of familiarity with your brand.

- ✔ **Improves your rank on search engines:** Because of the way search engines calculate their search results, the more broadly you position your brand, the better. Your name will show up closer to the top of the normal search results.

- ✔ **Encourages a sense of familiarity:** The more people see your brand, the more likely they are to get comfortable with it. When people have a series of consistently positive interactions with your brand, that familiarity normally turns to trust.

✔ **Keeps posers from faking your online identity:** Celebrities and public figures aren't the only targets for identity theft. Any disturbed person with Internet access and a grudge can create profiles with unflattering pictures in your name or your brand's name. You can prevent this by getting on those networks first, even if you don't plan on being active on that network. It's going to take several years before our legal system can address defamation issues online. It's just too new of an area. You are better off safe than sorry.

✔ **Eliminates risk of name squatting:** Name squatting (or cybersquatting) is a close cousin to the fake identity problem. Name squatters register accounts or domain names in your name or your brand name in order to profit from confusing consumers. Beat cyber creeps at their own games and save your time and money!

If somebody's using your image and information to create a fake profile online, you are well within your rights to complain to his domain registrar or the relevant social network.

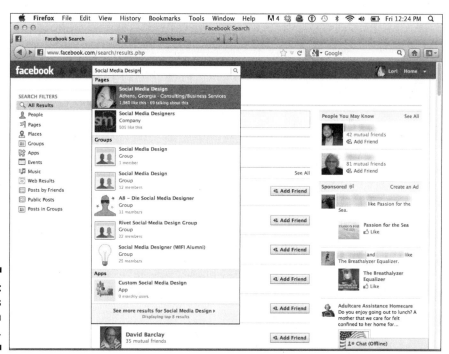

Figure 9-1:
Facebook's search function.

Being in the right place at the right time

Claiming your brand online often looks like a race. Sometimes it's just that simple, but even then you should take the time to do things right. Before you go on a name-claiming frenzy, then, make sure you do things in the right order. And what is that order? Glad you asked! Here it is:

- ✓ Research
- ✓ Decide
- ✓ Act

Research, research, research! If you don't research before claiming your name everywhere online, you could be in for some unpleasant surprises. Not all mistakes are easily reversible. If you find you've signed up with the wrong account name, for instance, you may find the right name has already been claimed.

Here's a step-by-step process for researching, deciding, and acting on your brand's exact identity online:

1. **Do a few web searches on your brand's name.**

   In Chapter 6 I go into much greater detail about SEO and how to work it to your advantage. For now, just search for your company's name and see how many other references come up besides the ones that are connected with you.

2. **Choose the best name to claim.**

   Did your research turn up a lot of similar references? It could be that you need to differentiate yourself from these others based on either of the following:

   - *Geographic region.* If "Bob the Plumber" is popular, try "Bob the Plumber of Guam." You may not believe how many plumbers named Bob roam the Internet, but my imaginary friend Bob the Plumber of Guam is showing up much better in Google's rankings because he differentiated himself by adding "of Guam," even if people searching for him don't live anywhere near Guam.

   - *A specific characteristic of your service or product.* For example, when I started Social Media Design very few people combined social-media consulting with WordPress design. So I combined the terms. This kind of wordplay is great, but don't be so clever that you leave people guessing about what you do. Because I differentiated, and because I often create new content online, my site remains number one in Google's natural results for *Social Media Design.* (See Figure 9-2.) For more about why this is essential, see Chapter 10.

3. **Now that you've decided on your best brand name to claim, establish accounts in that name in as many places as possible online.**

   Get your name out there in as many places as you can. And you'll do well to establish presences on brand-new, trending social media sharing sites before they become mainstream. If you have a nose for news and claim your brand early on those new sites, you will be thrilled by the return on investment (ROI) you get from your time and energy spent there. The time you spend getting familiar with (yet another) social site is normally well rewarded in new contacts and fresh perspectives.

Figure 9-2: A Google search for *social media design* shows the value of differentiating your brand.

Making a statement with your branding

It's true. You never get a second chance to make a great first impression. Within seconds, people decide whether they want to pay attention to your brand's message or move on. It's up to you to focus your message and put it in front of the people who need it most: your target audience.

There's no one-size-fits-all approach to styling your image, but it's important to differentiate yourself if you're going to enhance your reputation online.

Your branding bottom line must be the benefit that people receive from doing business with you. It's what you're known for, your trademark.

People make decisions about your brand with their emotions and justify it with their reasoning later. Use emotional triggers in your design decisions and your marketing. You can use emotional triggers ethically, as long as you're telling the truth about your particular service or product.

Make sure that your testimonials are typical results and are not exaggerated. It's the law!

Some examples include:

- ✔ **Security:** You've taken control of a worrisome issue. For example: "The most trusted name in (product or service)."

- ✔ **Prestige:** You've "made it" because you have this valuable product or service. For example: "We make the ultimate (product) for the ultimate connoisseur."

- ✔ **Luxury:** You feel pampered and indulged, especially when the product is something completely non-essential. For example: "Get away from it all with (your product)."

- ✔ **Trust:** You enjoy a predictable, measurable outcome, such as lower power bills. For example: "Amazing reliability."

- ✔ **Fear:** You feel like danger is imminent. The hottest research in how the brain works indicates that fear may well be the most powerful trigger of all. I try to use this in moderation because although it provokes an immediate response, it can be a drag over repeated interactions. People prefer a positive, energizing, informative online resource throughout a cyber relationship. And you want to create actual connections with people as much as possible to build a powerful reputation online. For example: "There are millions of infected computers conducting illegal raids right now. Is your computer one of them?"

For an interesting read on emotional triggers and branding, read Sally Hogshead's book, *Fascinate: Your 7 Triggers to Persuasion and Captivation*. You can also take her quiz at www.sallyhogshead.com/f-score-personality-test to see what your primary emotional triggers are. It's fun!

Using the New Media Shift to Your Advantage

Traditional forms of media, such as television, radio, and newspapers, haven't gone away, but their influence has waned. The most effective business model has flipped from being media-driven (creating something and then broadcasting to get results) to being consumer-driven (listening first, then creating and sharing). You must pay attention to what your target markets are saying in order to create goods and services that meet their needs. If you can succeed at this, your customers will reward you with loyalty and with positive word of mouth, which can help you in a number of ways: If a crisis surrounding your brand erupts online, for example, customers from around the world will automatically vouch for you. And, of course, word of mouth makes for priceless advertising: In a growing number of age groups, consumers look to their online friends' experiences with a brand or product before they buy.

The consumer-driven business model is a natural business model. After all, listening before you respond is fundamental to basic human communication. Picture two people having a conversation. Ideally, one person listens intently as the other person speaks. The listener does her best to interpret the message correctly (which can be wildly inaccurate if you consider the "telephone" game), takes the speaker's thoughts into consideration, and then responds with her own message.

This is far superior to the broadcast model. When two people talk at the same time, there isn't much higher thought being generated on a topic, and they're certainly not reaching any common ground, which is essential to establishing a real rapport. In this scenario, if real communication happens, it's a complete accident! You deserve better odds.

As with face-to-face discussions, listening online is a form of love. I know I do better when I listen intently first and then thoughtfully respond. Asking clarifying questions helps a lot too. In this attention-starved culture, listening is a gift, and it will draw faithful, responsive people to you online. By earning people's trust, you will gain clients, and you'll also gain friends — people who will speak up on behalf of you when you aren't around online. That's pretty powerful stuff.

Employing the familiarity bias to build trust

It's one thing to connect with people over the products and services you offer, and quite another to make connections so strong your customers feel like family. This is the *familiarity bias* — people will feel more comfortable about you and your brand when you make them believe they have more in common with you than a passionate love for knitting bicycle seat covers, for example.

The need to build familiarity especially applies when you're introducing a new technology or a new idea. Brainstorm to determine the characteristics of this idea most people are already familiar with (and feel positive about!). You may also consider forging relationships with thought leaders or already established brands to help your new idea seem safer.

Tailoring your message to short attention spans

Zzzzzzzzzzip! What was that, you ask? It's the average online reader's attention span! Experts agree that the average person spends less than one minute looking at a website but will spend hours flitting around on social networks because he can customize his experience.

Go with the attention-span flow and position yourself on as many social networks as possible. In Chapter 8, I show you simple, effective strategies for keeping your head above water while still claiming your brand on as many places as possible online.

If you want your message to be memorable and if you want to maintain your visitor's attention for longer than a second or two, you need to keep your message and branding simple. The more I work in design and consulting, the more I appreciate the value of communicating your real, unique value proposition in simple terms. It's more difficult than it seems, but well worth your effort. With people's lightning-quick attention spans online, you have to hook their interest immediately, and without guesswork. You want your page to have just enough distractions to keep visitors engaged, but not so many that they get overwhelmed and seek a more rewarding experience elsewhere.

Colorful, eye-grabbing graphics and effects have their place, but when overused they become distracting and can make visitors feel awkward and overstimulated. Still, when you're trying to attract attention, they can be hard to resist. Just say no.

Hiding your personal-blog identity

My friend Amy recently dealt with the complications of online branding. Amy, a college professor on social media topics, maintained two blogs: a professional blog in which she discussed current social-media trends and gave detailed tutorials, and a somewhat-outrageous personal blog in which she recorded the snarky opinions of a cartoonish version of herself, virtual martini in hand. Amy applied to write for an up-and-coming online social media magazine, but in the course of a background check, the magazine folks discovered her snarky personal blog and were horrified. Their resulting rejection was so harshly worded and insulting that

Amy gave up both blogs and even left her professorship to pursue other, non-Internet interests. She's brilliant, honest, and hard-working, but she's a sensitive soul. She wasn't able to set aside her concerns about future rejections based on her personal blog.

Takeaway: If you choose to express yourself creatively online, consider whether you're up to the criticism you'll get. Some people may love you for being your loveable, personable, outrageous self, but not everybody will. Keeping a completely separate, anonymous blog is your most secure approach to sharing content that may raise some eyebrows.

Instead, follow these rules to make your message instantly memorable:

- ✔ **Keep your message simple and clear.** Write in a style that's more conversational and less like a term paper without losing meaning.

- ✔ **Make sure that all the content you post is consistent with the overall goal of your branding.** Personal blogs are wonderful places to discuss shabby chic craft projects, dog-training techniques, and fantastic food finds. Unless your brand is specifically related to such hobbies, however, you're better off discussing something else. If you must talk about off-brand topics, get yourself a personal blog under a pseudonym and have at it. (See the nearby sidebar, "Hiding your personal-blog identity.")

Identifying your target audience

If you can't identify whom you want to influence, then all the time, love, money, and attention you're lavishing on your online reputation is being mostly squandered.

Identifying your audience is not just for niche brands. Even brands with huge marketing budgets spend a lot of time and money figuring out exactly who their customers are and where to find them. Wal-Mart, for example, owes a lot of its early success to the day somebody defined the target market as people who live from paycheck to paycheck. The rest, as they say, is history. Even if you don't want to emulate Wal-Mart's business model, you must agree the thoughtful attention the company pays to its target market is impressive and successful.

If you're a do-it-yourself (DIY) kind of person (like me!), I suggest the following time-tested advice for discovering who your primary target audience actually is. Although it's a lot easier to look at somebody else's brand and arrive at that "Aha!" moment. Mine remained largely elusive for long months after I transitioned from doing web design to brand (online image) consulting. After brainstorming and muddling through for months, I have finally put together this process that really helps:

Create a list of the most wonderful clients you've ever worked with. Really think about what makes them tick, why they were such a joy to work with, and why you'd clone them if you could, because the experience was so mutually beneficial and fun.

Now ask yourself:

- ✔ What do they love?
- ✔ What do they hate?
- ✔ Where do they hang out online?
- ✔ How did you communicate with each other?
- ✔ In what ways was your product or service exactly what they wanted?

This process can take months, but your answers to these questions will give you the most reliable start.

Protecting your interests

Don't assume that a disgruntled or sloppy web developer, web designer, or social media agency won't block internal access to your social media network and website. Before you do business, get a signed agreement that clearly states that all your social media network access and domain access must be in your company's name with your company's e-mail as the primary contact.

Sometimes even large, prestigious firms say they write code to fit their proprietary platform and (therefore) own all of it. If a client becomes unhappy with the process and goes elsewhere, he leaves empty handed and with no monetary refund. Read every contract you sign and look out for your own interests.

Co-creating your brand with your fans online

One of the reasons identifying your target audience is so critical to your online reputation is that your audience will be shaping your brand with you in the upcoming months and years. The new-media business model, after all, relies on listening to your customers and then making changes according to their wishes.

Because new media is in a constant state of growth and expansion, your online experience evolves by the minute, and the way you communicate your reputation needs to change with it. By staying close to your ideal client base, you'll hit the mark more often than you'll miss and you'll have a more enjoyable time in the process.

Your best branding should focus intently on the benefit that people most enjoy from associating with you (instead of what you think is the most valuable). Beauty is in the eye of the paying client, er, the beholder.

Being Seen in All the Right Places

To get the word out about your brand, you want to make sure you're seen in all the right places. Of course this means adding your online presence on Facebook and Twitter, current popular favorites, but history suggests these sites won't stay popular forever. Where else should you focus your efforts?

Change is the only thing we can depend on when it comes to online communication, particularly social networks. Your best approach is to become an early adopter of as many sites as possible without sacrificing too much of your time.

Being seen in the right places, then, is often a time-management issue. In Chapter 11, I explain more about time management on social media networks, but for now just know that there are strategies for keeping up your productivity as you engage on social networks. You really can engage successfully online and keep your "day" job!

Remember AOL?

Back in 1998, a movie called *You've Got Mail* charmed American movie audiences everywhere. It centers on an online relationship that gets started on an AOL (America Online) chat room. Moviegoers thrill to the familiar "You've got mail" sound as Meg Ryan and Tom Hanks log on to AOL in hopes of receiving mail from each other.

AOL was such a household name that nobody dreamed it would all but fizz out to make room for other Internet service providers (ISP). But it did. These are exciting times, and nobody knows what's going to happen with Facebook, Twitter, or LinkedIn, but one thing's for sure: Competition is fierce, and more networks enter the scene every day.

Learning about how proximity builds trust

When people see that you have a profile on the same network that they use, it builds a sense of familiarity, which creates trust. People who are one click away from you online tend to feel more comfortable with you than people who are a few more mouse clicks apart. It's a subtle way to reinforce your online reputation as they watch you interact over time.

The World Wide Web seemingly bursts at the seams with new social networks, new sites, and new profiles, so it's easy to overlook some lesser-known players. In this section, I cover the most popular (and promising) sites for you to explore, and explain why it's important for you to claim your brand on networks you may have never even heard of.

Here are some great reasons for you to claim your personal or brand name in as many places as possible:

✔ **It prevents squatters from taking advantage of you.** *Squatters* are people who claim web domains, social profile names, and social network business pages even though they have no relationship to the name or brand. They do this in hopes of making lots of money by basically holding the site hostage until somebody pays them enough money to transfer ownership. Establishing your brand presence on a network removes this threat.

✔ **It minimizes name confusion.** This is only going to get more confusing as more people engage online. David Meerman Scott, marketing guru and PR thought leader, used to go by "David Scott," but discovered that in search results his name got lost among the other David Scotts in the world. Adding his middle name helped make him unique and thus eliminated confusion.

✔ **It prevents people from using fake profiles to pose as you.** Celebrities and politicians deal with this all the time: Pranksters hijack their names to pull jokes or to make inappropriate comments. You never know when you or your brand could end up becoming a public figure for at least a limited period of time. Claiming your name as widely as possible protects you from unnecessary embarrassment.

✔ **It improves your rank on search engines.** There's nothing like having lots of terrific information about you "above the fold" in a search engine's results.

Diving in to popular communities

There are more online social networks than you probably ever want to know about, and new ones pop up almost every day. To stay on top of things, you don't need to exhaustively seek out every new site, but you do need to keep your ears open. New sites that people are genuinely excited about and engaged in create a lot of buzz (versus hype). You can spot the difference almost immediately: A promising new network feels energizing, while others feel forced.

Trust your instincts and spend the majority of your time in the networks that feel right for you and your target audiences. Visit the less effective ones only periodically. In Chapter 8, I share tips and tricks on how to keep up your social media strategy without losing sleep.

The following list offers a few places to consider claiming your brand online:

- **Your domain name(s):** YourName.com, YourName.net, and YourName. tv are all good starts.

- **Google+:** It's the fastest growing social network in history, reaching more than 25 million users in its first month. It's projected to reach 400 million users by the end of 2012. Google+ also will map into everything Google does, including Google Places.

  Figure 9-3 shows my Google+ profile. Note the About tab in the center area. You can customize this tab extensively with links and a lot of creativity.

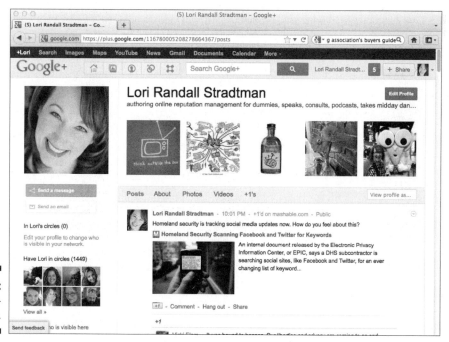

Figure 9-3:
My Google+
profile.

✔ **Facebook:** Hot contender for search dominance online. According to Alexa.com, in some weeks Facebook searches have outnumbered Google's.

✔ **Twitter:** Its unique link-sharing culture helps you to promote your brand to a large audience as long as you're willing to retweet interesting, helpful, or entertaining info from others.

✔ **LinkedIn:** This is the best place to develop your professional contacts and to reinforce your reputation by sharing achievements, recommendations, and more about your education and professional experience.

✔ **Pinterest:** Fun place to create virtual bulletin boards where you share your interests. Linking pictures on Pinterest to pictures on your blog is a great way to improve your search engine results.

✔ **Tumblr:** This informal blogging service pulls together WordPress-style publishing power with awesome Twitter integration. Great place to share images.

✔ **YouTube:** It's the largest video-sharing site on the Internet. Because YouTube is owned by Google, the site is integrated into everything Google (although the search algorithm is completely different), which means it's great for your SEO (as long as it's you posting the videos under your name) and a must-do for your reputation online.

✔ **StumbleUpon:** Social sharing site that gives you the ultimate site-hopping experience, all geared toward your preferences. As you share your favorite posts, people learn more about you and your brand via your profile.

✔ **Slideshare:** Uploading slide show presentations was never so cool or viral. Slideshare has 500 percent more traffic from business owners than any other professional website.

If your brand is confined to a city (if you're managing online reputation management for a restaurant, for example), by all means establish yourself on a geolocation service such as Google Places. I show you more about geolocation services and how to use them to your advantage in Chapter 17.

Great list resources for more networks

Another way to seek out networks is by using an automated service. Just paste in your profile information. The following sites automatically search for your name or brand in a great number of sites and social networks (so that you can find out where your name is taken or available). In addition, these services can help you set up accounts on any of these sites:

- ✓ **Namechk** (www.namechk.com): Complimentary service scans 160 social sites for your name, brand name, or vanity URL in less than a minute.

- ✓ **KnowEm** (www.knowem.com): Another free service, though it searches 590 sites and offers paid packages if you want them to automate your profile creation. (See Figure 9-4.) It's been featured in the *Wall Street Journal, The Washington Post,* and on Fox News, CNN, cnet, TechCrunch, and Mashable.

Copying and pasting your profile information takes only a minute, though you will probably have to resize your image more than once to fulfill the guideline requirements of certain networks.

Both of these sites have received good reviews, but neither worked for me as advertised. I suggest using them to check to see if your personal name, brand name, product, or service name is available on social and bookmarking networks — but sign up for each site manually so that you can be sure it's done correctly.

Figure 9-4: Knowem.com searches nearly 600 sites.

I really prefer to set up accounts manually because you get to fully customize them and take a moment to check out the community while you're there. You may find your target market there and be glad you discovered it.

Consider marking your calendar with periodic reminders to check for new networks every couple of months. I cover this more in Chapter 17, where you learn how to save time and energy with your social media engagement.

Chapter 10

Creating Great Messages

· ·

· ·

*I*n the online marketplace of ideas that is social media, there is no end to information. As social networks become more popular, they are becoming flooded with status updates, pictures, videos, press releases, white papers, and blog posts. Some of this content may be valuable, but valuable content can often be boring — and in this age of distraction, boring content gets lost in the shuffle.

The most compelling content online goes beyond being informative, helpful, thought-provoking, or entertaining. It's done in a way that builds relationships with people.

As the saying goes, "nobody cares about what you know until they know how much you care." The more you level with people as a friend instead of a "guru," the more they'll trust you and care about what you stand for.

The number-one reason why people respond to someone's online content isn't because of that person's popularity (although that helps). It's because of trust. I follow people for a variety of reasons, but the main reason I keep coming back to my favorites is because they deliver top-notch content that I know I can trust.

In this chapter, I show you how to transform ordinary, easily ignored messages into messages that can attract raving fans — no matter what venue you engage in online.

Balancing Meaning with Buzz

Organizations tend to release information to the Internet only when they want to say something specific — that is, when they have a message to broadcast. However, the Internet is a poor broadcast medium. It's a community of voices or at least a two-way dialogue that's open to others. Unless you can find a way to make your message attractive or "buzz-worthy," you don't have a hope of gaining traction with that message online.

When you strike a balance between infusing your content with meaning and making that content appealing enough to share, you become infinitely more trustworthy online. Many people, not realizing the impact of what they're doing, are treating their online content like sales propaganda. In the realm of online ideas and reputation management, the more trustworthy you are, the more people will align themselves with you — they'll sing your praises to friends, and come to your aid when your good name is slandered. You really do get what you give online, so give substantive content that's framed in a meaningful context.

With strong, well-communicated reasons for what you do (besides making money), your online reputation will soar.

The only way you can stand out is to create something truly valuable for your audiences and do it in a way that's charming, funny, expressive, powerful, or otherwise engaging in some way.

Here is my simplified step-by-step plan for engaging easily and effectively online:

1. Define your brand's voice.

2. Weave in your search engine optimization (SEO) keywords in a natural way.

3. Infuse your brand's messaging with meaning.

4. Demonstrate value (results) for what you do or offer.

Using your voice

In Chapter 8, I begin by telling you why having a clear and inspiring brand voice is important and I show you how to cultivate your own. Be sure you use it and adapt it along the way as you discover how people are responding to you.

Oftentimes, what we think we're delivering and what people are getting are different things. Try to put yourself in your audience's shoes as you progress and pay attention to them. You may be surprised to discover how much more enthusiastically people respond to your message.

Once you've defined your brand's unique voice, it's essential for you to integrate that voice consistently, within both within your organization's internal and external messaging, as follows:

✔ **Internal messaging:** This is the way you refer to things between departments. If you're calling something "Project X," it should be discussed as "Project X" via memos, departmental goals, and so on, so that your people can stay focused and rallied around what's going on at present, instead of an old policy or way of doing things.

✔ **External messaging:** This is the way you refer to things (like "Project X") online and via traditional media, such as in posts, updates, videos, press releases, and so on.

Be an original: Your joy of sharing what matters to you most will shine through.

Weaving in your SEO keywords

One way to balance meaningful content with buzz is to weave your SEO keywords into your message. (See Chapter 6 for more on how to research your keywords.) If you've researched well, you end up with a clear, heart-warming message that will attract lots of traffic.

Help people to find your great content by using your SEO keywords in post titles wherever possible. Don't be shy about using one or two of your SEO keywords in each post, as long as you can do it unobtrusively. What I mean is that it should flow with the ideas and with the tone of voice you're using. This needs to feel natural, so that it doesn't look so obvious. It's always better to focus on building relationships with people instead of search engines, but with a little practice you can do both.

Mark your calendar with a recurring appointment to review your SEO keywords every three months. As your listening campaign really dials in to what people are actually saying online about what matters to you (and your organization) the most, you likely will discover buried treasure in terms of how people think about your business and what to do about it.

The original purpose for filling in "alt" tags for website pictures is to give vision-impaired people an idea of what the picture is about. For instance, if your picture is of a dog running beside a girl, you might name it "Fluffy and Buffy," but your alt tag should say something like "dog running beside girl." Besides doing good in the world, you also get SEO benefits when you fill out these fields!

Infusing meaning

Sometimes the best way to explain something is to give an example. Pretend for a moment that you own an air-conditioning/heating service, and you want to tailor your message in the context of keeping air clean for your family, one breath at a time. Instead of saying "take advantage of our annual, duct checkup special," you can say something like "rest easy knowing the kids are breathing clean air with our annual, duct checkup special."

From here you could go further. You could donate a percentage of sales to an organization that helps people who have asthma or other breathing difficulties. Contributing to your community in a real way creates a strong online reputation like nothing else. If you haven't done this recently, brainstorm for what your core values are and how you can express them in a relevant way in your online content.

Giving something valuable

Build your strongest reputation possible online by contributing useful content to your audiences on the different social networks. These proven categories make your posts easy to understand, enjoy, and share:

- ✔ **Tips:** Give clear instructions with helpful screenshots.
- ✔ **Tricks:** Show people how to do something faster, better, or more easily than the standard approach.
- ✔ **How-to's:** Show people how to do something with step-by-step instructions. Include pictures whenever possible. For example, right after Facebook made huge changes to its privacy policy, I wrote a post with simple instructions on how to navigate those new but complicated privacy settings. My post spread like wildfire, and it helped to establish my reputation as somebody who knows how to navigate social media networks reliably. (See Figure 10-1.)

Figure 10-1:
Simple
steps to
control your
Facebook
privacy.

✔ **Timely news:** Be a reporter and break important news that matters to your audiences. If you're a political blogger, be among the first to report new developments in the presidential election and opine about what it means. Facebook especially rates content on how much it's trending at the moment. This gets you better coverage on Facebook's "Top Stories" feed. Twitter and LinkedIn also value timely news with their respective "Trending Topics" and "Trending" areas. You share the exact story a week later and get little, if any traction on it. Remember, timely news updates are much more likely to spread your messages far and wide.

✔ **Relevant trends:** Keeping in touch with trending topics helps your brand develop a reputation as being in touch. Organizations that can adapt more quickly while retaining their voices will build stronger reputations by virtue of having broader, more appreciative fan bases. Even if you aren't in a fast moving industry, you can tap in to trends as a way of keeping your message current. For example, let's say you're a dentist, and you discover that people are starting to use baking soda–based toothpaste more often, you can post about this trend and explain how it relates to your audiences. Show them why it's important. Figure 10-2 shows one way to quickly search for trends.

Rainy day relating

I admit it. Some days, I just don't feel the love as much as usual. If there's been a personal situation weighing on my mind or I didn't get enough sleep the night before, sometimes the energy doesn't bubble up to the surface like it does most days. When I feel less than inspired and couldn't care less about the latest social network that warrants exploration and investigation, I try not to force it.

When people are familiar with you, they pick up on your moods just from the way you post. On days when you're feeling down, don't feel compelled to fake it. Instead, say something authentic that doesn't drag people down, say nothing at all, or get somebody else to cover for you.

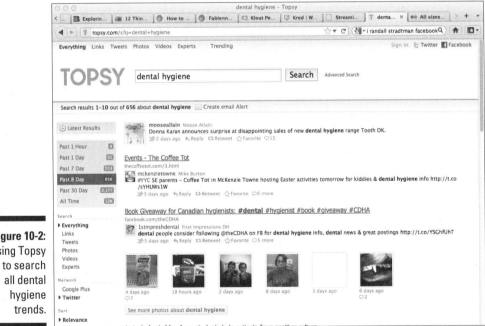

Figure 10-2:
Using Topsy to search all dental hygiene trends.

✔ **Numbered lists:** An oldie but a goodie. Human nature loves a numbered list because you can correctly anticipate what you're likely to get. There are entire blogs devoted to list posts, but I suggest you use them to spice up your content a few times a month. Variety is the spice of life, after all. Stay spicy.

✔ **Research:** Depending on your areas of interest, you may find that you engage in some pretty interesting research. Particularly if you want to establish yourself as a thought leader in your industry, do quality research and share it online via posts, articles, white papers, and e-books. Most people do not charge for these resources, but they make them a free download with e-mail newsletter subscription. Having a robust e-mail list is always valuable to your online reputation management; I include a section on this in Chapter 12.

Adapting Your Message

These days, it can be a little confusing when you are deciding how you want to relate with people online and build relationships via shared interests. It's helpful to understand the differences between social networks and online communities, like message boards, interest groups on LinkedIn, Facebook Community Pages, or forums. Just as there are different dress codes and expectations for places you go to eat, there are different virtual dress codes and expectations for social media networks and online communities. When you engage in these places in a way that's consistent with their culture, you can begin to have interesting discussions and develop relationships with people you respect.

✔ **Social networks:** It's personal. Family, friends, people we know from school, colleagues, and so forth. These personal relationships usually exist "on land" before they're expanded to include keeping up via social media. It's especially terrific for keeping up with friends who live far away from you and whom you want to keep up with. When you engage on social networks, remember that this is a friendship you're developing and it's important to share some personal things that have nothing to do with business.

✔ **Online communities:** It's about shared interests. Whether people in online communities are passionate about geographical location, their profession, hobbies, or even their favorite beer, people love to get together with like-minded others to discuss what they love most. When you engage in an online community, keep this at the forefront of your thinking and talk with people about this shared interest, rather than what movie you saw last night (unless, of course, that's the community's shared interest!).

LinkedIn combines social networking and professional online communities so that they go more deeply into a subject from the perspective of an experienced professional.

Organizing Your Team's Approach

Making a few decisions ahead of time about your team's approach to messaging can save you a lot of heartache later. In the heat of the moment, during an escalating online reputation management crisis, every minute counts. Having an organized team approach to messaging prevents most issues from developing into something unfortunate for your brand. The following are things you need to resolve ahead of time so you can spend the rest of your time planning your next paid vacation instead of worrying about what's going to happen online next.

Approval process

Smaller organizations have the easiest time with this issue. If you're a small-business owner and make all major decisions, you have it easy. Still, you should decide ahead of time what your policy is on different matters that typically arise online, such as requests for refunds, referrals, and requests for proposals.

Having to think on your feet all the time is highly overrated! Settle these questions in advance so you can share a clear policy that's been thoughtfully presented. Having things like this in place helps you to react better in the moment because you've already made that decision. All you have to do is share it in a timely fashion.

Deciding who's guiding

Larger companies may have several departments that are interested in creating a strong online brand reputation and leveraging it to meet their departments' goals. This sounds like a lot of fun until somebody has to make the sticky decision about who's actually responsible for your brand's social media team. Decide now what department is directly responsible for your online reputation management and who will guide the direction you want to go as you build your brand's influence online.

Even though it's wise to give each relevant department a voice in what happens online, you need to establish who's in charge so that you can enjoy a vibrant, healthy online reputation that's able to not only withstand attacks, but also take your business to new heights via online interaction with your customers. The following departments often have a stake in how social media is leveraged online:

✔ **Marketing:** Can help communicate the ways your product or service makes people's lives better.

✔ **Customer service:** Demonstrates how your brand supports customers by giving detailed information and quality service.

✔ **Human resources:** Help with recruiting staff.

✔ **Sales:** Develops relationships with existing and future clients.

✔ **Public relations:** Maintains relationships with journalists and gets the good news about your organization out there.

✔ **Product development:** When your brand has a defined, distinct voice it's easier to engage with people about what kinds of product developments would suit their needs and wants best.

It can be tricky to establish one department as your designated hitter for online reputation management, and yet give the others some time up at bat to take a few swings of their own. Here is my down-and-dirty guide to pleasing everybody at your organization. (Well, almost everybody.) The following is a useful process you can use and revisit as often as you like.

1. **Define which departments get to play.**

   Limit the number of participants to five so that you can keep your audiences engaged by retaining some focus. Nobody wants to know about corn on the cob, air-conditioning, sulfur water, lip balm, and the newspaper business from the same company, unless that brand focuses on entertaining people via trivia, hot trends, or funny stuff. The popular site "Holy Kaw!" (http://holykaw.alltop.com) shares "all the topics that interest us."

2. **Frame these departmental messaging streams as different aspects of the same topic.**

   For example, if you're a running-shoe manufacturer who wants to demonstrate that you care about the community, then "care" is the organizing principle for your messages. To further this message you could

   • Get your PR department to pass along the knowledge that your company has been giving away running shoes to underprivileged high school track teams.

   • Get your marketing department to talk about how your company "cares enough" to create running shoes to the highest standards of craftsmanship.

   • Get your human resources department to "demonstrate care" by hiring the very best talent.

3. **Unify your efforts by creating a shared mindmap document that holds up to five categories.**

   For more on mindmapping, see the nearby sidebar "Mapping your mind."

   Assign a different color to each departmental team involved. For example, Marketing may get purple assigned to its message flow. (See Figure 10-3.)

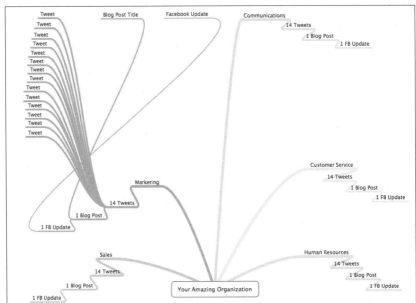

Figure 10-3:
Sample
mindmap.

At first glance, the mindmap in Figure 10-3 may look like multi-colored spaghetti, but it's really just a way to graph out and organize your thought process. Mindmaps are available for free in many places online.

The circle at the bottom of the mindmap in Figure 10-3, the one called "Your Amazing Organization," refers to your brand's voice and primary objective. Each department involved with social media (see the preceding bullet points) is represented on the map by a line with a unique color. Different activities are listed, such as

✔ Blog posts that are written by that department and are specific to their goals and message. All images that go with the post need to be attached, including attribution for photos, as needed.

✔ Tweets that are composed by that department, aligned with their message, and any attachments, such as blog post links, videos, or pictures.

✔ Facebook updates that relate to that department, aligned with their message, and any blog post links, videos, or pictures that relate.

Now that you have defined and color-coded your content streams, you can begin to farm out — er, *delegate* — responsible content creation. The following steps take you through a system that gives other departments full control and responsibility over their content. Everyone is empowered, and your life becomes easier.

1. **Each month, give every department a fixed number of status updates, tweets, and blog posts that it can use to promote its goals.**

   For example, on a weekly basis, this may amount to

   • 14 tweets (2 a day)

   • 1 blog post

   • 1 Facebook Page update

2. **Allow a week for each department to fill in a month's worth of online content on its mindmap.**

   Depending on the number of days in a month, it will amount to a little over the weekly output shown above. If your top online reputation management tools are a blog, a Facebook Page, and Twitter, you also need to specify a number of pictures and/or videos to accompany the blog and Facebook Page updates.

3. **Create a standby mindmap of standard content that can be used as a substitute in the event a department fails to provide all of its content on time.**

   Tardy submissions won't work because everything gets configured at one time to save lots of time and energy. You can reuse these backup content mindmaps monthly as long as your messages remain timely and awesome.

4. **At the end of the first week, combine all the mindmaps and have a designated person check them to make sure that they're complete and then copy them to the online publishing schedule for the entire month.**

   This involves

   • Scheduling tweets via HootSuite or another aggregator (see Chapter 5 for more on aggregators. I give you HootSuite specifics in Chapter 7.)

   • Formatting and scheduling blog posts. Optimize them with your SEO keywords wherever possible, and label your pictures and give them alternate descriptions.

   • Marking the calendar with manual Facebook Page updates.

For maximum visibility and engagement, post your updates directly to Facebook. You can schedule updates via an aggregator if you're pressed for time, but they can get lost in the Top Stories feed. Include pictures and videos whenever possible. They substantially boost your status update's status within Facebook's ranking algorithms.

5. **Toward the end of every month, ask your participating departments to assess their content. They will need to**

   • Review: Take a look at what traffic and responses looked like in the preceding month. Make a note of any messages that were unclear or that inadvertently sent the wrong message. Most importantly, take stock of all messages that were received well and shared the most.

   • Reflect: Decide which messages need to be reworked/omitted, which need to be repeated, and which new messages need to be created.

   • Reboot: Update the existing mindmap and turn it in within the first week of the current month.

6. **Make sure each department creates its own dialogue that clearly addresses each month's updates. It should give department members a place to collaborate on how successful the previous month's messaging was (or wasn't) so that they can adapt their findings when planning messages for the following month.**

   You get serious bonus points for stipulating that it needs to be a shared document on Google or via an internal network, because this makes it super simple for

   • Departments to update as new information becomes available

   • Social media team members to share meaningful notes, problems, and positive feedback that they're getting relevant to that department's messages

   • You, as online reputation management wonderworker, to see how things are progressing in a moment, rather than scheduling a bunch of meetings

Your social media team needs to understand the plan and be able to communicate directly to a particular department if that department's messages are attracting a lot of attention.

It's a good idea to allocate around five different areas of emphasis and to map out different messages under these headings, though you can certainly do less. Your brand's message can start to look a little fractured and complicated if you allow too many departments into the social media mix. If you encounter this problem, I suggest having a senior-level member of the crisis communications team make that decision.

Mapping your mind

I realize that if you're unfamiliar with them, mindmapping applications can sound like something from the cheesy, 1960s, sci-fi movie genre. They're actually quite innocent and are terrific brainstorming, organizing, and sharing tools. New ones come out all the time, but here are a couple of interesting picks that work on Macs and PCs.

✔ **Concept Draw's ConceptDraw MINDMAP:** It has a free trial version and features built-in Twitter functionality, which can be a timesaver. The only drawback is that you will have to use your own link shortener because it doesn't do this for you automatically, the way HootSuite or TweetDeck do. You can learn more at `www.concept draw.com`.

✔ **SimpleDiagrams:** Creates surprisingly easy and elegant diagrams and flow charts. Terrific tool for first-time mindmappers. Check it out at `www.simplediagrams.com`.

✔ **SlateBox:** A cloud-based mindmapping tool that's free for individuals, with plans for organizations or educational institutions. Cloud-based mindmapping tools make room for collaboration, should the need arise. Learn more at `http://slatebox.com`.

If you have a computer, there's no reason why you have to resort to jotting down ideas on the back of soggy cocktail napkins again. These tools streamline your brainstorming time like you wouldn't believe.

Keeping It Fresh

Keeping your online content fresh and vibrant is terrific for creating positive enthusiasm for your brand, which certainly elevates your reputation online. Amazingly, our love of discovering new ideas and information online actually causes our brains to release that delightfully pleasant hormone called dopamine. Yes, via your great messages online, you're now a brain-chemistry drug pusher. Not only are happy feelings good for the world in general, and your brand in particular, but a surge of dopamine also energizes you to take action to help you end up getting more accomplished. Used correctly, your messages can motivate people to do things that they may not have felt inspired to do before. By creating anticipation and by motivating people to share your content with their own audiences you can help keep your content fresh. I talk about each of these methods in the next sections.

Anticipation

Successfully creating a state of anticipation keeps your audience eagerly coming back for more. It's precisely this kind of dynamic that makes your reputation the strongest online. You're not shouting for people to come and pay attention to your brand. You've simply intrigued your audience, gotten it to anticipate what you'll publish next. They can't wait to talk about it with their friends. That's where all the great online sharing happens.

Posting regularly

This is how you create significantly higher engagement with posts. Have a regular posting schedule on your top three networks. Some people suggest that you post on the same day every week, but I suggest you experiment to see what resonates with your audiences. Play with it until you establish a regular publishing rhythm.

Creating excitement

After a period of time of experiencing rewarding boosts from your brand, a number of people feel confident to take the next step in getting closer to your brand, whether that's

- ✔ Sharing content
- ✔ Signing up for your e-mail newsletter
- ✔ Commenting on posts
- ✔ Signing up for a free download (course, e-book, white paper, and so on)
- ✔ Purchasing something low-cost
- ✔ Referring friends to your brand

Motivating people to play with your content

Creating the kind of content that gets people engaged is less about lecturing and more about connecting on an emotional level. You can engage with people on an emotional level while still keeping your facts straight and delivering something of value. It's the biggest difference between posts that get excitedly shared and those that remain undiscovered. People want to share things that they feel will genuinely entertain or help their own followers also. You can motivate people to play with your content by hosting challenges or by providing short-term rewards.

Hosting challenges

It's the "lose 10 inches in 10 months weight-loss challenge. Join with us to banish bloat and pummel pounds together." I'm kidding, but not really. People love a healthy challenge, particularly when they're doing it with others and can share notes and swap tips.

Providing short-term rewards

Motivating people with short-term rewards, however simple, energizes them. When I hosted a "Pages Gone Wild" networking game to build community, I promised (and delivered) linked profiles to the top-ten participants on a special "Hall of Fame" page on my site for the rest of the year.

People still send me testimonials and thank me for the event, because they felt so engaged, made so many new friends, and watched their business growth explode. All I did was to be like a chemist. Make good connections in a positive environment and watch them bubble up. Hosting that challenge and providing short-term rewards are what make events like "Pages Gone Wild" exciting and meaningful for people.

Maintaining a Sense of Humor

People love an original. Be authentic and put a little high-spirited fun into what you share with others. Your investment will be paid back with interest.

This boosts positive sentiment for your brand, plus it comes in awfully handy if a social media reputation crisis should emerge, because these people will automatically defend your brand to others. That's the viral beauty of true online reputation management in action.

The best way to lift your own mood is to do it for someone else first! Share something funny, genuinely wish people well, or engage in an anonymous act of kindness. The following list offers some tips on maintaining mood:

- **Post positively:** People come to the Internet to relax and solve problems. When you combine these pleasures, you have something powerful.

  Maintaining a sunny tone lights up readers and makes them want to learn more. Do this as you deliver solid content, and you will build a community of people who enjoy your posts and "get" you.

- **Respond to people:** Respond as quickly as possible and be upbeat. Even if somebody's in a rotten mood when she contacts you about something or makes a crabby reply to one of your posts, maintaining your sense of humor will cause others to be even more supportive and lighten the mood. You can be responsive without taking it too seriously.

- **Respond to situations:** It's unavoidable. Sometimes sticky situations develop, and there's no way around them. You have to go through them. Always remember that most sticky situations pass. As you maintain your sense of humor about a situation and deal with it directly, you discover that it passes much more quickly.

✔ **Laugh with others:** Although some people laugh at others online, I often observe a boomerang effect. You do tend to get what you give online, so I suggest laughing with the others over funny situations, maintaining a playful attitude where possible, and giving people the benefit of the doubt. I'm not saying that you need to agree with everything somebody says, but as you maintain your joyful self, you attract like-minded people. And that's great online reputation management.

The act of smiling actually releases deliciously happy, feel-good endorphins into your body. Take a second to smile really big right now and see how much it elevates your mood. Besides, if anybody's watching, it will keep her guessing.

Chapter 11

Tapping In to Focused Interest Groups

. . . .

. . . .

*W*hether you run a nonprofit organization, a small business, or a large corporation, establishing relationships on the web means engaging online, and in order to do that, you must go where the people are. Forging relationships with thought leaders and participating in online communities that care about the things you care about are the most effective ways to connect with people and to improve your online reputation management. A *thought leader* is simply an organization or person who is recognized by her peers for having innovative ideas. The most powerful thing you can do to promote and insulate your online reputation is to recognize that all online activity is really about interacting with audiences of audiences.

In this chapter, I show you not only how to establish relationships with respected influential leaders, but also how to find other resources online where people are talking about what matters to you most.

Defining Influence Online

There are lots of misconceptions about what constitutes *influence* online. Some analytical tools even try to measure your ability to be charming or persuasive online. However, true influence online means getting people to take action. If you can get people to do something online, you are a legitimate influencer.

How can you become influential? Cultivate an audience that can't wait to talk with you about the latest thing that you've posted. People love to share their impressions and experiences about what's important to them. Be that resource, that trustworthy person they love, and they will share your content like wildfire.

Don't aim for big numbers — aim for engagement. Engaged audiences are much more powerful than people who can barely remember your brand or why they wanted information from you in the first place.

I get a little dubious anytime somebody starts talking about a foolproof way to measure influence online. A few sophisticated services do a surprisingly good job of tracking retweets, comments, and more, and then shaping them into an influence score that you can use to compare yourself to someone else. The trick with using these tools is to keep in mind that scores fluctuate pretty rapidly, so you need to look at them over a large interval of time to get an average score. Going on vacation can be disastrous for one of these influence scores, but it doesn't really mean that his influence has suffered in any kind of meaningful way.

Don't be overly concerned with scores like these. They may not mirror reality. Some people post content as much as possible in order to "game" influence scoring systems, or use other tricks to improve their scores.

Blog, social network, and forum comments are terrific ways to get a feel for how engaged people are in your online communities without having to look at a number. These are the most influential influence-measuring sites available right now because they demonstrate whether somebody is really engaging and influencing others. Going by numbers doesn't give you an accurate picture of influence, in my opinion. It gives you an idea about how active somebody is, and there's a world of difference that can exist between those two things online.

No matter what your influence score is, if people love your content and believe that you stand for something meaningful, then you'll have amazing influence online. I can promise you that in the event of a social media crisis that influence scores don't matter. People do.

Now that I've told you all the reasons why you shouldn't worry about your own influence scores, I want to point out that they are great ways to assess how active somebody is online. Anyone with a high influence score is likely someone whose content is regularly shared online.

Klout

Klout (see Figure 11-1) is definitely the most influential ratings service online. You can check it out at http://klout.com/home. It looks at

✔ **Twitter activity:** Retweets, mentions, and replies

✔ **LinkedIn activity:** Comments and likes

✔ **Facebook profile activity:** Comments, wall posts, mentions, shares, and likes

✔ **Google+:** Comments, reshares, and +1

✔ **Foursquare:** To-do's and tips done

Klout also allows you to connect Facebook pages, YouTube, Instagram, Tumblr, Blogger, WordPress.com, Last FM, and Flickr accounts. According to Klout, these networks don't automatically impact your overall score. They are responsible enough to evaluate your involvement on these platforms and then apply it to your score. My advice is to take a few minutes to connect every social media network you're on into Klout. You can only win. Here's how

1. **Sign in to your Klout account.**

2. **In the upper-right corner, locate your account name and picture. Click on your name — it's a drop-down menu.**

3. **Choose Settings in that menu.**

   Now in the left column is a menu.

4. **Choose Connected Networks. You can add your other social networks here by clicking Connect Now next to the icon and entering your login information.**

Figure 11-1:
A Klout page.

REMEMBER

HootSuite automatically lists your Klout score whether you are logged on to Klout or not.

Kred

Kred (see Figure 11-2) is a relative newcomer in the social influence-rating arena. You can check it out at www.kred.com. I am impressed with how well it evaluates the influence and outreach levels. Another terrific benefit is that you can meet and network with other influencers, which is hugely helpful in establishing your reputation online. Kred rates the following

- ✔ **Twitter activity:** Retweets, mentions, and replies
- ✔ **Facebook Pages:** Posts, mentions, comments, shares, event invitations, and likes

Figure 11-2: How Kred rates influencers.

PeerIndex

PeerIndex is another influence-ranking service that is worth looking into. I like that it takes a more thoughtful look into social activity online, which helps to bypass the "gaming" effect. You can sign up via your Twitter or Facebook accounts, and it takes about three minutes to connect your accounts. It tracks Twitter, Facebook, LinkedIn, and Quora in much the same way as the foregoing services, but I like that it also breaks down influence into the following

✔ **Authority:** The measure of trust, calculating how much others rely on your recommendations and opinion in general on particular topics.

✔ **Audience:** Your audience score is a normalized indication of your reach, given the relative size of your audience.

✔ **Activity:** Your activity score is the measure of how much you do that is related to the topic communities you are part of. By being too active, your topic community members tend to get fatigued and may stop engaging with you; by taking a long break on a particular topic, community members may not engage with somebody who hasn't been contributing lately.

Considering Individual Influencers

Being an influential person online doesn't just translate into being an active user. You may spend a considerable amount of time online and may even be influential among a small circle of people, and still not be truly influential. Everyone's voice is important, of course, but because of influence some people's voices are more important than others.

All kinds of different personalities captivate people's attention online. They come from multiple and varied industries. From crunchy-granola organic crowds to the most high-tech bloggers, thought leaders range in every possible way; yet, there are four basic categories of influencers. They are

✔ Celebrities who charm, entertain, or otherwise capture people's attention

✔ Experts in a given field

✔ Trusted resources for news, tips, or technical know-how

✔ Curators of the funny, fascinating, or fantastic

You can spot an influential individual by how often other people respond to that person's presence online. In particular, pay attention to how often people do any of the following:

✔ **Read/view that person's material:** Check blog traffic, subscriptions, or search-engine rankings to get a sense of how often people are visiting that person's site or blog.

✔ **Respond to that person's posts:** Check Likes on Facebook, plusses on Google+, and comments on any blog, forum, or social network.

✔ **Shares or reposts of that person's material:** Retweeting on Twitter, sharing via Facebook, and forwarding via e-mail all qualify as reposts here.

Cultivating relationships with influencers

Cultivating relationships with online influencers is rewarding from many different perspectives. As you look for and value what makes other people influential, you learn from them and begin to express what you've learned in your own unique way. Cultivating these relationships also can be a practical way to promote your content and to improve your search engine optimization (SEO): Linking from influential sites is SEO gold!

Invite influential people to help you build communities that will benefit them also, so that you are combining your resources and audiences.

Valuing and supporting thought leaders online help define you or your organization and strengthen your voice and the things that matter.

Online, as in real life, people tend to get what they give. The most effective way to become recognized by an influential person is to value and share that person's posts (or other material) with your audiences. Building relationships with thought leaders online evolves with trust over time. Nevertheless, smart influencers pay attention to who's paying attention to them.

Meeting Brian Solis

Brian Solis is my all-time favorite expert in online reputation management. He's smart, he freely shares top-level research, and he writes informative books on the subject of online reputation management. For me, he is the thought leader with whom I want to associate my own brand.

Over the past few years, I've retweeted his content, given warm shouts out for his books, and even chatted with him via Twitter about his latest book, *The End of Business As Usual* (2011; John Wiley & Sons, Inc.). I resonate deeply with the messages in his books. As chance would have it, I ran into Brian (in person) at an author's party. As I shyly approached him to say hi and introduce myself, he surprised me by recognizing me first! "I know who you are!" he said. With characteristic finesse, I blurted out, "No, you don't! You have over a quarter-million fans online! How could you possibly know who I am?"

Turned out that Brian did know who I am because he's smart enough to look at who's talking about him online to see what they're interested in and why his content appeals to them. Now I'm even referencing him in this book. Pretty smart guy!

When you want to cultivate an online relationship with someone who's influential, try the following steps. Over time, you may end up having conversations with them and begin to develop a relationship.

1. **Follow people you genuinely appreciate, and make upbeat comments about them online:**

   • Mention them via Twitter.

   • Comment thoughtfully on their posts. Give some thought to the conversation you want to have instead of just writing, "I love this!" It shows that you really do understand where they're coming from and resonate with their messages or perhaps even have something to contribute that they may not have thought of.

   • Be positive. Even if you totally disagree with something, you can frame it in a way that's productive and positive.

2. **Share their content via your major social networks, such as Facebook, Google+, and LinkedIn.**

3. **Link to their sites in your blog posts. Mention them by name.**

Checking out Community Groups

Community groups are a gold mine for tapping in to focused interest groups online. When you consider that true online communities are groups of people who just love getting together on forums or chat rooms to discuss your area of expertise, it's crazy not to shop around for a group that's a good fit and then get involved.

These days, you can find an online community for just about anything you can imagine. Search by using your keywords and other relevant terms, and see what surprises turn up! It's also helpful to search for thought leaders on these topics to see what turns up. Get creative because search engine results can be deceptive. You may need to dig in order to find the right fit.

Discovering groups on larger social networks

Many people don't realize that there are smaller, more focused communities that you can join or request to join on both Facebook and LinkedIn. Depending on your subject, either of these social networks may provide you with established and lively communities where you can contribute.

These are some of the most trusted social networks for meeting like-minded people and chatting with them about what matters to you most. As you socialize, you'll discover people who are most influential. Check out their sites and cultivate relationships with them if it feels like a good fit.

- ✔ **LinkedIn groups:** LinkedIn groups are an amazing place to meet professionals who share your interests. Many of them are influential with their peers, if not online. Many people even get jobs via their LinkedIn communities. Don't overlook this powerful resource. You can search for them by going to the top right Search window on LinkedIn. Some of these groups will want to approve your entry into the group, so just

  - Introduce yourself.

  - Explain why you're interested in the group.

  - Wait a few days for a response and then either join in or move on if you haven't heard back yet. Odds are good that if you haven't heard back that it's an inactive group.

- ✔ **Facebook:** A fabulous place to find communities of people who are engaged in your subject area and have audiences of their own who are interested in the same things. Just go to the search window at the top of Facebook's screen and search for your keywords or for the pages of thought leaders. You will find communities and pages for almost any topic.

  Facebook changes its structure and rules about as often as some people change their hairstyles. Understand that these groups are fluid in concept, but no less powerful. If you anticipate that there will be changes, you'll be much happier and fast on your feet when they occur, instead of trying to hang on to the old ways and missing out on the advantages that come from being an early adopter online. All I'm saying is, when it comes to Facebook changes, go with the flow.

- ✔ **Google+:** A social media playground for technically minded nerds like me these days. But that doesn't mean you can't start using it creatively to discover other people who share your passion for tropical fish or practicing law. You never know.

  - Go to the search window at the top of Google screens and search for your keywords over the names of influential people.

  - Create a circle with those people in it, and choose to only look at their newsfeeds when you go to Google+.

  - Host regularly scheduled Google hangouts, which feature live videoconferencing, concerts, webinars, or simply a group meeting of the minds.

Answering questions on Quora

Sometimes you can meet up with amazing people via Quora, a question-and-answer–based community of users that you can find at www.quora.com. As with most sites, you may find people who are using it in a spammy way, but don't be put off. A lot of great discussion and thought appear on there by some of the most influential people online. It never hurts to check Quora out to see if people are talking about your favorite subject, and if so, what they're saying. It's also a great place to ask questions. You may be surprised by the level of detail and scope of the answers you receive.

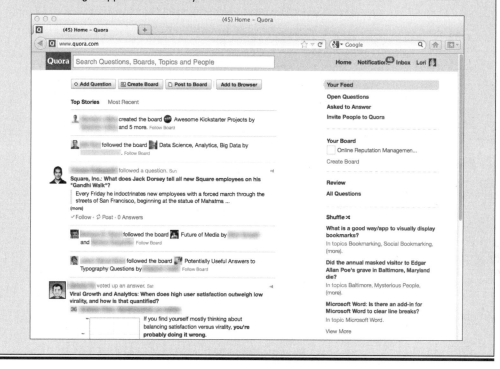

Searching for dedicated social networks

Can't find a community group that fits your needs? Create your own! Create a dedicated social network of your own without needing to pay for a fancy developer by using services like Ning and Yammer. Apart from hosting forums on your own site, Ning and Yammer provide powerful platforms that give people a place to discuss what they love most. I encourage you to check out these services so that you can either discover an open group that already is talking about your business or create one of your own.

✔ **Ning:** Quite literally a place where you can create your very own social network for anything. Check it out at www.ning.com. (See Figure 11-3.) It includes

- Photo slide shows

- Member profiles

- Discussion forums

- Videos

- Interest groups

- Real-time activity stream, which is nice for keeping conversations going

- Capability to paste in external widgets

- Capability to paste in widgets with your branding on them that facilitate sharing for your visitors

- Facebook Page integration

The price ranges from

- Ning Mini is now free for eligible North American K-12 and Higher-Ed Ning Networks

- Plus groups with advanced features at $24.95 monthly

- Pro groups that are built for scale at $59.95 monthly

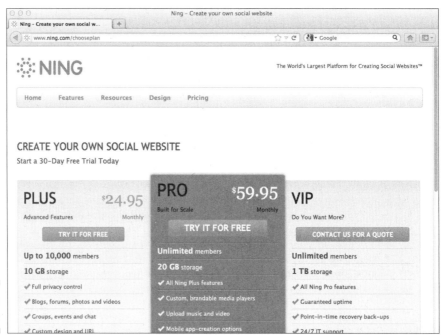

Figure 11-3:
Ning.

✔ **Yammer:** A very involved, enterprise-level, social network service that gives you a private forum to brainstorm, collaborate, and discuss ideas in real time. You can also deepen relationships with customers and partners by maintaining a private community with them. You can find it at `www.yammer.com`. (See Figure 11-4.) Some of its many features include

- Member profiles
- Status updates
- Real-time activity feed
- Interest groups
- Videos
- Discussion forums
- Events
- Private messages
- Polls

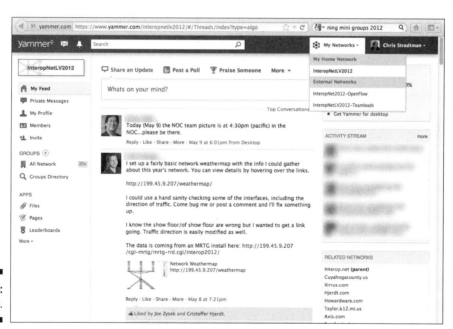

Figure 11-4:
Yammer.

Review Sites

Review sites tend to be trusted resources for buying decisions. Most people feel that they learn more from individuals, rather than professional copywriting on an organization's website. People value

✔ More objective content

✔ Limitless variety of opinions

✔ Sincere results testimonials

If you run a business online, it pays to pay attention to review sites periodically. You never know who's commenting on your business. Reward your satisfied customers when they leave positive comments online so it will not only bury any unfair feedback, but also help to establish your positive reputation.

Angie's List

Angie's List is a growing, online consumer-reporting community that is quickly becoming one of the most established and well-respected review sites online. It's been repeatedly touted by national media in both broadcast and periodicals. Angie's List insists that its employees review each testimonial and that no anonymous ratings are allowed in order to help ensure consistently accurate results. It also limits ratings to once every six months for any company so negative reviews can't get buried under positive ones. If your competition is simply covering up their negative reviews instead of doing something about them, a classic online reputation blunder, this is a great way to get ahead of your competition. Building a positive reputation online is much more effective and widespread. Besides, it's good karma!

Yelp

If you own a business in an urban area, you need to look at Yelp. According to its FAQ, it's "an online urban city guide that helps people find cool places to eat, shop, drink, relax and play, based on the informed opinions of a vibrant and active community of locals in the know." People dish about what they love about businesses and what they've don't love, often in colorful terms. They share their opinions about how much goods or services cost, what the atmosphere is like, and even how clean the places are. I occasionally discover the most amazing places and deals via Yelp.

Reviews on Google Places

Google Places is a review site that can be used by businesses with storefronts or by those who work from home. (See Figure 11-5.) It's another phenomenal, free tool via Google and offers the following

✔ **Service areas:** If you travel to serve customers, you can now show which geographic areas you serve. And if you run a business without a storefront or office location, you can now make your address private.

- ✔ **Local advertising:** A little advertising never hurts.

- ✔ **Business photo shoots:** You can upload your own storefront photos. In select cities, Google is even providing free photo shoots of the interior of your business. You can investigate this at `www.maps.google.com/help/maps/businessphotos`.

- ✔ **Customized QR codes:** A *QR code* is a matrix barcode that can be read by smartphones, mobile phones with a camera, and QR scanners. They're very popular in Japan, and many companies are trying to make them more popular in the United States.

  From the dashboard page of Google Places, businesses in the United States can download a QR code that's unique to their businesses, directly from their dashboard pages. You can use this on business cards or advertisements.

- ✔ **Posting real-time updates:** New feature where you can post real-time updates to your Place Page. You can use this to promote a sale, special event, or anything else that deserves a real-time mention.

If you work from home, be sure to hide your Google Places address by selecting the Do Not Show My Business Address on My Maps Listing option within your dashboard. If you don't hide your address, your listing may be removed from Google Maps, which would be bad for business. More importantly, you don't want your personal address out there!

Figure 11-5: A review on Google Places.

If you aren't on Google Places and would like to get started, here's how:

1. **Go to** `www.google.com/places.`

2. **Click Get Started Now.**

3. **Enter your e-mail address and password for your Google account, preferably one associated with your business.**

4. **Enter your phone number and follow the steps from there that relate to your business.**

   You will receive a physical postcard that you need to mail back to prove that you're a real person with a real business.

I suggest showing your clients exactly how to review your business on Google Places. Now that it's integrated with Google+, you get even more great exposure for your brand. Here are the steps your clients should follow for writing reviews:

1. **Search for** *(your awesome business)* **on Google or Google Maps.**

2. **Click the More Info link next to** *(your awesome business)* **in the left panel.**

   More options pop up.

3. **Click Write a Review.**

4. **Give your review a title and rating.**

5. **Click Save.**

Deal of the day websites

"Deal of the day" sites like Groupon (`www.groupon.com`) or LivingSocial (`www.livingsocial.com`) feature discounted gift certificates you can use at local or national retailers. A new deal is available every day, but the purchase price is good only for that day, and only if a certain number of people commit to buying that deal at the advertised price. Once you have paid for the deal and the minimum number of people have participated, you receive a voucher via e-mail that confirms your purchase. Vouchers are generally good for at least a couple of months and have become very popular in some markets. If you're new in town and offer tangible goods for sale or a service, such as automotive tune-ups, this may be a good way to get your name out there by a trusted authority.

Chapter 12

Writing Your Way to the Top

Sharing written content is probably the strongest thing you can do to create a strong, vibrant, positive online reputation. Individuals and organizations often start blogs, e-mail newsletters, or the like with the best of intentions, but when success doesn't arrive quickly, they give up. However, when you know how to write and optimize content for the web and how to use social media, you can get maximum traction. After all, if you research and write content, it's awfully nice to have somebody read and share!

Although this chapter applies to any kind of written content online, my primary emphasis here is on blogs because at the moment they are the most popular way of sharing written content online.

This chapter gives you a system for planning and carrying out an effective campaign to write and share great content online. No matter whether you're planning to write blog posts, white papers, press releases, or e-books to share, this chapter walks you through the process of creating written content that people find irresistible and want to share with their audiences.

Infusing Your Content with SEO Keywords

In Chapter 6, I show you how to research your keywords and explain why the exact same posts and white papers can either languish on page 3 of Google's search results or pop much closer to the top. One of the smartest things you can do to write great content that gets discovered and shared is to get in the habit of using those juicy little search engine optimization (SEO) keywords in your blog posts, e-books, newsletters, and white papers.

Create an SEO keyword glossary that you can refer to at a glance when you're writing. It will make integrating them easier.

To be most effective, however, you should follow some guidelines. For example, if you load a blog post with too many instances of the phrase "best plumber in town," Google's algorithms will judge your post to be weak content and actually list your post *lower* in its rankings.

Remember, Google's number-one objective is to provide rankings that put the very *best* content on top. That's where I want you to be. So here are a few guidelines for spicing up your blog content with keywords:

- ✔ Make sure the keywords are relevant to the subject you're writing about.
- ✔ Use them in an appropriate context.
- ✔ Try to use at least one keyword phrase per post. It's great to use your keywords in both your title and your post headings, as long as they're going to read well and make sense to your readers.

The most important thing is for you to write engaging content that people will enjoy and share. Google ranking is a second consideration, though its algorithms especially love popular content.

Whenever possible, use your keywords in post titles. For example, if one of your SEO keyword phrases is "ferret fashion," you get more SEO bang for your buck if you begin your post title with "ferret fashion: 5 unforgettable looks."

Why? Here are a few good reasons why this is a great post title:

- ✔ The keyword is at the front of the title.
- ✔ The title has fewer than 72 characters, so the full title appears in search results.
- ✔ The text clearly explains what the post is about. When people link to your post on their blogs, that title helps to show readers what they'll be getting. You get visitors who are genuinely interested in the latest runway looks for ferret couture. Also, Google's ever-changing algorithms seem to consistently like this and rate it higher.

Most seasoned bloggers start with the title before they ever write the post.

Capturing Attention with Catchy Titles

Most online readers will never read past the title you put on your work. It's often said that the dust jacket sells the book. The same thing applies to e-books, white papers, e-mail newsletters, and most definitely blog posts. You want your titles to be as attractive and attention-getting as possible.

In this section, I share the most proven and respected ways to get people to click those titles you create. When you invest your time, resources, and attention into creating great content, you deserve for it to be read.

Humans are genetically primed to notice something out of the ordinary. Stand out by creating post titles that explore something new or do it with a fresh interpretation.

Be careful, however. It's easy to create outlandish post titles. Eye-catching? Sure. A good idea? Not always. When they're too outrageous, those wild titles that beg to be read can actually harm your credibility. Have fun and make only promises you can keep.

Create a list

List posts may well be the little black dress of blog post writing. Or if you don't wear dresses, perhaps the best way to describe list posts is to say that they're like a great pair of blue jeans. They never go out of style. Even though current fashion may involve boot-cut legs instead of skinny or straight-cut legs, they're still blue jeans and they're still awesome.

List posts always deliver because they give you a clear opportunity to make a promise and absolutely deliver on it. People know what to expect when they're looking to get solid, applicable information.

Here are my favorite styles for writing list posts. Hopefully, you'll find a couple that look good on your site and feel comfortable for you to write.

- ✔ **"5 Kinds of Ferret Fashionista: Which one are you?":** Keyword loaded up front and invites your visitors to play along and see which category they think they belong in.

- ✔ **"5 Familiar Ferret Fashions we can't live without":** Keyword loaded up front again, also piques your reader's curiosity. Will it be hats, gloves, belts, knitted booties, or aprons again this year?

- ✔ **"Free book gives you 55 ferret treat recipes":** "Free" is usually attention getting, as are targeted recipes. You can make this even more specific by saying "Free book with 55 ferret fashionista treat recipes," but that would be a pretty long title. Shorter works better most of the time.

- ✔ **"5 ways to build ferret fashion runways":** Combines time-honored list-building (pun intended) approach with the ever-popular "how-to" post. As a bonus, you can include ferret fashion week spoilers. Of course, there's no such thing as ferret fashion, but you get the idea. I like writing this with the number "5" instead of writing out "five" online because it reads faster and takes up less space on a tweet or update.

Tell 'em how to do something

I feel a little funny introducing a section that tells you how to write how-to posts, but there really is more than meets the eye to this clever little art form. A casual look at the most popular and influential blogs in any genre online confirms that "how to" posts never fail to get readers to click on a post title when there is good content involved.

It's another great way for you to establish your credibility with visitors. You get to make a promise to your readers, and then keep it.

The most important thing to remember when writing a how-to post title is to take something complicated, unpleasant, or downright intimidating and make it easier, faster, or better. Here are some examples with commentary on what works and why. I use unicorns here because they're fun and I won't accidentally steal somebody's content. Of course, if you breed and show unicorns, I deeply apologize if my sample post titles resemble yours and give you full permission to steal mine as long as you send me unicorn pics. I love the white, sparkly ones that have a rainbow-colored horn.

- ✔ **"How to groom unicorns in half the time":** Saving time is always sexy

- ✔ **"How to spot wild unicorns and attract them":** Two benefits for the price of one

- ✔ **"How sparkle suds make unicorn bath time fun":** Another way of promising something specific to readers that you can deliver

- ✔ **"5 ways to photograph your unicorn":** This irresistible title combines a timeless list post with the promise of five photography "how to's." Bonus points for popping it out with an unexpected adjective, such as "5 surprising ways to photograph your unicorn."

Use your words carefully

Here are some tips for writing great post titles of your own:

- ✔ **Never say *always*:** Think a little bit like a lawyer. A blog post title is a kind of promise. And if you're promising that something "always" or "never" happens, then you're setting yourself up to break a promise. Besides, it tends to sound cheesy — and you are a class act, my friend.

- ✔ **Use the 5 W's: who, what, where, when, why:** These eternal questions almost never fail. Examples:

  - *"Who's mentioning you online?":* Ambiguous as to whether this is a good or a bad thing, so readers will assume it's what's already on their minds. Not a bad tactic if you answer both perspectives on this question.

- *"What online reputation crisis can you prevent right now?"*: Giving it a clear time frame is sexy because it's another promise that you get to keep.

- *"Where to find great For Dummies books"*: Shameless plug for this book series and a promise to deliver something valuable. Especially useful for hard-to-find items, like sparkly suds, unicorn bubble bath.

- *"When you feel like throwing in the towel: 5 reasons to fight"*: A little long, but combines a list with an emotionally compelling title.

- *"Why most people will read your blog posts"*: Intriguing promise of tips to make your blogging experience easier.

✔ **Badly kept secrets:** These always tickle me because writing a (hopefully) viral post on the Internet pretty much guarantees that any "secret" there is about to be exposed. Builds anticipation. Examples are

- *"Secret trick to learning how to speak Greek overnight"*: Promises two things: a method and a time frame. Though these are popular on social media, be careful you don't stretch your credibility. I suggest you build your online reputation by sticking to promises you can deliver on.

- *"Tax secrets the IRS doesn't want you to know"*: Intriguing promise.

- *"Secret way to sing in the shower without being overheard!"*: Combines "how-to" with promise that it will be an unusual method.

✔ **Social proofs:** Social proofs are extremely compelling online. They're the basic idea that if everybody's reading, liking, or sharing something with his friends online, then you can trust this content. Examples of using social proofs in a title include:

- *"Why everybody thinks . . ."*: You and I both know this is quite a promise that can't be delivered on. Try "Why almost everybody thinks . . ." and then give at least one other perspective.

- *"Who else wants . . .?"*: Works nicely because it assumes "everybody" is on board but doesn't say it explicitly. As long as one person actually wants this, you're telling the truth, which is always important when you're interested in maintaining credibility online.

- *"What everybody needs to know about . . ."*: Effective approach if you genuinely believe this. I use it from time to time when I'm just dying to protect people from a common mistake that can really hurt them. Say it only when you really mean it, and people will respect you for it.

The larger the audience is, the greater the assumption that what it's doing is legit and that you can trust it.

✔ **Fear of missing out:** Limited-time offers add dramatic tension, but I suggest you use this one sparingly and always truthfully. Many people also use this tactic to induce people into reading their posts for fear of missing out on what all "the cool kids" are doing. You can earn bonus points by saying, "All the cool kids are . . ." because it intrigues and makes a joke at the same time. I repeat, though: Use this one sparingly.

✔ **Fear of negative consequences:** I also call these "why you stink" posts. If you've spent any time in the blogosphere, you see posts that say something like "5 reasons why your blog posts stink" or "7 ways to spot a loser at dog grooming." A classic is "Why you're never going to suc- ceed (unless you buy our product)". I suggest you either avoid the entire genre or use it playfully and write a positive post with fantastic tips.

Negative posts do attract traffic, but they don't build relationships or attract loyalty unless you provide terrific content in a humorous (or snarky) way that people enjoy.

✔ **Love of new:** It's a natural inclination that works in your favor. Whenever possible, frame your titles with the most novelty possible. It entertains and captivates just enough to get somebody to read the first line of your post, which needs to captivate enough to get her to then read the second line. You get the idea.

Surf trends

Try to think like a reporter who wants to break an exciting story before all the other papers get wind of it. Figure 12-1 shows how to apply one of the trend-spotting tools I show you in Chapter 1 — Topsy — in order to surf the trends for attention-getting, blog post titles.

Figure 12-1: Topsy photo search for ferret fashion.

Be sure to give photo credit for any images you use from other sites. Ask site owners for permission first, just to be safe. You can do this at the bottom of posts and link back to them.

Artfully combining these trending topics with your content spices up your blog post titles and makes them a lot more compelling to open and read. This also works with celebrities in the news. For example

- ✓ **"Rock your ferret fashion like Elvis":** He's always in the news. Besides, you get bonus points for using clever wordplays.

- ✓ **"Now you can have hair just like ___'s":** Effective if you're selling hair products. Saying "now" makes another promise that you need to keep. I'm just letting you fill in the blank on this celebrity quiz because it's too much fun coming up with possibilities.

- ✓ **"What _____ (trend) taught me about ferret fashion shows":** Linking a current trend (Elvis is an easy target) to your ferret fashion show discussion not only ignites interest in your title, but it gets you more traffic.

More general themes work as well. For a while, "Ninja" was the word du jour for most A-List bloggers and social media savants. Everybody either was a Ninja or had several at her disposal. It was all quite heady. Some people even designed their sites, logos, and company names to feature the term "Ninja."

I highly caution you not to get caught up in using trendy terms for your branding, however, because trends always fade, and linking one to your brand will automatically outdate your brand's message in a short period of time. You want to be influential online for years to come, not just for the next month.

On the other hand, it's perfectly okay to make your blog titles trendy! Blog post titles are about as permanent as a bouquet of fresh-cut flowers. I love flower arrangements, but I'm very aware that they only last for a few days before they start to wilt. It's the same with fresh blog posts, though they are sometimes searched and enjoyed by new visitors to your site. That's why it's important to have accessible archives on your site.

The majority of blog posts receive 99 percent of their traffic within the first couple of days of being published.

Keep it short

Many people likely experience your content via a mobile device instead of a desktop computer. I tell you more about this in Chapter 8, but just remember that a lot of people are looking at your site, updates, and newsletters via a pretty small screen. Create a reading experience for them that's cleanly formatted and easy to navigate.

Google predicts that there will be more mobile users than desktop users by 2013.

Saying a lot with only a few words is powerful.

Priming Your Audience's Anticipation

For your audience, your posts should be like a powerful reward. One sure way of becoming truly influential online is to train — er, *prime* — your audience to anticipate the reward of your next post. Make them happy. It's human nature to love looking forward to something happy. Some experts even believe that the happy hormones released (chiefly dopamine) from anticipating something are often greater than actually receiving that something!

Armed with this awareness, do everything you can to build anticipation for your posts by sticking to a regular publishing schedule where readers can look forward to having you make and keep a promise that makes their lives better, easier, or more fun.

Solving stresses

Whenever you sit down to write, remember that people come to the Internet to find information that either will help them or will entertain them for a few minutes. As you become your own online reputation management expert, your job is to create content that meets their needs and even exceeds them with cool answers to questions they didn't even think to ask.

People don't search Google for aspirin; they search for headaches and how to fix them. The most popular posts you ever write will probably help people in one way or another.

Creating a series of posts

Creating a series of posts (a sequence of posts on a related topic that link to each other) is one of the most powerful things you can do in creating great messages online. Not only can it provide a reliable source of pain-solving posts on a particular topic for your readers, but it can later be repurposed into helpful free e-books, Facebook notes, and discussion topics for groups on LinkedIn, just to name a few ideas. The following are some more compelling reasons to consider writing a series of posts on a topic near and dear to your reader's hearts and minds:

✔ Terrific for boosting your search engine presence when you incorporate your SEO keywords

✔ Useful for engagement: Great way to build a conversation around a topic that meets a shared need

✔ Great method for going deeper into a topic

✔ Builds momentum with your writing flow

If you're interested in writing a series of posts, I suggest the following system:

1. **Identify one area of your audience's needs.**

   For example, if you're writing about dentistry, people may want to learn a lot more about what happens when they open their mouths for a routine teeth-cleaning appointment. You can alleviate their fears by explaining exactly what happens in a step-by-step process.

2. **Brainstorm your list.**

   How many procedures are done during a routine checkup? What is the experience typically like and how can you explain it simply?

   Writing a series of posts is a fantastic way of creating a very shareworthy list post when you're done.

3. **Craft a catchy title.**

   "10 reasons your smile sparkles from teeth cleaning" is a good starting point. It tells people what you're going to write about and why it's valuable for them.

4. **Announce your series.**

   Share with your friends online and ask them to share a link with their audiences. Reciprocate when they ask you to share a quality series of their own posts.

5. **Follow through!**

   Here are some approaches to writing a series of posts. Always follow a predictable schedule so you follow up on your promise to deliver content people want and need

   • Pre-write them and schedule them on your blogging platform.

   • Pre-write drafts and mark your calendar for time to tweak them and then publish on a predictable schedule.

   • Write and publish each post on the same schedule.

6. **Link, link, link!**

   Did I mention that linking back to your own posts in a series is important? You never know when readers are going to discover your blog, and realize that your series of posts really addresses the problem they're having and they can't wait to read more. By linking to previous posts in a series, you give people a trail of breadcrumbs to follow that's more reliable than search engines. Besides, it's a very search engine–friendly thing for you to do in order to boost your SEO ranking.

7. **Tie it all up with a bow.**

   Finish strong by creating one central post that summarizes what the series is, why you wrote it, and who it's for, and includes all the links in a numbered list. People love to share something this informative and easy to understand.

Discovering your audience's needs

Sometimes the best way to get a straight answer is to ask your audiences for one via asking a question on social networks or at the end of one of your blog posts. I've gotten everything from enthusiastic responses to proverbial cricket chirps, as do most bloggers. Unless you've heard from the masses and they're passionate about their desire for certain content, it's usually more effective to do your own research via Google keywords to discover what the online public is searching for.

Surveys and polls are still a great way to get your audience's opinion. There are some pretty useful tools out there for the give and take of taking polls and giving surveys. There are

- **Poll plug-ins that are built right into your blog:** PollDaddy is a popular WordPress plug-in, though I must admit that I haven't seen it used in quite a while.

- **Web-based polls that you can link to from your site or any social network:** It's really fun to use them when they're optimized for smartphones. This is just starting to happen, and I predict that polling will once again be cool when it can be done easily via mobile devices.

Repurposing other web content

Twitter and Facebook conversations get repurposed into useful and lively blog posts all the time. This may seem strange or redundant, but remember that the Internet is a huge space! Nobody is everywhere all the time. Fascinating conversations erupt all over different "corners" of the web. It's perfectly legitimate to share them in the form of a blog post and add your own interpretation to them while asking people to share theirs.

Every season feels fresh and alive, yet you get the same four every year. Each one is fresh because it plays out differently every time. You anticipate the new sights, smells, and sounds, because you don't exactly know when you are going to see them. It's pure pleasure.

Keep your posts fresh by giving your own interpretation to current events. It's easy to stand out when you're an original.

Bringing in guest bloggers

There's nothing sweeter to an aspiring blogger than to be invited to create a meaningful post for a prestigious blog. Don't worry if your blog isn't internationally famous yet! Fake it till you make it (as long as you research your topic and deliver value) with aspiring bloggers who think that your brand's message is awesome and meaningful to them.

As they direct traffic to your blog and you share posts written by these other bloggers with your audiences, everybody wins, good search engine optimization and karma are achieved, and you get a day off from writing.

The following are effective sample guest posting guidelines for prospective posters. Please remember to give them a byline with a link back to their site, as well as to share their post with all your audiences.

- ✔ Post length should be 250 to 500 words.
- ✔ Include a suggested post title.
- ✔ Include images to go with the post and add a photo credit as needed.
- ✔ Include a numbered list or bullets where applicable.
- ✔ Break content up under different subheadings.
- ✔ Understand that some editing may be required in order to make the post more consistent with the body of work already on the site.
- ✔ Don't post this anywhere else, though you can link to it from anywhere.
- ✔ When the post publishes, check back periodically throughout the next couple of days to respond to comments and questions.
- ✔ Share this post with your audiences.

Create your guest posting policy now so that you can easily share it when it counts. You are welcome to use my list and add to it as needed.

Weekly Schedules for Blogs

Putting yourself or your organization on a writing schedule can really free up your time. When you dedicate a time slot to writing online content and publicizing it online, you will seldom ever panic over a forgotten post or forget to respond to questions and comments that your readers are kind enough to leave.

You don't have to do all this writing by yourself! Options abound.

Many blog communities feature

- ✔ **Regular contributors:** These can be from different departments, or a few designated hitters who understand your goals and your brand's particular voice.

- ✔ **Guest bloggers:** Variety is indeed the spice of life, and it also can give your blog the fresh visibility by attracting traffic from your guest poster's social media audiences. It's also good SEO because your guest posters will tend to link to their articles on your site from elsewhere. Establishing relationships with guest posters contributes toward making you a great web citizen because you're giving guest bloggers perhaps a larger platform (and linking) than they're used to. (See the section, "Bringing in guest bloggers," earlier in this chapter.)

- ✔ **Hired writers:** Sometimes it's most effective to hire professional web copywriters to breathe life into your organization's message online.

Sharing write on time

Bad pun, huh? I can't resist because I want you to remember how important this is to getting your posts opened and read. You may be shocked to learn that the very same post can have dramatically different traffic rates depending on what time of day you shared it with your social networks online.

Pay attention to when your most-involved followers tend to post online. This is your prime time to post links to your written goodies. Reciprocate by paying attention to their posts whenever possible. Reward people or at least thank them for supporting your writing.

Peak sharing days for different kinds of content

Every few months, some group publishes a study telling when the best sharing times are. It's interesting to note that Tuesday, Thursday, and Saturday tend to be great sharing days.

Deciding how many days a week you will write

There's no perfect answer to the question of how many days a week you should publish blog posts, though once a week should be your minimum standard if you're going to build a credible reputation online as an engaged thought leader.

I suggest starting by writing once a week until you get the hang of writing for online audiences and formatting posts. Give yourself a couple of months to get comfortable, because I want you to be able to easily accomplish more in just as much time. Everything gets faster and easier with practice.

By month three, I suggest you increase your posting to at least two or three times a week. You may never want to increase it from there, but if you're running online reputation management for a large organization, I strongly urge you to publish at least five times a week: Tuesday through Saturday or Monday through Friday.

Decide now what days and times you will dedicate to blogging. Now set a recurring appointment in your calendar to make it happen.

Editorial Calendar

If you use WordPress, you're in luck because there are several good Editorial Calendar plug-ins available. As with all WordPress plug-ins, work through the following steps whenever installing something new:

1. **Back up your website entirely (there are great paid plug-ins for this such as Backup Buddy, but I digress).**

2. **Read through the details on the Editorial Calendar you want to try before you install anything. Check to see if it's been updated recently or if it's compliant with the version of WordPress you're running.**

3. **Navigate to your plug-ins page.**

4. **Search for your Editorial Calendar plug-in of choice.**

   It's often a good bet to go for the ones with the most recent date and the most stars, though there are always oldies that are goodies. Figure 12-2 shows you how this looks.

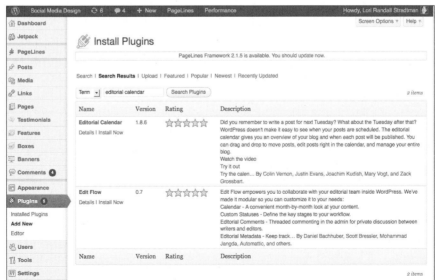

Figure 12-2: Choosing an Editorial Calendar plug-in.

5. **Hold your breath. (Not really.)**

6. **Click Install.**

7. **Check how your site looks via another tab and make sure everything looks and works properly.**

   All kinds of people write all kinds of code for plug-ins and WordPress themes. When you think about it that way, it's no wonder plug-ins and themes don't always play well together.

8. **If everything looks good, rejoice! And start using your Editorial Calendar to organize your blogging schedule.**

9. **If your site looks strange or isn't behaving properly, uninstall that plug-in. That should fix the problem.**

   In the very odd chance it actually broke something, reinstall the safe copy of your site that you squirreled away in Step 1.

   Congratulations! You either have an Editorial Calendar installed or you are set to try another Editorial Calendar plug-in to see if it will play nicely with your theme. Worst-case scenario, scrap the whole plug-in idea and simply create a shared calendar in Google Calendars or via your in-house network. There's more than one way to do just about anything online!

In Chapter 10, I share a detailed plan for weaving in content from up to five departments.

Periodic Schedules for E-Books

Self-publishing is becoming a serious industry and a fantastic way to write your way to the top of search engines and social networks. Amazon is the most popular platform.

Say you are considering writing a series of minibooks that solve people's pain. If you know about the care and maintenance of Mexican jumping beans and there's a lively community of people who yearn to learn more, write a series on the care and maintenance of Mexican jumping beans that establishes you as an indispensable authority on the subject.

  ✔ Make it relevant.

  ✔ Write a catchy title using one of your keywords if at all possible.

  ✔ Use compelling cover art, even if it's a free or inexpensive e-book. Just use the same cover every time with a new title if it's a series. (I share more about using effective visual imagery in Chapter 13.)

  ✔ Make sure your e-book's branding is consistent with the rest of your branding online (more on branding in Chapter 9).

Making e-mail newsletters personal and effective

E-mail newsletters are slightly different animals from any other kind of written communication online. They arrive in your e-mail box. They're typically more personal. Newsletters need to have a personal voice because most people are eager to delete every single piece of e-mail that crosses their path unless they have a compelling reason to open it.

Many people read their e-mails from a preview window, so you really have to make a useful great impression right away. Promise to solve a problem, and then link to a blog post that delivers on that promise. Always treat your readers like special guests or friends whom you are inviting into your home.

In this age of distraction, most people only follow a handful of blogs regularly. Your best shot at getting noticed, read, and getting some community engagement on your blog is to provide people with something they would want or need and then link back to it in your newsletter. Establish a regular posting routine so that people begin to look forward to getting your newsletters and feel like they're missing out on something if you haven't posted recently.

The value to having an engaged e-mail newsletter list is infinite when it comes to establishing and maintaining your reputation online. If you must ever face a crisis with your reputation online, you can post to your list and give your followers the opportunity to come out in droves to support you because you've been so generous and trustworthy with them.

Fanning the Flames of Positive Engagement

A few years ago, it seemed like I was always teaching new bloggers how to get their content shared online. I really wanted them to succeed but realized very quickly that it was going to take more than a well-designed site, great writing, and a cute personality to cultivate influence online. It requires having a system that works and using it consistently.

I've discovered that this system works for every kind of blogger I've shared it with. Whether you're looking to build an online reputation for a cooking blog, a solar energy online community, or a celebrity fan club, this method works. I call it my Blogging Jump-Start Project. Anybody can do it. "Writing Your Way to the Top" involves getting to the top of the rankings, so you need some social media engagement to get you there.

Many people assume that whenever they post updates on Facebook that all their friends can see it. This is just not true. Facebook has worked out some pretty impressive algorithms that rank users according to perceived influence on Facebook. They keep these algorithms under lock and key, but

Facebook does share some basics about the things it looks at when it decides whether your post is going to make the newsfeed or not.

Facebook calls this *EdgeRank,* its algorithm that determines the updates, posts, photos, and so on you will see in your Facebook newsfeed.

Your job is to take the status updates that you use to spread your blog posts and make them show up a lot more often than a tiny percentage of the time. In order to understand how this works, consider the three basic categories that Facebook uses when figuring EdgeRank:

- ✔ Affinity
- ✔ Weight
- ✔ Timing

I discuss these more fully in the next few sections.

Affinity

Affinity has to do with how close you are to people via Facebook. For example, I have many friends on Facebook whom I seldom relate with. It doesn't mean that I don't care for them, only that we don't often interact via Facebook. This is an important distinction.

When Facebook talks about affinity, it is specifically looking at how often you and I "like," comment, and share each other's updates. If you and I visit each other's profiles often and interact a lot, odds are very good that your updates will show up in my Top Stories feed. Facebook deduces that we are close friends and want to be updated about what the other person has to say.

If you and I aren't Facebook friends, or if we became friends last year and haven't commented since then via Facebook, then odds are good that I won't see your updates on my newsfeed.

In another example, let's say our mutual acquaintance Bill wants to get to know you better and comments on your profile a lot. His updates are less likely to show up in your newsfeed than if you respond back to him, because that's what friends do.

Facebook determines affinity only on the basis of what happens on Facebook. You and I can be great friends on Twitter, but never make each other's newsfeed on Facebook if we don't interact there.

Weight

The best way to throw your weight around on Facebook is to post things that people are likely to interact with. Sometimes a status update alone is clever enough to provoke a response, but most people respond really well to the following, in order of preference. The following tips show you which kinds of updates Facebook attaches positive weight to. This is the stuff that makes your updates more likely to be seen and enjoyed there.

✓ **Videos:** Uploading your own video directly to Facebook is probably the most strongly favorable things you can do to get your update on the top newsfeed. Adding videos from YouTube and Vimeo, for example, is also good, though not quite as strong.

✓ **Pictures:** Uploading your own pictures directly to Facebook is the most effective way to boost EdgeRank by sharing pictures. You can also share links to pictures or share someone else's Facebook update that has a picture.

Make an even bigger impact by uploading pictures directly wherever possible, instead of using a link. The image appears much, much larger.

✓ **Links:** Links are the third most highly rated kind of status updates on Facebook. Be sure to always link directly to your blog posts instead of your general blog page, so that the pictures you so carefully choose correspond with your subject.

✓ **Status updates:** By now, I hope I've convinced you to spice up your status updates with links, pictures, and videos whenever possible.

Timing

Timing is everything when it comes to Facebook and rank. For example, trending information has a freshness date with Facebook's EdgeRank. When you post up-to-the-minute news on trending topics, your links to written content have a much greater likelihood of being seen in the top newsfeed.

If you want to post something about Thanksgiving, for example, Facebook will pay a lot more attention to it if you post during the last couple of weeks in November, because it's more relevant at that time. Americans talk about Thanksgiving in November more often than any other month of the year. If you create that same provocative update with the same glistening, delicious-looking turkey on it during the month of July, you will hear a proverbial chorus of crickets because it will be a miracle if it makes the newsfeed. Figure 12-3 shows what a typical Top Stories feed looks like.

Don't forget the "time decay factor" of Facebook's EdgeRank algorithms. If your friend posts on Wednesday and you don't log in until Tuesday, you may not see her post. It's too old. This is why posting often is a good idea if you want to establish an effective presence via Facebook.

Under the Sort button, select Top Stories instead of Most Recent if you want Facebook to EdgeRank to try to anticipate who you want to keep up with more closely. Most recent posts automatically appear in the upper-right window anyway, so you can still see updates in real time.

People use a couple of strategies to make their posts appear more timely. One school of thought says to only post links to your blog posts when your most influential users are typically online. This may look like 8:30 in the morning, 12:30 in the afternoon, and 9:00 at night.

The other school of thought is to update your status with blog post links when fewer people are logged on, so that there will be less competition on the newsfeed.

I personally believe in posting links to your blog when your most engaged users are active on Facebook. Because you will not only get ranked for their interaction, but your post may well make the newsfeed for their friends, because it's an activity. These days, I often get feedback via Facebook from people I've never met on there.

Figure 12-3:
Facebook's
Top Stories
feed.

Play with your approach and see what works for you, but the greatest likelihood is that you get better results by sharing while people who share are online and active.

It pays to pay attention to when your most influential followers are active on Facebook.

Jump-Starting Your Blog

Now that you have a better understanding of how Facebook's EdgeRank works and how to get the most out of your activity on there, I'm ready to share my Blogging Jump-Start Method.

The method's general idea is to create a group of people willing to share other members' posts with their own online audiences. Since true social media influence is about inspiring people to take action and reaching out to audiences with audiences, this method enables you to build Google ranking and Facebook EdgeRank very quickly, not to mention getting lots of new visitors to your blog, which is the primary reason to jump-start your blog.

To use the method, first create a group of five to eight people who want to fully participate with you in this blogging jump-start project.

Details are important here to ensure that you have a system that works to everyone's mutual benefit. Here's how the method works:

1. **Either join an online community of bloggers or begin approaching other bloggers whom you like and respect.**

   This is essential because you are going to be sharing their content with your friends. This demands a lot of credibility . . . and just a little charm. It's always more enjoyable to share something uplifting and useful.

2. **Decide whether this will be an ongoing project or whether you'd like for it to last for a fixed period of time.**

   You may, for instance, plan to do this just prior to a book launch, campaign, or any major event that you want to publicize online. It primes Facebook's EdgeRank to be especially kind to you in the Top News feed, which helps a lot.

   I suggest leading this for just a month, with weekly checkups. Review what's working and what needs refinement at that point. If somebody's consistently not reciprocating, you can refrain from sharing his content until he shows you a little link love back.

This is strictly voluntary and can be a lot of fun for all participants involved as they get lots of new, appreciative visitors to their blogs!

3. Agree to an evenly balanced writing schedule.

For example, if everyone else in your group posts only once a week and you post three times a week, it's a terrific deal for you, but the others in your group may not be quite so eager to share every one of your posts. Another option is for you to share every one of their weekly posts and for them to share their favorite post of yours from that week. This keeps everything fair and evenly balanced.

4. Subscribe to each other's RSS feeds.

As soon as you see one of these five to eight posts arrive in your mailbox, share a link to it with your audiences on Facebook and Twitter with a helpful, funny, or otherwise interesting little introduction.

If your group includes designers or artists, you may want to share pictures (that link to their blog posts) on Pinterest instead of Twitter and check the Share on Twitter box because Twitter doesn't penalize you by hiding your posts. They share them all in chronological order. This way, you can gain exposure on three social networks with the same amount of effort as just Facebook and Twitter.

5. (Optional) Comment on their posts.

You don't have to write an epic response or dig deep for the world's greatest inspiration on every topic, but this can still be a significantly greater time commitment rather than simply sharing via your social networks, because you can do all that in a minute once you get the hang of it.

This step is optional because it doesn't affect social media involvement as much as directly sharing on social networks, though all the major blog commenting systems are incorporating social media sharing into their systems.

I suggest you put it up for a vote and do what everybody feels comfortable doing.

This system works for people of all different backgrounds and interests. Blog subscription rates, commenting rates, Google ranking, Facebook Page likes, Twitter follows, and more always climb fast among committed group members who create quality content. Good luck!! Please inundate me with your success stories!

Chapter 13

Using Visuals to Spread Your Message

There is something powerfully primal about the way the human brain responds to visual cues. Marketing studies tell us that people make decisions with their emotions and only justify those decisions with rational thought later. Using pictures is a natural way to grab people's attention on a direct, emotional level. That makes pictures great tools for maintaining your online reputation.

Whether you use photographs, illustrations, cartoons, or cocktail napkin scribbles, visuals can communicate complex messages in an instant. In this chapter, I show you the world of infographics, and explain how you can use visuals to communicate, and even to lure people back to your blog or website.

Working with Infographics

Knowledge is power, but let's face it: Some kinds of knowledge, like statistics, can be pretty boring. Visual representations of statistical information, on the other hand, are much more engaging. That's an *infographic* — a graphical representation of related (often statistical) information. A true infographic (instead of interesting looking graphic) shows percentages or numbers according to scale so that your reader can immediately get a sense of scale.

Popular subjects for infographics include

- Social media trends
- Mobile device use trends
- Nutritional information

Any discussion where you want to demonstrate how a bunch of things relate to one another is ripe for an attention-getting infographic. The key difference between an infographic and a simple list of items is the emphasis on the connections and comparisons among those items. To make a good infographic, you need to illustrate relationships among items by making them look larger or smaller on a percentage basis. This usually requires a little help from a spreadsheet.

Infographics are a great way to share your branding online. Every good infographic gives source credits, and you should always include your own brand among them. I suggest inserting the name of your brand below the title so that it can't easily be cropped out. Add a link leading back to your site on all your infographics.

If you aren't a designer (and don't want to pay for one), you can still create fun infographics using any of these five free tools online that vary from interesting to tons of fun.

You can create attention-getting infographics fairly easily via the following sites, though I recommend getting a graphic designer friend to do this for you because they can do it more comfortably. If not, just allow yourself a little time to create a few versions so you can get the hang of it. Once you've created your first one, the rest are easy.

- **Visual.ly** (`http://visual.ly`): Super fun storytelling visualizations in minutes. It's also a great place to scroll through a wide variety of compelling infographics. It's fully optimized for social media sharing, which can save you a lot of time. Figure 13-1 was created via Visual.ly in about three minutes.

- **Hohli** (`http://charts.hohli.com`): Great resource for creating charts, including line charts, bar charts, pie charts, Venn diagrams (my favorite), scatter plots, and radar charts. You can choose from a variety of backgrounds and color combinations. It's also optimized for social sharing.

✔ **Google Public Data Explorer** (www.google.com/publicdata): Lets you use the power of Google to harness existing data sets. It's going to take more time and attention to detail to create an infographic with this tool, but you can go into significant detail and know that you are representing something accurately.

✔ **Many Eyes** (www-958.ibm.com/software/data/cognos/manyeyes): A research tool experiment hosted by IBM research. Like Google, it gives you access to data sets, but the visualizations look a little more compelling and are easy to create. It also gives you the opportunity to participate in communities where people discuss different topics. This can be a terrific way to meet your target audiences.

In the next section, I show you where infographics are a good fit and give you tips for making images a more powerful sharing tool for you online.

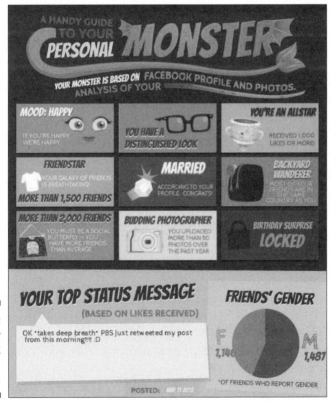

Figure 13-1:
My
Facebook
"Monster"
infographic.

Improving Your Images

Images are important to your online reputation because they often demonstrate your authority and understanding in your subject area, as well as your willingness to share what you know with the community.

Google's Image Search function enables people to find your posts via pictures. However, online culture tends to revere the new and different, so to stand out, your images need an element of novelty. In this section, I show you how to optimize your images for sharing and where the best places are to showcase your work.

Popping their peepers

This section can also be called "Making your pictures compelling," but eye-popping posts and status updates that beg to be investigated further are one way to catch people's attention.

Another way is to include an intriguing image. Believe it or not, an image that's a little "off" gets more attention than a slick, technically precise image. It pays to be a little offbeat.

Some tips for making your pictures more intriguing:

- ✔ **Go nuts:** Surprise your viewers with something unexpected, like a pig wearing a tiara.
- ✔ **Use animals:** Internet users are famous for their love of animal photos (such as Figure 13-2, which shows my dogs lounging in the sun). Be playful and use animal pictures with funny expressions.
- ✔ **Use primary colors:** The human brain is hard-wired to take action when it sees primary colors.
- ✔ **Play on words:** For example, "Writing with a broken pen is pointless" or "a backward poet writes inverse" may make cute titles for a writing-related image.
- ✔ **Be authentic:** "Real" pictures (as opposed to professional, touched-up looking photography) engage visitors for much longer periods of time than fancy stock photography.
- ✔ **Be inspiring:** The most compelling images online build people up, inspire them somehow, or make them laugh.

Figure 13-2:
My
esteemed
co-authors.

Bringing sharing savvy back

Whether you're sharing a picture to enhance your blog post or launching an exciting infographic, your strongest online reputation boost comes from identifying that picture as yours. When people share your images online with their own audiences, then, a little bit of your brand spreads around the virtual world.

As your pictures get shared and spread across the Internet, you can generate more traffic for yourself by doing a few simple things. Optimize your pictures for sharing by

- Including your name in the title
- Including your name in the caption
- Using your Twitter hashtag (for example, #Dummies) in the title
- Using your Twitter hashtag in the caption
- "Watermark" the image before you share it. A watermark is a faint logo or line of text visible within the image. You can add them by using
  - Plug-ins that can automatically watermark uploaded images
  - Photo-editing software

Photo-editing freebies

I continue to be amazed at the quality of free photo-editing software online! If you're new to using photo-editing software and don't want to purchase Photoshop, the premium brand used by many professionals, consider downloading a free open-source application called Gimp. It's highly useful and respectable, and has been around for many years. It just keeps getting better. You can get it at `www.gimp.org`.

Protect your original photography and artwork with watermarks. If the images you use aren't yours, give credit where it's due. And make certain you have permission to use them. Just crediting the photo source may not protect you from copyright violation.

Sharing Your Images on Social Networks

Okay, you've created an eye-grabbing image and added your branding. Now where should you put it? Social networks and photo-sharing sites evolve by the minute these days; in this section, I list the main players. Individual mileage may vary, which is why it's important to understand differences in how the community values and shares pictures. Here are the strongest picture-sharing sites today.

Blogs

It's usually a good strategy to save your best pictures for your blog pages. Hopefully, these are the images that people are going to turn to again and again as they check out your Services, About, and Contact pages. Including an image also helps people to share your posts via Pinterest, Facebook, or Tumblr, where images are shared quickly and easily.

The most important thing to keep in mind about using images for blogging is to not step on anybody's toes in terms of copyright infringement. There are even scams going on right now involving "free" photography downloads. When the unsuspecting customer uses the image, the scammer demands money for the image and threatens to sue, citing copyright infringement.

I prefer to use my own random photography, pictures from friends who have given me permission to share, or to find them on safe places online like

- ✔ **Flickr creative commons** (www.flickr.com/creativecommons). You can find more on them a little later in this chapter.

- ✔ **Veer** (www.veer.com) offers free and paid images, in a variety of browsing categories, as well as fonts. (Fonts are digital typefaces that help to tell the story of your site and images.)

- ✔ **stock.xchng** (www.sxc.hu) says it's the world's leading, free, stock photo site. Offers safe, reliable images and an engaged community.

When you're crafting a blog post, place your image on the left side of the screen. It's often said that people spend more time there because most people read from left to right.

Facebook

Listen up, everyone, this one's important: Facebook claims an ownership interest in every single image (photo, graphic, illustration, infographic, and so on) that gets posted there, whether you designate it as "private" or not.

Yes, you read that right!! Facebook makes good on exercising its ownership interest, too. In a recent case, Facebook used a photographer's images in a series of Facebook ads without any prior notification — and without paying the photographer a dime. Beware!

That's the bad news. Now the good news: Despite this, Facebook is still a terrific place to share pictures accompanying your blog posts. The more your picture gets shared via Facebook's sharing feature, the more your blog post gets put in front of interesting people who may not have ever heard of you before.

Facebook changes its settings often, and the rules will always fluctuate, but when it comes to sharing images, you can't go wrong keeping these tips in mind:

- ✔ Upload pictures that are linked to one of your blog posts.

- ✔ Avoid infographics — unless they're very small. Long infographics may aggravate your friends instead of intriguing them.

- ✔ Share something surprising.

- ✔ Upload something colorful.

As with any online activity, follow up on any responses and engage with people. You may be surprised to learn how many Fortune 100 companies don't reliably monitor their Facebook pages. People will love you for taking the time and attention to relate with them.

Also, when it comes to images on Facebook, it's important to remember those Facebook basics — the profile picture and the Timeline cover. For your profile picture, remember to

- ✔ **Smile from the heart.** It really comes through.

- ✔ **Look into the camera** so people can get a good look at you. It's often said "eyes are the window to the soul."

- ✔ **Wear something appropriate and that you don't mind sharing** with the world (including potential business contacts).

As for the Timeline cover, remember the profile picture and the Timeline cover are the same size, which is 851 pixels wide x 315 pixels high. Facebook cautions people against advertising via these Timeline covers. People who violate these rules may end up getting their pages removed without warning. To make sure you're compliant, avoid putting onto your Facebook Timeline cover graphic

- ✔ Calls to action, such as "tell your friends"

- ✔ Contests

- ✔ Promotions

- ✔ Any kind of contact information (though you still get to share this in your page's "About" section)

- ✔ Requests for people to "like" or "share"

Google+

Google+ is an extraordinary community for professionals of any kind to share images and collaborate, but I especially appreciate the work there by professional photographers. They often post beautiful images and include information about the equipment they use and how they achieve their special camera effects. Google+ is a terrific place to learn tips and appreciate fantastic work.

Unlike Facebook, Google+ says that you retain ownership of any intellectual property rights that you hold on your images.

At the moment, desktop version of Google Plus looks different than the version for mobile devices, but it won't be long before you can enjoy a prettier and easier-to-navigate mobile version of Google+, according to Google.

Pinterest

Because Pinterest is a "virtual pinboard," it's an image-poster's paradise. It lets you post and organize images from all over the Internet. If you like images, Pinterest is for you.

Pinning for SEO

Pinterest has been around for a few years, but it suddenly became super popular as a tool to boost search engine marketing. Originally, everything you "pinned" included a link to your site containing the image. Now those links are "no follow," which prevents search engines from passing that link love back to your site. You can still add followed links into the description of a pin, however, so it can still be valuable to your image-sharing strategy.

Pinterest's popularity is growing fast. In the first half of 2012, Pinterest generated more referral traffic than Google+, YouTube, and LinkedIn combined.

When posting images on Pinterest, keep these tips in mind:

- **Use a hashtag so people searching for your content can find you.** For example, if you are a food blogger and have a juicy fruit salad picture you want to share, name it something like "Juicy #Fruit Salad" so people can find it more easily.

- **Upload a picture that links to your blog post that tells more about it.** For example, pictures of food are very common on Pinterest. When you click on the item, you can normally click through to a blog post that has a recipe or story about that item. I love it!

- **Use your search engine optimization (SEO) keywords as board categories, as appropriate.** Figure 13-3 shows you a few of my Pinterest boards. Please note the use of one of my obvious keyword terms: online reputation management. When people search for this term via Pinterest, they are very likely to find me. I use pictures from my blog posts and link them from my site so that visitors can click on them to learn more.

Slideshare

Slideshare is becoming an increasingly popular image-sharing venue. It's a well-respected professional platform, and you can find an amazing array of presentations to absorb that never would have been possible without traveling to a conference. (See Figure 13-4.)

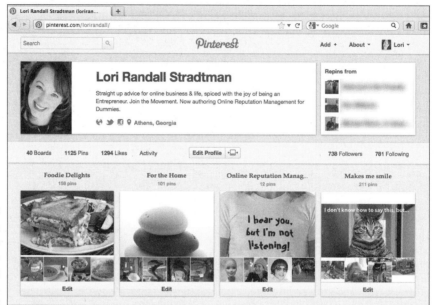

Figure 13-3:
Note the key
terms on my
Pinterest
boards.

Although I have only shared a couple of my speaking presentations on it, many people are creating and uploading slide shows that they haven't even given in front of an audience. It's really smart if you do a polished, professional presentation that delivers meaningful value. Some online reputation benefits are that

✔ You can embed your presentation onto your Facebook fan page or send links to your Twitter account, to really make the most out of your presentations.

✔ It gives you a great place to use those SEO keywords that you research in Chapter 6. Name your slideshare account after yourself or your brand, but be sure to use your relevant keywords in the tags to get Google's attention.

✔ They offer instant transcription, which is great because it picks up some of the SEO keywords that you use in the presentation.

✔ If your slideshare presentation is captivating enough, the slideshare community will feature you on its site, which results in amazing exposure and is a solid endorsement to your online reputation.

Figure 13-4:
Slideshare.

Flickr

A lot of professional and serious amateur photographers post on Flickr. It features different sharing distinctions that protect your rights if you only want people to see your work, but not share it easily. These designations make it really fun to share on Flickr and can contribute toward protecting your ownership of an image, though I must tell you that any time you post a picture, somebody can figure out a way to copy it. Period.

Flickr's privacy settings can be set at a default level or can be customized per image. You can change your settings for the photography or artwork you upload at any time. The settings are

- ✔ Public
- ✔ Private
- ✔ Friends
- ✔ Family
- ✔ Friends and family

Flickr's Creative Commons is a gold mine for blogging post pictures! Just give attribution at the bottom of your post, and you're set. (See Figure 13-5.) Always remember to protect your reputation by giving image credit to other photographers and artists and ensuring you have permission to use their works at all.

Navigating Flickr in search of free images can be a little tricky, so I want to show you exactly how to get your hands on Creative Commons pictures that are free to use with no copyright infringement worries. Figure 13-5 shows what your profile looks like once you set it up. Please note that on Flickr it greets you with "Hello" in different languages. It's a fun way to remember that you're on the Internet and that almost anybody in the world can see your images if you use the default view.

Navigate to the top menu bar and look for Explore. From the drop-down menu that appears, click on The Commons. Figure 13-6 shows what this should look like. Even if Flickr changes its layout a little, the steps will be the same.

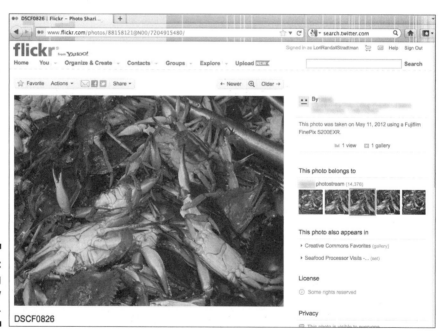

Figure 13-5:
Feeling
Crabby
Gallery Pic.

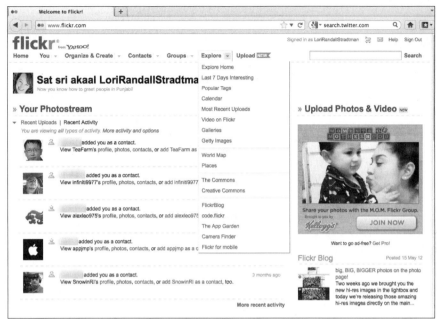

Figure 13-6:
Flickr
Photo-
stream
Home
View.

Inside The Commons are many different licensing categories, including

- **Attribution License:** It lets others copy, distribute, display, and perform their copyrighted work — and derivative works based upon it — but only if you give them credit. You can include a photo credit link at the bottom of your blog post to satisfy this requirement.

- **Attribution-NoDerivs License:** This is the same as Attribution (see preceding bullet) plus No Derivative Works, which means it lets others copy, distribute, display, and perform only verbatim copies of their work, not derivative works based upon it. You can use these images and include a photo credit link at the bottom of your blog post if you don't change them in any way.

- **Attribution-Noncommercial-NoDerivs License:** This is the same as Attribution-NoDerivs (see preceding bullet), plus Noncommercial, which means it lets others copy, distribute, display, and perform their work — and derivative works based upon it — but only for noncommercial purposes. I play it safe and avoid using these for blogging when it's a business blog, but you're wide open to use them for hobby blogs where nothing is being sold.

- **Attribution-Noncommercial License:** This is similar to Attribution-Noncommercial-NoDerivs (see description above) except without the NoDerivs clause. You can use these images and include a photo credit link at the bottom of your blog post if you aren't selling anything on your site.

✔ **Attribution-Noncommercial-ShareAlike License:** This is the same thing as the preceding category, except that ShareAlike means it allows others to distribute derivative works only under a license identical to the license that governs their work.

✔ **Attribution-ShareAlike License:** This combines the Attribution and ShareAlike licenses. As long as you include a photo credit link and accept that if you've changed the image in any way that people only need to give you a photo credit link as well, then this will work for you too.

The bottom line for me is that I tend to only use the attribution license for my business blog, and I don't change the images in any way. I supply a photo credit at the bottom of my posts and link not because I have to, but because it's a nice thing to do. It's how I say thank you.

Tumblr

Tumblr is the mainstream social media home of NFSW (not for the kiddies) content, as well as a number of mainstream blogs and cute fashion profiles. I have a profile on Tumblr and it's quite tame, though it's quirkier than my LinkedIn profile. See LinkedIn down below for something more mainstream and professional looking.

I suggest using Tumblr for spreading brand awareness if your brand is about fashion, photography, or art, because those communities thrive there since it's primarily an image-sharing platform.

Instagram

Instagram is a photo-sharing service that links to prominent social media networks, so this makes it an especially interesting tool for sharing images with an eye towards spreading your brand's name online. It also gives you some pretty nice, instant photo-editing filters, such as inkwell, toaster, earlybird, and sutro, that can enhance the personality of your images. It's fun to check them out, but it's certainly not necessary for photo sharing successfully.

Facebook purchased Instagram in the first half of 2012, and it's unclear whether Facebook will allow Instagram to continue as a separate service or just exactly what Facebook will do with it. I suggest that unless you're already a huge user with an established audience, it's best to promote your online reputation with a site that's more stable so that you can reap more long-term benefits by building an audience via a more long-lasting social network.

About NFSW content

No discussion of sharing pictures online is complete without at least acknowledging the startling fact that at least 75 percent of the Internet is devoted to pictures you don't show your kids, according to top network engineers.

Some of my research for online reputation management includes interviewing artists who work with nudes, for example. Photo-sharing networks like Tumblr and (believe it or not) Pinterest do not moderate content, so these may be places to share artwork, though Pinterest communities tend to be less edgy than Tumblr.

Twitter

Even though Twitter is a huge, social media network with more than 140 million users (as of March, 2012), sharing images via Twitter goes in and out of vogue. It's always an available option for adding interest to your tweets if your content is well chosen and you introduce it with something attention-getting. I think it's pretty terrific to link to a great infographic via Twitter because it delivers a lot of relevant content for one easily sharable link.

You can upload pictures directly via Twitter, or any application that posts to Twitter, such as HootSuite and TweetDeck.

LinkedIn

Because LinkedIn is a "professional" network, it should be your least quirky or surprising profile, unless it's to demonstrate how surprisingly accomplished you are in your profession. Use a profile picture that's been taken within the past year or two. Always represent yourself the way you would want a potential client or employer to see you. This isn't the most appropriate place to share your offbeat humor or cutesy images. Save those for Facebook!

Concocting Viral Videos

One day, a friend of mine who works as a social media strategist told me that his employer was instructing him to "create a viral video for us." This is a worthy goal, to be sure, but it's an almost impossible one to achieve.

If I knew how to reliably create viral videos, I'd be too busy counting my money to write a book on online reputation management.

Forty-eight hours of content is uploaded to YouTube every minute of the day. How can you get your video to go viral? You may not be able to do it reliably, but you can at least improve your chances by using these tips:

- **Drop your video on Friday:** Most videos that go viral peak the highest on Fridays.

- **Appeal to tastemakers:** Many of the most popular viral videos are first uploaded in obscurity.

   But then something awesome happens. A late-night pundit or taste-maker, like Jimmy Kimmel, Jon Stewart, or Stephen Colbert, gets wind of this video and shares it with his or her own particular perspective on what it means.

   Suddenly, thousands of people who are watching this on TV check it out on their mobile devices, laptops, or desktops and then share with their friends on Facebook, YouTube, and Twitter as fast as they can with their own comments. (An example, the "Double Rainbow" video, appears in Figure 13-7.)

Figure 13-7:
The famous "Double Rainbow" video.

✔ **Remix an existing viral video:** The only thing more fun than sharing a running joke is to embellish it.

Take the "Nyan Cat" video, for example. (See Figure 13-8.) If you have a high tolerance for looped animations and music, this one's for you! People have had a wild time recreating this simple video with

- Embellished music

- Artistic effects, such as sepia, which gives it a vintage look and feel

- International Nyan Kitties, with different themes

- Video of a cat watching Nyan Cat

- A girl dressed up as the Nyan Cat and playing the theme on her violin

There's even a three-and-a-half-hour extended version of Nyan Cat that has been downloaded close to 5 million times. Remix well and you can get a lot of attention.

✔ **Add surprises:** Focus on creating something with a unique, unexpected twist.

One such totally surprising viral video features a guy promoting the need for protected bike lanes in NYC while riding a bike into unsafe situations because he's paying too much attention to the camera. I hope he's a stuntman because he keeps getting into accidents, which proves his point. (See Figure 13-9.)

Figure 13-8:
Nyan Cat.

Figure 13-9:
The bike
lanes video.

Chapter 14

Discovering and Inspiring Brand Evangelists

*F*ew things are more wonderful than discovering that you have a fan. I'm not talking about the new guy on Facebook who liked your business page — although that's good, too — I'm talking about real fans, people who consistently share your blog posts, comment on your updates, and demonstrate that they really "get" and appreciate your brand. Fans like these are more than just followers — they're *brand evangelists*.

Relationships with your fans, as with face-to-face relationships, flourish when they're reciprocated. Returning your brand evangelists' appreciation nurtures those relationships and pays big dividends for your online reputation.

In this chapter, I show you how to discover your most influential brand supporters, and how to deepen your relationships with them.

Understanding Your Brand Evangelists

In order to attract brand evangelists, it helps to understand why they care about you in the first place. What motivates your brand evangelists? Simple. They're after meaning. Something about your brand or your message resonates with them, and they want to learn more. They want a relationship with you because they see something special in you or your brand.

Psychologist Abraham Maslow created his (famous) Hierarchy of Needs to explain the motivations of human development. I created a similar hierarchy to explain the motivations of your brand evangelists. The hierarchy goes as follows (see Figure 14-1):

WHAT ENERGIZES YOUR BRAND EVANGELISTS?

Recognition

Involvement

Belonging

Trust

Knowledge

Figure 14-1:
My
Hierarchy
of Needs
for brand
evangelists.

✔ **Knowledge:** In Maslow's hierarchy, our most basic requirements are for physiological basics like air, food, and shelter. For brand evangelists, this is more about informational basics, or knowledge.

When you provide quality information that is specially tailored to your audience, you are giving your brand ambassadors something unique, powerful, and meaningful for their audiences.

Be generous. Give your brand ambassadors the tools they need to become experts. This doesn't mean you have to give away free consulting or proprietary information, but showing people what's important and telling them why it is huge.

✔ **Trust:** The next level up on Maslow's hierarchy includes safety needs like law, order, and stability. For brand evangelists, this means trust. People need to know they can trust your product or service. You can help to foster trust by being

• *Reliable:* Under-promise and over-deliver.

• *Consistent:* Blog on a routine schedule so people can fall into a rhythm with hearing from you.

• *Stable:* Clarify your message and stick with it. Focus is essential to success.

• *Predictable:* Think about some of your favorite brands. Odds are that they've evolved throughout the years while still retaining their essential uniqueness. It's a form of predictability that's very endearing.

✔ **Belonging:** Maslow's hierarchy lists belonging and love needs next. These involve things like affection, family, and other relationships. In terms of your brand evangelists, this translates to belonging — you need to create a sense of community where people belong because they share a common interest or passion in the same thing.

✔ **Involvement:** The next level of Maslow's hierarchy includes esteem needs — things like achievement, responsibility, reputation, and status.

Your online brand evangelists want to be involved with you. They don't need bribes or gimmicks to do so. They don't want your free T-shirt: What they really desire is to develop more of a relationship with you because they admire what you're doing.

You can help to foster these relationships by listening to these people. Acknowledge them privately, appreciate what they're doing online, and express genuine appreciation when they've helped to influence your next move.

You don't have to give away private information or do anything that makes you uncomfortable, but as you give people the same sort of recognition that makes you feel good, your relationship deepens, which is the essence of creating and maintaining a strong reputation online.

Your brand promoters are storytellers who spread the heart of your idea. Give them a story that's engaging and easy to share.

✔ **Recognition:** Self-actualization sits at the peak of Maslow's hierarchy. It involves personal growth and fulfillment. This may seem like a tricky concept to apply to your brand evangelists, but you can do this very simply by

- Identifying and linking to them in blog posts
- Sending them an occasional personalized message or tweet
- Commenting on their Facebook pages
- Inviting them to write a guest post for your blog
- Naming and linking to them in e-mail newsletters
- Publishing their reviews of your product/service
- Approaching them for advance feedback on your upcoming books, white papers, projects, products, and so on
- Sending them an occasional personalized gift or card for the joy of it

Love the one you're with: It costs five-to-seven times more to reach a new fan or follower than it does to cultivate an existing one.

Being a brand evangelist shows you've got good taste and that you want to contribute to your community in a meaningful way. Don't just court your own brand evangelists — be one yourself!

Discovering Them Online

It's often easy to spot your brand evangelists. You see their retweets, blog comments, and status update comments. Sometimes they post directly onto your Facebook page with something interesting or they share your content.

As you set up your listening tools, you will begin to see even more about what people are saying about you, your brand, and your industry online.

It would be wonderful to have enough time to validate each and every fan for your brand, but once you get to a certain point online, there are more cool people to chat with than the time that you'd like to spend chatting with them. After all, there are lots and lots of people online!

Savvy online reputation managers identify their most influential brand promoters by looking through the blogosphere, Facebook, Twitter, LinkedIn, and Google+, for starters. (The next few sections discuss this in detail.) If your brand holds more visual appeal, such as if you're an artist, photographer, or designer, you need to check out their influence on photo-sharing sites like

- ✔ Pinterest
- ✔ Google+
- ✔ Tumblr
- ✔ Flickr
- ✔ Picasa
- ✔ Instagram

Targeting your message to your best brand promoters is a handy shortcut to creating your ideal client profile. They tend to be the same person!

Blogs

You can assess whether a blogger is influential by how large his number of followers is, but I believe the stronger measure is how much that blogger's audience is paying attention to what he says. If your brand ambassador consistently gets blog comments and shares, people value your ambassador's integrity, opinion, and passion.

Number of blog posts is also a good indicator of a blogger's trustworthiness.

Anybody can blog into a vacuum without getting much response, but these days blog comments are getting more and more scarce, and therefore more valuable. Look at a few posts before you decide whether you think someone is influential or not, because some posts are hot and some posts are not. Experimentation is allowed and encouraged.

Be sure to look at any social media–sharing icons to see how widespread their posts are whether they tend to get many meaningful comments. It helps if these comments are positive, but that isn't always necessary. It's better to be engaging and interesting, even if you're controversial, than to be plain and unopinionated. Blogging requires stepping out on a limb.

The blogging holy grail involves lots of followers and lots of engagement.

Facebook

Facebook followers, friends, likes, and shares are all indicators of interest, influence, and participation there.

I want to clear up some common misconceptions before we go any further into assessing somebody else's influence on Facebook. When you sign up for Facebook you automatically receive a "profile" that you can use to add friends and share lifestyle events with them. If you want, you can create a "Facebook Page" from there by answering some more questions and identifying the kind of page you want to create. Facebook treats its profiles and pages very differently, because profiles are supposed to be strictly personal. You can't have a profile named "Betty Sue's Cut & Curl," for instance, because it's a brand name.

People will occasionally create both a Facebook profile and a Facebook Page in their own name. This can be misleading when you're trying to figure out how much influence somebody has online because anybody can round up 5,000 Facebook friends over a weekend. Figure 14-2 shows my Facebook profile, which is in my own name. On this profile, I limit the number of people I'm friends with.

It's much more difficult to get people to like a Facebook fan page, so it's a better indicator for genuine interest in that person's brand. Figure 14-3 shows my Facebook Page, which is in the name of Social Media Design.

Figure 14-2:
My
Facebook
profile.

Figure 14-3:
My
Facebook
Page.

Lots of people are investing time and energy into creating social media analytics sites for Facebook fan pages. A few include:

- ✔ **AgoraPulse:** Offers Facebook Page management, marketing campaign applications, social CRM, lead management, and more. Check it out at `www.agorapulse.com`.

- ✔ **SproutSocial:** Social media aggregation tool (I share more about these in Chapter 5). It also offers comprehensive reporting and analytics. It can be found at `http://sproutsocial.com`.

- ✔ **BlitzMetrics:** Comprehensive service offering uniquely detailed info, such as geographic mapping of fans and monitoring Pages of competitors. Learn more at `https://blitzmetrics.com/content`.

Twitter

It's a good idea to look up your brand evangelists and influencers on Twitter. Check to see

- ✔ How many followers they have
- ✔ How often they're listed
- ✔ What kinds of lists they appear on
- ✔ How often they're retweeted
- ✔ What categories get retweeted most
- ✔ If they regularly participate in Tweet Chats (If they do, note the category to see if it meshes with categories you rank in.)

LinkedIn

If your brand evangelist has a LinkedIn profile, look it over carefully. See if it's been filled out completely. Check out her work history and education, as well as any testimonials that tell you a little bit about her personality and what she's known for.

The number of followers she has may not be important if her relationships run deep. I suggest you pay more attention to quality than quantity. Figure 14-4 is a screenshot of my LinkedIn profile.

You can visualize your own spheres of influence on LinkedIn with a cool LinkedIn tool called InMaps (`http://inmaps.linkedinlabs.com`). (See Figure 14-5.)

Figure 14-4:
My LinkedIn
profile.

Figure 14-5:
LinkedIn
InMaps tool.

Google+

The best way to tell how influential somebody is on Google+ is to first Google her name and then check out her profile. Look to see how much feedback she's getting on what she posts. The following Google+ tools help you to take a closer look at your influence on Google+ as well:

- ✔ **SocialStatistics:** Features the Google+ "Top 100" and more. Find it at `http://socialstatistics.com`.

- ✔ **CircleCount:** Shares people with highly engaging content on Google Plus, most followed profiles, most followed pages, and my favorite "Today's Cream of the Crop," which features a particularly interesting and popular profile. Learn more at `www.circlecount.com`.

- ✔ **FindPeopleOnPlus:** Offers a cool filtering tool so that you can look for interesting people to follow based on different demographic criteria, such as education level, relationship status, gender, and age. Check it out at `http://findpeopleonplus.com`.

Recognizing True Influence

True social media influence is impossible to measure. There are infinite approaches to measuring different aspects that may well add up to something interesting, but nothing you discover via any listening platform can top doing a little manual searching around for the following kinds of activities.

Speaking at conferences

Check this person's site or social media platforms to see if he has spoken at any conferences within the past year or two. He gets bonus points for keynoting. Pay attention to the venues where he speaks. I've keynoted for conferences with hundreds of people in Las Vegas and New York City, but I've also given intimate little seminars to 30 people crammed in a room.

Take a look at what kind of conference she is addressing. If your brand is all about macramé potholders and your brand promoter is presenting at a macramé convention, you've got a serious gem of a follower!

Authoring books

Have a look at his site and social profiles to see if he has authored any books. Although indie publishing is gaining popularity, you can be sure that if he has written a book that's been published by a traditional publisher, he has been thoroughly checked out as having influence and being known as an expert in his field.

Some other influential authoring categories include

- ✔ White papers
- ✔ Podcasts
- ✔ Video series

Participating in groups

If your brand evangelist lists a number of professional organizations related to your brand, group, or local meet-up group, it is a definite sign that you have discovered a fantastic brand promoter. Look for clues that will show you how active this person is within the organizations or groups.

Comments on blogs and periodicals

The line between blogging and journalism gets fuzzier by the day, both in legal terms and in how people use them online. Blogs often contain serious news, and professional news sites now feature social media connectivity and commenting. You can get amazingly useful information about your existing (and potential) brand evangelists when you check out popular websites for your industry. Investigate what their commenters are saying. It's likely that you will see more assertive, informed people surface who seem likely to appreciate your own brand, based on their preferences.

Blogs

One of the coolest things about blog commenting is that there are platforms that allow you to search for everything a person has said online via blog comments on that platform. You can learn a lot more about your brand evangelists by checking out where they comment most and how they feel about your industry. In the following list I've included the most popular commenting platforms — these give you the most information about commenters:

- ✔ **Gravatar:** An image that follows you around from site to site appearing beside your name when you comment on a blog post. You can look up a brand ambassador on Gravatar to see what kinds of comments are being made and where they are being left. This gives you a great idea about where this person's interests lie and how influential he may be for your own brand. I suggest reading several comments to get an accurate feel for his tastes. Figure 14-6 shows you what a Gravatar profile looks like. You can find Gravatar online at `https://en.gravatar.com`.

✔ **Disqus:** Another platform that does much the same thing as Gravatar, except that Disqus offers site moderators a lot of spam prevention features to make managing a site more convenient. Enables users to share comments on Facebook, and Twitter. Check it out at `http://disqus.com`.

✔ **Livefyre:** A relatively new social commenting platform that leverages Facebook and Twitter very well. Includes the same features as Gravatar. Learn more at `www.livefyre.com`.

✔ **IntenseDebate:** This has similar features to Disqus, Gravatar, and Livefyre, and also has a nice spam filter. Works on a variety of platforms, so this is great for checking out comments on more than WordPress. Discover more about IntenseDebate at `http://intensedebate.com`.

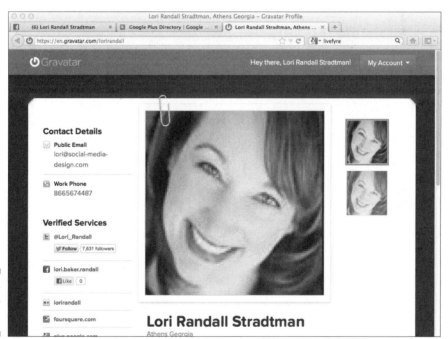

Figure 14-6:
My Gravatar
profile.

Periodicals

Services like PeekYou (see Figure 14-7) can index information about you and your brand promoters if they identify themselves while commenting on these sites. (For more on PeekYou, see the section "Rating Influence," later in this chapter.)

✔ *Huffington Post:* Not only features sharing on Facebook and Twitter, but it also indicates when posts on each of those networks are "hot." Also notifies you when a friend has published a post right there on the *Huffington Post.*

> ✔ *New York Times:* You have to log in or create an account in order to comment, but the *New York Times* does connect with Facebook, Twitter, and Google+.

Figure 14-7:
Peek in on
PeekYou.

Participating in forums

Google definitely picks up activities like participating in forums. When you do a Google search for your brand promoter, go through a few pages of results and see if any forums related to your industry pop up. You may even discover some forums that are new and interesting to you.

Wikis

A *wiki* is a website on which a community of users are invited to add, remove, or edit any page they like via a web browser. It's super easy for people to jump in and revise pages. Wikis are becoming known as the tool of choice for large projects involving lots of people. Wikipedia (www.wikipedia.org) is the most well-known wiki online, though people create wikis surrounding almost any topic.

If you are involved in a growing industry, there may well be wikis that you or your brand promoters are active on. Take note of active, insightful wiki

community users and then search for them online to see if they have websites or social profiles. You may well discover interesting competitors, key
influencers, and your own brand evangelists.

Online followers and friends

It's always fun to have friends and followers online. There are so many social
media sites that I don't have room to name them all. Still, because you're this
far into the book, you know the big players. Some other popular sites include

- ✔ **Quora:** Question & Answer forum. Find them at `www.quora.com`.

- ✔ **Foursquare:** A geolocation application. Located at `https://
foursquare.com`.

- ✔ **GetGlue:** A social network for sharing with friends what you're watching, listening to, or reading. Learn more at `http://getglue.com`.

- ✔ **Goodreads:** Keeps track of what you've read and organizes your books
into virtual bookshelves. Check it out at `www.goodreads.com`.

Rating Influence

While nothing beats a manual, check into what your best brand promoters
are all about online; it's pretty great to have tools available that can drill
deep down into the information in seconds while you check your e-mail.

These tools are also useful for discovering new influencers to follow who may
be helpful to you in the future:

- ✔ **Followerwonk** (`http://followerwonk.com`): Followerwonk (see
Figure 14-8) is a surprisingly robust platform for evaluating followers.
Within only a few hours, you can pull up an astonishing amount of qual-
ity information. The free version lets you

  - Search Twitter bios

  - Compare Twitter users

  - Analyze followers/follows

  - Overlay your social graph from other accounts to find overlaps in
followers

  The paid version does much more, and subscription prices range from
$40 to $2,000 a month.

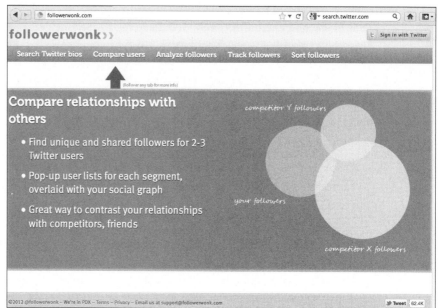

Figure 14-8:
Follower-
wonk.

✔ **Klout** (`http://klout.com/home`)**:** Klout just keeps getting better and better. It started by tracking Facebook and Twitter alone, but now it includes LinkedIn and many more platforms. Check out your brand promoters' profiles on Klout, if they have one, and see what areas they're influential in and how they're rated.

✔ **Traackr** (`http://traackr.com`)**:** Traackr is a much more sophisticated tool than Klout and has a $399 monthly subscription rate to go with it. Tracks "A-List" individuals who are thought leaders about a specific topic. This is a very good tool if you can justify the business expense.

✔ **eCairn** (`http://ecairn.com`)**:** Listening platform that creates influencer lists of bloggers. Has a lot of flexibility for more in-depth searches. Average user spends $99 a month. Main features include

- Brand monitoring and reputation management

- Tracking social media initiatives

- Identifying brand advocates or influencers

- Improving customer insight and market research

- Gathering competitive intelligence

✔ **PeekYou** (`http://peekyou.com`)**:** If you don't mind looking past a few ads, this free influence-rating tool is a real gem for checking out who your brand ambassadors and influencers are, as well as to assess their online influence. You can use it to search according to

- Name

- Interests

- Work

- School

- City

- Phone

- E-mail

- Google

PeekYou also allows you to track comments made to periodicals. See the earlier section, "Periodicals," for more.

Deepening Your Relationships

Social media dynamics are all about relationships. Social media have a more face-to-face feeling than any other form of media because you're expected to converse one to one. It's about a million times more intimate than a noisy infomercial blaring out of a TV set. Because of that back-and-forth, there's a lot of growth potential.

The following points show how you can maximize that potential to improve your relationships with evangelists — and everyone else — online.

- ✔ **Listen intently:** The more you pay attention to what people say about you, your brand, and your industry, the more intelligence you have to make smart decisions about what you will do with your business. Listen to the way people describe their problems so that you can articulate answers to those problems in a way that they can better understand.

- ✔ **Make sure people "get" your message:** The best way to make sure people "get" your message is to share a compelling, results-oriented story that makes your point. However, this isn't the only way.

    This morning, I read an excerpt from a CNN interview with the founder of Klout. The interviewer asked him whether it was true that the whole idea for the Klout platform came out of the founder's love of burritos. It had, sort of, and that's just the kind of memorable, surprising detail that makes stories more interesting.

    Clearly, sharing that you got the entire idea for a social influence platform while musing about your love of good burrito places makes a startling first impression. Any time you can combine two ideas that don't go together into one statement, you've got an attention getter. A few other methods:

    - *Use rhymes or alliteration:* Alliteration constantly crushes consonants, for example.

- *Create a common enemy:* Like bad breath, sticky keyboards, or slow load times.

- *Insult someone or something:* Not my favorite, but a trusty standby for certain personalities and brands.

- *Use pop-culture references:* Linking popular songs, TV shows, movies, or celebrities to your content draws attention.

- *Use lists:* A time-honored favorite, featuring a periodic "Top Ten" post can be quite appealing if you research your topic well.

- *Use over-the-top statements:* Using terms like "ultimate," "life-changing," or "never-fail" can be a fun attention grabber for your readers — but only if you use them sparingly.

Become a master at paring down your message to its rock-bottom essentials. Getting messages this clear takes a lot of discipline. Sometimes you can get straight to the heart of your message by answering some basic questions. Ask yourself these questions and be honest about the answers. You may end up with a message clear enough to share with anyone:

- Who am I? (not as a human being, but just as a person representing a brand. No mountaintop retreats required)

- What do I do?

- Whom do I do it for?

- Why do I do it? (What is your larger purpose here?)

✔ **Share concrete results:** Nothing inspires people to share the love of a brand faster than supplying them with measurable results. Instead of featuring testimonials that say something like "My new Flitzer 5000 makes me so happy," ask your satisfied clients for something more concrete, like "My new Flitzer 5000 makes me so happy because it got me ten new, ideal clients last week."

Of course, this approach works best when you can actually substantiate your numbers with more than an artistic flair for the truth. It's the Internet. People need more reassurances here than they do with local, brick-and-mortar businesses.

Give people a touch point so they can imagine themselves getting a similar result. Being "happy" is great, but it can be pretty subjective. Give them something specific to daydream and talk about.

✔ **Keep in touch:** Perhaps the most effective way you can deepen relationships with your brand promoters and influencers is to create an e-mail newsletter and publish something with a personal touch regularly.

Respond to people on the same social network or blog that they use to contact you most frequently. And always, always treat people the way you want to be treated in the same situation. Mutual respect is the "golden glue" that holds healthy relationships together, on and off-line.

Part V
Responding to Crisis

The 5th Wave   By Rich Tennant

"Somebody got through our dead end web links, past the firewalls, and around the phone prompt loops. Before you know it, the kid here picks up the phone and he's talking one-on-one to a customer."

In this part . . .

In Part V, it's time to grapple with crises online. Chapter 15 shows you how to spot and manage escalating issues as quickly and easily as possible. If you just want to cut to the chase to see what happens during crisis management, turn to Chapter 16, where I share the most current tips and considerations as I show you how to work through a true crisis situation as efficiently as possible. Everybody likes a happy ending, and in Chapter 17, I give you tips for promoting goodwill and turning lemons into lemonade as online issues arise and after they are resolved.

Chapter 15

Managing Escalating Issues

. . . .

. . . .

*N*ow that you've assembled your everyday, social media team, created your crisis communications team, set up your monitoring tools, and published top-quality content about you or your brand online, you have created a solid foundation for yourself. Now you're ready for the hard stuff: How can you best manage an escalating online crisis?

These days, an online crisis can blow up quickly, but when you understand how to manage an escalating issue effectively, you can avoid an online reputation catastrophe. Crisis aversion is an invisible art: When done correctly, no one will ever know that you did anything. Your reputation will remain untarnished, and no one will be the wiser.

In this chapter, I show you how to deal with such an escalating issue. The main difference between an escalating issue and a full-blown crisis is the passage of time. An emerging crisis is one that is just developing on a few social media channels and hasn't reached a general level of outrage. Most crisis situations don't come as a total surprise because they arise from long ignored vulnerabilities or issues. In Chapter 16, I explain what to do if the unthinkable happens and your escalating issue blows up to crisis proportions.

Assessing Your Situation

Preventing an escalating, social media crisis is a delicate situation. It calls for a greater degree of delicacy and research than normal day-to-day engagement online. In order to assess the situation, you need to

- ✔ Understand the conversation surrounding the issue. Look for identifiable themes and people whose content is being shared the most.

- ✔ Identify which social media channels are affected so you can respond on the same channels.

- ✔ Research the issue that's being discussed in case it's an issue you've dealt with before, one for which you have a ready solution.

If you feel like you are dealing with something that continues to escalate as you research and as you begin to take action, you may be dealing with a full-blown crisis. In that case, it's time to get help. Turn to Chapter 16 for advice on how to turn the situation around as quickly as possible.

Learning More About Your Commenters

Under normal conditions, as you use your listening tools, you track your commenters in general terms (although it can be really useful to identify your biggest fans). In those circumstances, you don't need to research every commenter. Now, however, you need to learn all you can about the people commenting. This gives you a better context in which to

- ✔ Understand what's going on
- ✔ Make an educated guess about what these people want from the interaction

It's also really important for you to find out how broad a network your commenters have and on which social networks they're most popular. Routinely listen across relevant channels for words like "hate," "sucks," "bad," "not working," and so on, in conjunction with your brand name. Google Alerts can be very handy for setting up these routine searches. (For more on Google Alerts, see Chapter 7.) You should also track who is linking to your site and read that person's blog posts and articles. When you locate your commenter, take a few moments to figure out what's going on. Carefully read the content, whether it's a tweet or a long blog post, and try to understand the commenter's point of view.

Approach commenters in good faith, with the intention of helping them. If you discover that your commenters aren't acting in good faith (in other words, if you have trollers) remain calm, and don't let them get to you emotionally.

Do you have a relationship with that person? Is he your brand's customer? The answers to these questions affect how you should respond. Your decisions get a little trickier when your commenter turns out to be

✔ **An anonymous profile:** I mean someone who isn't logged in or who isn't using any sort of traceable name or ID, not Anonymous, the hacker group. (That would definitely qualify as a full-on social media crisis.)

✔ **An obviously fake profile:** When people use obviously fake profiles they aren't typically dealing honestly with your brand. Spotting a fake profile can be very difficult and time consuming. You need to cross reference that social profile with others using that name, follow up with links, and look up key phrases they use in order to spot a pattern online. You can use the following information to help you spot a fake Facebook profile, but please remember that these are just guidelines Questionable profiles can often be legitimate. Use your best judgment. You can also use these guidelines to assess profiles you encounter on other social networks.

  • 97% of fake profiles use women's names (58% of those claimed to be interested in both men and women).

  • 15% of regular profiles have never posted status updates, but 43% of fake profiles have never updated their Facebook statuses.

  • Regular profiles tag (link the image to another user on Facebook) an average of one person for every four photos posted. Fake profiles average 136 tags for every four photos uploaded!

  • Regular profiles average about 130 friends, whereas fake profiles average about 726 friends.

✔ **One of a set of multiple profiles:** The escalating "conversation" can be the product of a single commenter using a number of different names.

✔ **Part of an echo chamber:** An *echo chamber* exists when a person repeats an erroneous point (or set of points) made by another source, often a source with some degree of reliability. Often the commenter is a well-meaning person simply spreading someone else's message. But because he's making a point he believes comes from an authoritative source, he gains confidence — even though he's wrong — and won't back down easily. Typical echo-chamber comments tend to include

  • Bullying or just plain mean comments

  • Accusations or condemnations of the actions of others

  • Personal attacks

  • Unreasonable demands

  • Well-meaning people spreading somebody else's message

Dealing with online echo chambers

Online echo chambers can impose chilling effects on any individual brave enough to post contradictory opinions. Insults and accusations fly quickly.

The same dynamic is sometimes at work when established thought leaders in the same industry work to promote one another. It's great to have a group of online colleagues/competitors that you respect, but when the people in that group start following each other blindly and carelessly repeating messages, this can quickly become an echo chamber. When such people find an erroneous point they want to make and decide to "spread the word online," it's difficult for anyone to correct them. And worse, all this attention can drive up Google ratings for the conversation (because it's so interesting and juicy) and bring fresh traffic right to you when you appear to be at a terrible disadvantage.

When the echo chamber "flames" on your blog, you can choose to turn off comments, but that can backfire if your group is determined and has sites and audiences of their own to galvanize.

Often, echo-chamber commenters are just riding a bandwagon and simply trying to get a rise out of you. In most cases, you can ruin their fun simply by keeping your cool. The best thing you can do is to take decisive action, even as you take the high road. State your case sensitively and in clear terms. Respond only to legitimate questions. If necessary, announce a follow-up post as soon as possible to discuss the issue further (and intelligently). Time is of the essence when you're dealing with an escalating issue online.

Determining motivations

As you are doing your homework to check out your more prominent commenters in this escalating situation, ask yourself what may be motivating the main people involved. Most often, people will start agitating online in order to

- ✔ **Get attention:** Trolls derive a sense of power from getting negative attention even.
- ✔ **Driving traffic back to their blog:** This is a sneaky tactic used by many bloggers interested in stealing attention from one conversation in order to draw attention to themselves and their blog. If this becomes a routine problem, I suggest modifying your commenting system's settings so that people can't leave links or share videos on your site. This cleans things up nicely and won't subject you to derision, because every blogger should know that this is a questionable tactic anyway.
- ✔ **Being a sneaky competitor:** Sometimes competitors poke around just to discover perceived weak spots in your customer service or expertise.

✔ **Desiring some good old-fashioned customer service:** Serve it up in style and demonstrate that they matter.

✔ **Wanting more information about your service or product:** Depending on the size of your organization, you need to either handle this yourself by referring them to more informative resources that they can read/ watch on their own time, or have someone in the sales department contact them via the same medium they contacted you on. In other words, if they contacted you via Twitter, answer via Twitter.

✔ **Expressing concern about a mounting issue:** Definitely let them know that you are there, you're listening, and tell them what's being done about the issue and that you will publish updates if they want to check back with you. Again, make sure it's the same medium so that you aren't asking somebody to migrate the issue over to somewhere else. Besides, it's more considerate to your visitor to make it more convenient.

✔ **Venting outrage over a current event involving your brand or industry:** This is a situation where you may want to start thumbing your way over to Chapter 16, where I tell you about crisis communications. But if there are only a handful of hot comments or updates, then it probably isn't time to call in reinforcements. Sensitively ask them what they want to see done about the issue. This will help take the guesswork out of you understanding where they're coming from.

✔ **Getting even:** Sometimes a disgruntled employee (even a former one) can be a terrible source of angst online for your brand. These people will normally post via fake or anonymous profiles to cloak their true identities so they can avoid legal trouble. If this person (or group of people) is posting regularly and doesn't respond to reasonable discourse, your best bet is to hire an online security expert who can determine who is actually behind the attacks and how to legally confront them once unmasked.

Beware of irrelevant, emotional, "oh, pity me" appeals (citing special circumstances that sound illegitimate and can't be verified) urging you to bend the rules for them or give them something special, such as your extra time.

Deciding What To Do

In responding to an issue, you must strike a balance between implementing a strategy quickly and slowing down long enough to engage in a coolheaded analysis.

Always consult your everyday social media team and relevant insiders who are key decision makers so that you can make the most informed decisions possible. Use these pointers to keep you on track:

✔ **Determine how urgent the situation is:** Don't allow a couple of hot comments to get you anxious that an online crisis is actively brewing, because that information alone can be very misleading. If you believe this is an urgent situation, discuss the solution with all internal parties involved as soon as possible.

Bring in the right people: Consider who from your organization should be brought in on this situation. Contact customer service, sales, or marketing, if those departments are involved. If you need more help, turn to Chapter 16 and familiarize yourself with more in-depth guidelines to crisis communication. Move quickly, though — time is of the essence.

✔ **Determine a solution:** Once all the parties involved have been consulted, it's time to determine and begin implementing a strategy to communicate your solution.

Different situations call for different solutions. Sometimes you must come out swinging — and sometimes you just have to take one on the chin. For instance, if suddenly one Thursday all the red widgets you sold turned out to be pink, you should apologize to the affected customers and offer to make things right (in whatever way that makes sense) as soon as possible.

✔ **Keep your back-up teams on standby:** Notify your crisis and executive teams that an issue is brewing so that they can step in if they determine that the problem has a larger scope than you realized, given the information that you have to make a decision. They may have a different perspective that sheds further light on the topic.

They also need to be mentally prepared as much as possible so that if they are called into action they will be ready to move fast.

✔ **Craft your response message:** Take a little time to carefully consider how you want to respond to the issue at hand. For example, you can apologize about something a few different ways. Frame your message most effectively by making it short enough to tweet. Some other key considerations include

- Understand how social media can explode a topic in hours.

- Create trust by maintaining transparency, even if doing so is embarrassing for you or your organization.

"The dog ate my homework" didn't even work in grade school. Advise your team about blame shifting. It can seem like an effective tactic, but if your brand is at all responsible for the situation at hand, it can easily make problems much worse. When your brand is (or isn't) responsible, acknowledge that responsibility honestly.

- Discover your silver linings to this storm cloud, such as gaining a new perspective on your brand's persona, learning about problems that need to be fixed, and converting critics into fans.

Validating concerns

Look for opportunities for when you can do something about the situation at hand, if only to express concern. If reasonable people are making negative comments about your brand, apologize and offer them something special, such as a trial use, bonus item, or special discount.

People want to be heard, understood, and to have their concerns validated. I call this the Triumvirate of Online Reputation Management. Some ways to address this triumvirate include

- ✔ Following people who complain and comment
- ✔ Being sensitive
- ✔ Apologizing when necessary
- ✔ Looking for common ground
- ✔ Taking it offline as quickly as possible
- ✔ Discerning the source of their objections

Engaging just enough

Don't bother trying to please everybody online. It simply can't be done. Occasionally people on your social media team may be inclined to respond to the same commenter or group of commenters back and forth, comment for comment, instead of making a statement and then reinforcing it with your other fans and brand advocates online.

Overengaging is sometimes the worst thing you can do for your online reputation. It signals to people trying to provoke you that they're "getting to you," which only fuels the fire.

It also signals to search engines that something interesting is going on and needs to be elevated in the page rankings. Believe me, you don't want this kind of attention online.

By responding immediately and often in a state of "false alarm," you can actually escalate your own issue and transform it from a flakey series of comments to a full-blown online firestorm.

 The best way you can know if you're overengaging is to check out the online influence of your commenters. If they don't have much influence, just say one kind, accurate, balanced thing to let them know you are listening to them. Then just let it go.

Responding Effectively

After you've assessed the situation, tracked down the commenters, and decided on a plan, you're ready to make your response. First, let me state the obvious. When you have an online reputation crisis escalating and threatening to go viral, you need to act quickly and thoughtfully. Remember, however, to

✔ **Know when to take the conversation private:** Upon initial contact, it's appropriate to acknowledge the problem in a public channel. After the initial public tweet, you should reach out in a private channel to really dig in and see if you can make a difference. Under no circumstances should you ever exchange confidential account information in an unsecured or public channel.

✔ **Offer an individualized solution:** In customer service, there's no "one size fits all," because each case is different. Offer an individualized solution, which may require you to work with the right people within your own company. Don't just tell this poor person to call the 800 number — go to bat for him.

To dissipate the high emotional energy, respond by following these simple steps:

1. **Respond back in the same social media channel where the conversation originated.**

2. **If the conversation is on the brink of a crisis, offer to take the conversation offline.**

   This is especially important if she's a customer.

3. **When offline, involve executives in the conversation to ensure they're hearing these issues.**

4. **Continue to discuss the issue offline until it is resolved.**

5. **Follow up when you have a solution or update to share.**

   Maybe this person's feedback has prompted a change in your product or a new feature that you're soon releasing.

Remembering your purpose

During the normal course of monitoring social media networks and the blogs, you may have commenters try to drag you into a discussion that's off topic and undesirable. The Internet is filled with all kinds of people who engage for

any number of reasons. Most are regular people, but you may occasionally
run into those who are

✔ **Confused about what brand they're talking to:** For example, they may
    be steamed about a fast-food incident that happened with one chain and
    start ripping on another chain without realizing their mistake.

✔ **Looking for attention:** Some people get involved in online controversies
    because it's a way to get attention from brands and feel heard.

✔ **Emotionally disturbed:** Respond respectfully and in an even tone. Then
    move on to monitoring and representing your brand's reputation online.

Even though some people may now have a legitimate issue with your brand,
accuracy doesn't matter nearly as much as kindness and professionalism. In
these cases

✔ Remember that this is not a counseling session

✔ Stay grounded in fact versus "what if's"

✔ Stay proactive

✔ Maintain the high ground

✔ Stay positive

If somebody is pushing your proverbial buttons, get a breath of fresh air and
come back to the issue refreshed and confident in what you're doing and the
brand that you're representing.

Turning bad reviews to your advantage

Bad reviews often contain helpful criticism. When you're prepared to make
changes accordingly, reviews and review sites can be a gold mine of information and influence. A *review site* is a website on which people can post
reviews about businesses, products, or services. Some notable review sites
include

✔ Google places (www.google.com/places)

✔ Yelp (www.yelp.com)

Sometimes a bad review happens because somebody is misinformed about
your brand. When this happens, it's a great opportunity for you to give people
a clearer look into the four W's:

✔ Who you are

✔ What you do

✔ Whom you do it for

✔ Why you do it

The most important thing you can possibly convey is why you got into this business in the first place. I don't want to buy music from a musician who heard that you can make a lot of money in that industry and who follows a formula that he heard about from somebody else. I want something with soul, something that comes from the heart and reflects a grasp of true technical ability. I want to be swept up into the experience of somebody really sharing a piece of herself, whether it's just for fun, is soul stirring, or makes a political statement. It just has to come from an authentic place and be done well.

People feel the same way about you and your brand. They want something that they know you really care about. I have a friend who is a professional illustrator, and she pours so much love and passion into her work that it's impossible not to love it. Some ways that you can reflect your love of craft online are to

✔ **Ditch wimpy marketing ideas:** Wimpy marketing ideas typically make little sense, are gimmicky, and aren't targeted toward people who are likely to be your customers. They're hot for the person trying to sell them to you, but you need something that shows your authenticity and why you're worth a look, or maybe even a great review.

✔ **Write a great About page on your site that tells your story:** This is a great way to get people to understand why you do what you do. People want to understand what makes you special and unique.

✔ **Take that great About page message and abbreviate it into a quick sentence or two to add to your profile on these review sites, your Facebook Page, and elsewhere online.**

✔ **Share videos:** Where possible, share videos that demonstrate your love of the craft. Show before-and-after stories, where applicable.

✔ **Share pictures:** Use pictures of you or your team at work that reflect your pride in what you do. Cooking is fair game here, as are other more service-related businesses.

It all comes down to demonstrating integrity in what you do. When your message matches the four W's I list above, you get better reviews almost overnight if your business is run well, because the confusion is over.

Confusing messages cause bad reviews. Keep it clear, and show some heart for your brand, and your reviews will get better.

Asking for positive reviews

Because most people only go to review sites in order to find out whether they want to go someplace or to let off steam about a negative experience they had, it's your job to ask for positive reviews.

This may feel awkward. A few simple, effective ways you can approach it that may feel more comfortable are

✔ Thank your customers and ask them to leave a review if you have made them happy with your work.

✔ Send special customers a postcard asking them to go online and share a review.

✔ Ask for positive reviews at the bottom your e-mail newsletter.

Make your request look more like a fun way to contribute to the community as somebody "in the know," rather than stating a whiny appeal. I notice major brands putting it out there like a desperate plea and have to wonder about their results.

Make it fun, and people will be much more likely to post a positive review for you.

Making lemonade out of lemons

Once you've cleared up any misinformation or confusion about your brand, it's time to roll up your sleeves and take action on consistently negative feedback. Take your clients by the hand and lead them through the four W's. It's your job to educate them and to set guidelines. Do so, and things should go smoothly for everyone involved.

Clients can be your biggest efficiency experts, and satisfied customers who were once disgruntled are your brand's best sales people.

You may need to roll up your sleeves and get down to changing a few things in your organization, such as

✔ **Customer service:** Take a deeper look into the dynamics of your customer service team and assess what kind of message your customers are receiving. Revise as necessary and then share that good news with your audiences.

✔ **Product offerings:** If people are leaving negative reviews about your product, it's time to take action to correct the issue, particularly if a consistent theme arises. Sometimes, I see brands attacking the person complaining, rather than trying to fix the issue. Clearly, those folks don't stay in business as long as they would if they treated people with more equity and respect.

Take the high road while not letting people take advantage of you.

✔ **Day-to-day operations:** Negative reviews can alert you that there's a better way to do things.

Chapter 16

Managing a Crisis

. . . .

In This Chapter

▶ Understanding what fuels the fire

▶ Crafting your strategy

▶ Admitting it when there's a problem

▶ Responding effectively

▶ Rewarding your team

. . . .

On Easter Sunday 2009, few customers were patronizing the Domino's Pizza franchise in Conover, North Carolina, and the kitchen staff had time to kill. Bored and armed with a cellphone, the two seriously misguided employees shot a two-and-a-half minute clip of themselves goofing off in the Domino's kitchen and uploaded it to YouTube. In the video, the two are shown doing *highly* unsanitary things to some Domino's menu items, to the accompaniment of giggles, and the video's narration makes clear that the tampered-with food will soon be eaten by unsuspecting Domino's customers.

Playing off widespread fears about food safety in fast-food chains, this cinematic masterpiece spread like wildfire. Bloggers blogged about it. People shared it on YouTube, Facebook, and Twitter. It was even discussed on national television. And of course, Domino's Pizza experienced a social media meltdown of epic proportions.

Domino's Pizza dealt with the catastrophe fairly well (see the section, "Examining Domino's Pizza's successful strategy," later in this chapter), and you can learn a lot from its example. In all likelihood, you will never have to face a crisis of this magnitude. Still, if you represent a brand that has significant reach or an organization with controversial ties, you should have a fully developed crisis-management strategy in place. Online meltdowns often strike out of nowhere and spread amazingly fast. Without a strategy in place, you may not be able to respond quickly enough to limit the damage.

In this chapter, I help you craft your strategy — so you can be prepared when PR nightmares become reality.

Understanding What Fuels the Fire

Online media is a strange new animal that we are all still trying to figure out. In Chapter 13, I list some tips about what makes a video go viral, but the fact is that nobody really knows why it happens. If anyone did, he could make quite a lot of money creating videos for companies with deep pockets.

I believe that the reason why so many social media firestorms happen is that most people online want to do good or to share stories that they feel are newsworthy. When an organization doesn't respond to the growing number of complaints, questions, and comments concerning the issue at hand, it leaves room for lots of speculation.

Savvy bloggers understand how to boost their blog traffic by picking up on online trends and writing about them. When that first post creates buzz, another blogger picks up the story, adds a fresh perspective, and creates even more buzz. Soon everyone is discussing the story.

Often, these buzzworthy stories are controversial, or simply incite passionate responses. In a real crisis, those passionate responses are directed at you. The best way for you to dissipate that high emotional energy is to address the issue with

- ✔ **Honesty:** You are seriously playing with fire if you think you can create a fake profile in order to infiltrate what inflammatory groups may be saying about you on their private forums. It's a huge breach of trust that has a huge chance of getting found out over time.

- ✔ **Respectfulness:** You can be kind, respectful, and engaging without being a pushover.

- ✔ **Transparency:** Explain what's being done to resolve any issue to your audiences as it happens.

Some brands even set up special Facebook Pages to address issues, but using your own site for updates is better because Google indexes it. You want to be found online by everybody who's looking for you. Lots of people don't have Facebook accounts and can't see information on there.

- ✔ **Efficiency:** Time is of the essence when you're confronting a fiery echo chamber of dissent.

- ✔ **Consistency:** This is why telling the truth is so handy. Be honest and keep a consistent message across all your affected channels, while keeping an eye on other social media channels, such as Twitter, Facebook, and YouTube at least every 15 minutes in a true crisis.

✔ **Comprehensive action:** Spread your message across all social networks that are affected.

✔ **Dogged persistence:** Don't take off for the weekend or go to sleep thinking that everybody else online is taking off from this issue too. Some of the biggest brand blowups I've seen are with companies that "took the weekend off" and assumed that bloggers work only Monday through Friday, too.

If you've gone through the steps in this book, you already have crisis communications and executive teams chosen and trained. Call them in as soon as you realize a true crisis is brewing.

Crafting Your Strategy

In the early chapters in this book, I show you how to create a solid online strategy that can support you and protect you during an online crisis. If you have gone through those chapters and created your online reputation management foundation, please just take a second to refresh yourself with the main steps below. If you haven't had the opportunity to build your teams and formulate your strategies, it isn't too late. Just use your best judgment as you read through this process and apply where necessary.

1. **Alert your everyday team.**
2. **Review your nightmare scenarios and solutions.**
3. **Call in your crisis team.**
4. **Bring in your executive team.**

Factor in the following considerations for your team:

✔ Make sure you have adequate coverage for your everyday team. If somebody's out sick or on vacation. Call in backup if necessary.

✔ Make sure everyone at your brand shares the latest info so that your messaging is accurate and consistent.

✔ Get the best out of your social media team during a crisis: Exercise patience, kindness, and lead decisively.

Remember, however, that every situation is different. It's tempting to improvise and rely on your feelings when you don't see the answer in front of you, but I strongly suggest you get some professional caliber help so that you can navigate through this process as smoothly as possible and bring it to a close.

Examining Domino's Pizza's successful strategy

The Domino's food-tampering-video crisis offers a great example for study. Representatives at Domino's surely never wanted to deal with a crisis like the one the food-tampering video caused, but their response was masterful. They responded to their nightmare situation quickly and wisely.

This case study explores just what Domino's did to rescue its online reputation from certain death. Here is a rough timeline narrative of the most significant steps in its recovery process:

1. **Domino's management was informed about the video less than an hour after it was posted to YouTube.**

   Domino's became aware of the situation via a tip from a consumer advocate blog called The Consumerist. These folks discovered the video on YouTube and posted it on its site, where it immediately went viral, and then contacted Domino's communications vice president to share the news.

   Set up Google Alerts and Yahoo! Pipes for your brand information so you don't have to rely on the goodness of strangers to protect your interests. (Step-by-step instructions for this appear in Chapter 7.)

2. **Tim McIntyre, Domino's Pizza's vice president of communications at the time, had already implemented many of the precautionary measures I describe in this book, so he was in a good position to move decisively. He immediately forwarded the information to**

   - **His trained social media team:** They needed to be on the lookout for this story spreading via blogs, Twitter, Facebook, YouTube, and LinkedIn.

   - **Domino's head of security:** Security was informed in the event of violent retaliation against the company.

   - **Senior management:** Ideally, senior management would have already pulled together an executive team, consisting of a lawyer, PR professionals, and human resource professionals, among others, who had long ago brainstormed nightmare scenarios and were ready with strategies to address the situation and minimize damage.

3. **Within a few hours, enthusiastic fans of The Consumerist blog figured out where the video had been filmed. Using clues in the video, they tracked the clip to the specific store.**

   This shows how useful an online audience can be!

4. **Using computer records, the Domino's team discovered that at the time the video was shot, the Conover store hadn't had any customers at all. The employees had never served the tainted food to anyone, and the video was a hoax.**

   At this point, you may be asking yourself why they felt like they had to do anything more. If tainted food had never been served to customers, there was no crisis, right? Wrong. I discuss this in the section called "Perception Is Reality," later in this chapter.

5. **Domino's identified the employees involved and contacted the independent storeowner, the local police, and the health department.**

   Domino's quickly fired the losers, er, employees who made the video and immediately closed down the restaurant so that it could be thoroughly cleaned and sanitized.

   By this time, TV stations were breaking the story, sharing the video, and adding to the furor.

   Domino's knew at this point that the video was a hoax. Does that mean it should have contacted TV newsrooms to explain the hoax in advance, before the story broke? It's true that this move could've prevented television media from spreading the story. On the other hand, before the story reached TV news, Domino's hadn't known that TV was going to get involved at all. If Domino's had informed TV stations in advance, Domino's may only have ensured the widespread TV coverage it was seeking to avoid. Bottom line: There's no such thing as a perfect formula, only guidelines.

6. **By Tuesday, roughly 48 hours since the video was uploaded, the clip had received more than 250,000 views. Domino's response team was communicating with key influencers and with the most relevant audiences online.**

   Note that Domino's was doing a smart thing by not talking about this issue on popular sites like Facebook or Twitter. Doing so would only have served to throw gas on the fire. By Tuesday night, however, the news started showing up on Twitter. At this point, with its hand forced, Domino's began responding on Twitter as well.

   Keep your response short, sweet, and easily retweetable. For example: "Yeah, we know. Domino's has found them. It's a hoax," in reference to the employees involved.

7. **By Wednesday, more than 1 million people had viewed the video. Instead of releasing a formal press release, Domino's decided to take the unusual step of creating a YouTube video to respond in kind. That afternoon, the company president, Patrick Doyle, returned early from an out-of-state vacation to appear as official spokesman in the response.**

In his clip, Doyle explained that the original video had been a hoax, that no tainted food had been served, and described how Domino's was handling the situation.

Domino's was right to work fast here. People aren't looking for a polished, professional response. They're looking to be reassured that your brand cares about what's happening and that something is being done about the situation.

This is why you should have your executive team designate "on call" times when they can be reached in the event of an online emergency. Even if your "on call" executive team member is on vacation, you should at least encourage him to record an agreed-upon message through his phone, upload it right to your YouTube account, and then let somebody on your social media team add the appropriate title and description.

Videos recorded by executives can be great responses to crises as long as the executive demonstrates genuine concern. Just make sure he doesn't record the video from The Masters golf tournament or some other swanky event.

8. **By the following week, the episode was fading into obscurity. Domino's tracking charts showed that online discussion about Domino's had returned to its pre-crisis level.**

Domino's reputation certainly had been injured and wasn't yet healed. For a long while afterward, the pizza company endured sales aftereffects — but it had at least staunched the flow of blood. The response team could congratulate themselves on a job well done.

New assessments to make during a crisis

In Chapter 15, I cover the basic important considerations you need in assessing your situation. I tell you how to address an escalating situation in hopes of preventing it from becoming a full-blown social media crisis. These primary points include

- ✔ Understanding the conversation.
- ✔ Identifying which social media channels are affected and responding on the same channels.
- ✔ Researching the issue in case it's a repeating theme where you have a solution that has already been figured out and implemented.

These assessments are still relevant now that a crisis has occurred. However, in addition, you'll need to take a few additional steps. Depending on your circumstances, make sure you

- ✔ **Search the blogosphere for relevant discussions.** When issues spill over from social media, blogs are usually the first place they'll appear. Handle this by

  - *Searching for blogs:* Check out `http://www.google.com/blog search` to look for blogs that focus on you, your industry, or your market in order to search for relevant discussions, if they exist.

  - *Discovering what they're saying:* Look at the kinds of examples and proofs they are using to support their statements. They may just be identifying a problem for you that others on Twitter and Facebook are just alluding to, but aren't really giving any concrete information. Dedicated bloggers tend to provide some kind of references, if only anecdotal instances that you can look into. Pay attention to how much attention they're getting.

  - *Responding in a friendly, constructive manner:* If you are just fact-finding and haven't yet arrived at a response strategy, you can comment that you represent the brand and that you're getting more information and will get back to them with your brand's plan of action as soon as you have one. Always keep your promises and respond with updates as soon as may be.

- ✔ **Take special care of your more talkative social networks.** They're your defenders, after all. Take care of them and let them help spread any message you may have. Be sure to

  - Make your social network audiences feel understood.

  - Keep your social network audiences informed.

- ✔ **Contact prominent online influencers.** As you assess your online crisis, remember your prominent online influencers. Facing a genuine crisis online means that it's time to contact all of your influential blogging and social media friends and people you know well enough to reach out to in good faith. Take care that you don't abuse the privilege by sending them too many messages and making this a job for them, no matter how dire circumstances may seem. It isn't their problem, but they may well help you out if they feel strongly about the situation.

Maintain the enthusiastic support of your prominent blogging and social media friends by respecting their time.

Everybody does better when there is a little incentive involved. As you broach the situation with each influencer, it's a good idea to share numbers for how high traffic is spiking concerning this issue and related terms. Writing a post about an issue like this could drive a lot of traffic and new visitors to the influencer's blog, which is exactly what every influential blogger wants. Consider

- Offering to give your most prominent blogger an exclusive personal interview for her blog, podcast, video channel, and so forth, with somebody noteworthy in your organization who's connected with the story.

- Offering to give your influencers more detailed information than you are sharing with the general public because of their special status.

- Asking influencers to share with their social media audiences directly.

Don't be shy, but keep it personal. Your participating influencers benefit in boosted rankings and exposure to new audiences from the buzz. You're kinda doing them a favor, too, so it can be mutually rewarding.

Learning even more about your commenters

In Chapter 15, I explain how you can understand the different types of commenters whom you may encounter during a heated crisis. In this section, I show you how to look even deeper.

Searching blogs

I want to start this little section by telling you about my friend Alexa. You can find her online at www.alexa.com. She isn't a blogger, but she certainly knows how to measure bloggers' traffic and influence — important considerations when you're assessing an online communication crisis. The more influential a blogger is, the more you need to pay attention to what she's saying and respond to her directly.

Alexa isn't the only web traffic metrics service out there, but she, er, the service, ranks 30 million websites worldwide and is still considered one of the best for accurately determining how much traffic a blog gets. Anybody can post fictitious follower counts online, but you get much better information if you use a service like Alexa to look at that blog's rankings. Here's how you use it

1. **Go to** www.alexa.com **and log in, either by creating a new account (click on "log in" in the upper-right corner) or by signing in via your Facebook profile.**

2. **Click the Home tab in the upper-left corner.**

3. **Type your search term into the search window at the top of the screen (see Figure 16-1). I suggest you perform searches for**

- Your name.

- Your industry.

- The current crisis, by different names and details. Try to anticipate what may be coming next, if you're familiar with the subject that's being contested. Odds are good that you're already aware of the topic and related issues. Search for them.

- Relevant thought leaders.

- Active commenters who may well have blog audiences of their own.

- News blogs that report on issues relevant to this crisis.

If you don't know the names of all the prominent blogs raising the temperature of your reputation online, it's a good idea to turn to Google.

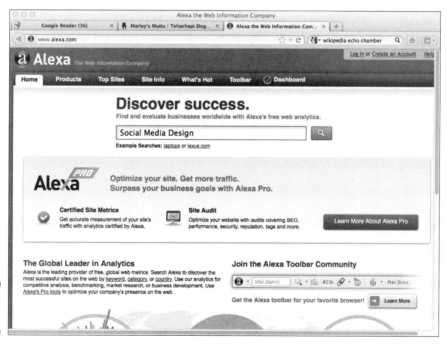

Figure 16-1:
Alexa.com.

You can easily search Google for blogs, specifically, in order to do some more deep research on any blogs that are talking trash about your brand. Sometimes a crisis is legitimate, but it's also good to know about a blogger's influence and reach so that you can frame your solution and apology in a way that will resonate with that blogger. It's always a good idea to speak to people in their own languages, as much as possible. It cuts down on the confusion.

If you are in the midst of a genuine crisis and are here to reach for help, please do search the blogosphere for posts relating to your subject matter. See what people are saying and who the main players are who are saying it. Meanwhile, in the following list, I chose to search for blogs that write about the subject of "hedgehogs," because that's more fun than crisis terminology.

Here's how you can search for blogs on Google.

1. **Go to** www.google.com**.**

2. **On the search page, find the links menu on the left (the one that begins with Web). Click the last link in this menu, More. (See Figure 16-2.)**

   Clicking More makes several other link options available in that menu.

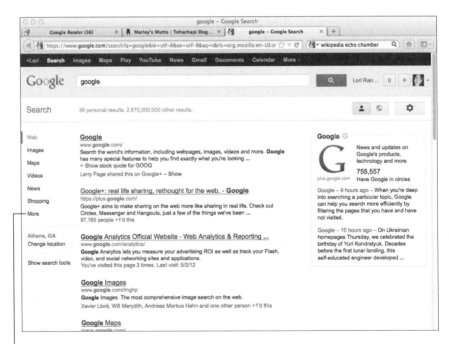

Figure 16-2: The More link on the Google search results page.

The More link

3. **After you've clicked More, click the newly exposed Blogs link.**

   Google's search results page now shows blog-related results for your search term. (I'm using *hedgehogs;* see Figure 16-3.) This is probably the best place for you to check out what bloggers are saying about your brand and this situation. Click the "homepages" link to see the most recent posts for your search term.

   Check out a blog's influence without having to take the blogger's word for it so that you're much more informed about your more talkative commenters.

4. **On this page, enter a series of searches. Use operators on your original search term, or use entirely different search terms. Be creative. (See Figure 16-4.)**

   You can improve your results by using the "super secret" Google search tips I share with you in Chapter 7.

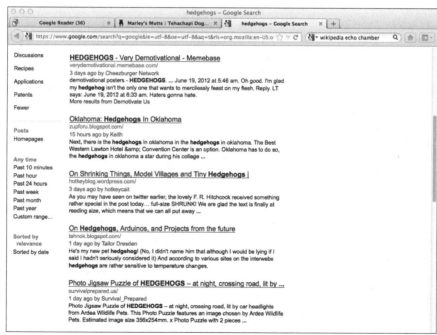

Figure 16-3:
Google
search
results
for recent
blogs about
hedgehogs.

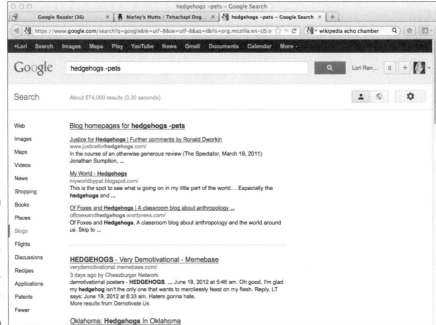

Looking into their profiles

Believe it or not, some commenters, if not many, will have thoroughly fake commenting and social media profiles. I am even aware of some highly visible online personalities who use a fake profile picture to hide behind instead of using their own likeness. I use all my own, real, current pictures and suggest you do the same as an issue of trustworthiness. Check out Chapter 15 for more information on how to assess fake profiles.

I bring up this issue because some people dream up online personalities for fun (and ill-gotten profit) and then use them to stir up trouble online. Please be aware that somebody may just outright lie about his blog numbers, education, and job experience, and online followers, for starters. Always qualify your sources before you believe in their supposed influence.

There actually are people out there who will create an overjoyed video review of your brand . . . for $5. Don't take appearances that seriously. Do your homework.

It's important to note that some people pose a threat greater than just trashing your good name online. Some disturbed individuals are willing to resort to real-world violence, such as destroying property or even worse, threatening physical harm. It's sad to say, but in rare cases uncontained online reputation management issues can extend to physical outcomes. I suggest reporting any alarming activities to the relevant law enforcement authorities about what's going on, cooperate with them, and give them frequent updates.

Notify law enforcement authorities if anybody threatens you or your organization. If you're worried the threat isn't credible, notify them anyway. They can advise you about your particular situation and help you in more ways than you may realize.

Use Google searches and other approaches to find out more about any threatening commenter. Also, if you have a photograph of the commenter, try TinEye, a "reverse image search engine." (See Figure 16-5.) You can use TinEye's reverse image search engine to help to verify whether somebody's being honest about his multiple identities online, and also to find out more if any of his other online activities relate to your crisis situation. The more information you have about lead commenters the better able you will be to create a smart plan of action.

All you have to do is go to TinEye at www.tineye.com and upload the image. TinEye tells you where that image appears on the Internet. It even offers browser plug-ins to speed you along on your way to ferreting out fake profile pictures. Oh, and did I mention that this is a free service? I love the Internet! I do want to mention, however, that TinEye is merely an image search and is not a facial recognition service (which uses different search algorithms), so you may find a number of images in its results that have the same sorts of colors or distance between the eyes. Still, TinEye is better at this than Google Images (which you can find at http://images.google.com), though you may want to use both tools to see what you can discover.

If you're dealing with a disgruntled employee who is making dangerous threats, you can do what Domino's did in the above example. It was lucky enough to have video that included the relevant employees' faces so it could run the pictures through its human resources department.

If you find you're dealing with a known violent offender, contact the police. Law enforcement agencies maintain databases with image files of people who have been arrested for violent crimes, so you can also turn in any images you discover to them, in the off chance that this is a potentially dangerous situation. Unfortunately, death threats are more common than you may think, even though the vast majority of them are (thankfully) idle threats. Be safe. Be proactive.

When you're dealing with a voluble commenter making threats or at least making a lot of waves online, you're in a much better position to make good decisions about how to proceed if you have accurate information about her actual audience reach and credibility among audiences that matter to you and your brand. If necessary, you can use that information to discredit your noisy commenter in a blog post, but only if it's relevant to debunking any important, false claims she's making that may be fueling the discussion. If she's just being insulting, it's best to just leave her alone.

Figure 16-5:
TinEye is a
handy little
tool.

Make sure your response is appropriate to the threat. A person posting with a fake profile from the public library can raise a little trouble for you, but when you treat him like a serious threat by paying lots of attention to him, he becomes a credible threat simply by virtue of the Google rankings you cause from all the interactivity.

Deciding what to do

When deciding what to do, you must strike a balance between moving fast to implement a strategy and slowing down long enough to engage in a cool-headed analysis with your crisis and executive teams.

If you've done your homework and created those worst-case scenarios I ask you to complete in Chapter 4, a lot of your work is probably done already. Find the scenario that fits best and begin implementing the solutions you brainstormed. Please keep in mind that every context is different, and even your best-laid, worst-case scenario plans deserve close attention to detail. Stay flexible as you consider your wisest course of action both now and in how it will impact your brand five years from now.

Try to put some emotional distance between you and the problem so that you can fully engage your critical thinking without getting flustered. Sometimes it helps to take walk by yourself for five minutes so you can release some of that pent-up stress and cool down to some nice problem-solving productivity.

Assessing whether you need to call in professional help

If you can't afford to hire a pro, you can always call in a few favors. Ask any of your social media savvy blogging friends to pitch in and help you through this crisis. A makeshift team like this can help by monitoring your brand (and crisis topics) and by reassuring online parties. Educate them about exactly what you want them to do and encourage them to ask you if they have any questions about how to proceed. Advise them to always err on the side of caution. If you're really on your own, I suggest appealing to online communities where people share your point of view. I tell you more about discovering and tapping in to focused interest groups in Chapter 11.

If you're fortunate enough to have an existing team and good resources, I suggest you at least research and then start talking with a PR agency about hiring it navigate this crisis with you (refer to Chapter 4). If you have your ducks in a row already, you're saving valuable hours. Hours don't sound like much for normal workdays, but during a fiery media crisis, every hour can matter.

Communicating with Your Audience

Dealing with a crisis is a lot like dealing with an escalating situation, as I show you in Chapter 15. You assess the situation, learn what you can about the commenters involved, and then decide what to do. When you have your response ready, you can first respond to the commenters involved. For guidance on framing that response, follow the steps I share in Chapter 15.

The following list contains the basic steps for communicating with your audience in a crisis. Keep in mind that every scenario is unique, so every step may not apply to your situation. Use your best judgment.

You don't have to get everything right to turn a crisis around. Just be proactive, seek to understand, and be decisive. Eventually you will come out on top.

1. **Double-check to be sure that this is indeed a crisis situation.** If it isn't, you risk making a mountain out of a molehill or, worse yet, creating a real issue by talking so much about it online.

   The next section titled "Perception Is Reality" tells you more about this issue. Don't worry; here are clear indicators that it's time to kick your online crisis communications strategy into gear. Remember, if you've done the planning work that I show you, you will do just fine.

   - **Something strange is going on:** You're seeing a new kind of (heated) complaint or information that you've never seen before. Perk up your monitoring "radar" and check for similar references on other social media channels. Ask about this issue from within your organization for more clues into what's going on. Check out any news stories against credible news organizations to be sure that they're legitimate.

   - **Something truly shocking has happened:** Case in point: the Domino's case study I discuss earlier in this chapter. Consider the potential impact and range of effect.

2. **Admit when there's a problem.** I show you more about how to do this at the beginning of this chapter.

3. **Respond effectively via the channel(s) where it's happening.** For example, if the issue is heating up via YouTube, respond to the people who are talking about it there. I give you more details later in this chapter in the section titled "Responding Effectively."

4. **Create a special crisis FAQ page on your site.** (If you don't have a site, skip to Step 5.) People will be going to your site anyway for more information, and putting a page up on your site (or repurposing your homepage for this emergency) shows people that you're taking the situation seriously, that you're being transparent, and that you're taking action. Include the following, as appropriate to your conditions

   - Response video made by a senior-level employee, if you've made one. (I share more about response videos in Chapter 15.)

   - Admitting to the problem (in detail) and apologizing for your brand's role in it.

   - How you came to learn about the problem.

   - What you're doing to resolve the problem.

   - How you're notified and how you've cooperated with the authorities, as applicable.

   - How you're making sure this problem never happens again.

   - Contact information; such as a dedicated e-mail address (speeds your response time) and your social media channels. Include a phone number only if you have enough people to answer those calls effectively.

5. **If you can, get your IT person to dedicate a fresh e-mail address (like** `FixingCrisisEvent@yourfiercelyawesomebrand.com`**). You can use it to**

    • Create a bulk mailing list.

    • Create an e-mail auto responder that routes incoming e-mails to a specific department (like PR, legal, or human resources) so that it can track and respond effectively.

    • Create a sensitively worded auto-responder that tells people that you will share more information is it becomes known.

6. **Provide a grounding place for charged emotions.** People who are emotionally triggered build up an emotional "charge" that needs to be grounded or else they will pass it on to other people online. It can spread like wildfire. People need to feel heard during a crisis and to get the latest information. When you provide a place where people feel like they can unburden themselves and release some of that stress without judgment (instead of angrily sharing it on other networks), you benefit for several reasons:

    • You get the issue custom delivered to you as it unfolds, so you won't have to search so hard for it.

    • You provide a place for people to neutralize that emotional charge, which demonstrates trustworthiness and transparency. Plus, it makes people feel good about your brand, which is essential to turning this crisis around.

    • You get to keep track of conversations more easily.

    • Your brand evangelists can participate and provide moral support all in one place, which gives a stronger impression than a few people trying to communicate on every social and blogging venue of the entire Internet.

7. **Make lemonade from the lemons.** Congratulations! The crisis is over. Hopefully you'll take at least a little time away from work to decompress. While you're gone I suggest you get somebody in your organization to document all this valuable information (such as a timeline of the events, copies of all e-mails, tweets, updates, and so on) so that you can analyze your performance for future crisis avoidance and reference. Your organization also needs to fully investigate what happened and why. This information may be very helpful. Also make a priority to

    • Thank people like thought leaders, brand evangelists, and your regular audiences, for sticking with you through the crisis and sticking up for you (as applicable).

    • Thank your employees for rising to the occasion.

Managing a crisis is about damage control, not winning an argument. Once you've addressed the issue with somebody a couple times, let it go and move on.

By all means, share any videos or general statements your executive team has released, so that the word can get out as efficiently and personally as possible.

Sometimes an event occurs in connection with you or your brand that never should have happened. It's unfortunate, but sometimes mistakes are going to be made. Even though you may be following all the steps I share for building an ethical, fantastic reputation online, something out of your control happens, like the Domino's video disaster, or you mess up and there's a wildfire of crisis communication igniting all around you. Focus on

✔ Admitting it and framing an apology that makes sense. Make sure your entire executive team agrees fully with what you are about to share with millions online. There's no taking it back. This is why I highly suggest including legal, public relations, and human resource professionals in your executive team for crisis management. Each department offers a perhaps slightly different, but still highly important, perspective that can save you and your brand a world of trouble. Listen to them and let them make the decision to admit there's a problem and to frame an apology.

✔ Dwelling on any positive aspects to the situation.

✔ Sharing a response plan on how your brand is taking corrective action.

✔ Demonstrating how your brand is carrying out the response plan.

Be the first to break bad news about your organization so you can frame the discussion.

Perception Is Reality

With online crises, the truth isn't always relevant. Let me explain. It would be wonderful if the truth about any online issue were able to rise to the top in a timely manner without any help. But that isn't the way it works. Sometimes the truth gets obscured by attractive, all-too-believable lies. This is human nature. That's part of how propaganda works.

In the Domino's case, the video was a hoax. The truth was that no one was served the tainted food. But that didn't matter because the general perception was that people had eaten the food. If Domino's had just assumed that the truth would eventually prevail over these rumors, the company would've been relying on slim odds. Rumors and lies are stubborn things, and they can often be indistinguishable from truth. Domino's did the right thing by responding the way it did.

As the person responsible for crisis communications for your brand, it's up to you to figure out how to get the truth out there. Put the truth into a brief message that can be expressed in a 120-character tweet, so that it can be shared quickly online by your wonderful brand ambassadors, influential friends, and bloggers.

Online firestorms aren't entirely rational, but they are manageable.

Responding Effectively

In order for you to resolve this crisis more effectively, consider authorizing your employees within more relevant departments, such as human resources or marketing, to engage during a crisis. People who have demonstrable people skills and who already have your brand's best interest in mind are powerful allies.

On a totally practical note, I just want to point out that your existing employees are already on the payroll. Just saying. Very few companies can comfortably afford to hire large outside PR agencies on an emergency basis and not have their bottom lines suffer. As long as your employees are kept in the information loop, treated with respect, and given the extra time to do what they were normally supposed to accomplish during the crisis, there probably won't be any backlash from asking them to help during an online crisis. Just be sure to send your employees a copy of the following ten commandments of community.

The Ten Commandments of Community

- ✔ Be transparent
- ✔ Be helpful
- ✔ Be trustworthy
- ✔ Make it right
- ✔ Share solutions
- ✔ Stay calm when you're provoked
- ✔ Be sensitive to people's sexual orientation, as applicable
- ✔ Respect religious differences while staying neutral, as applicable
- ✔ Keep quiet about your political views, as applicable
- ✔ Be a friend

Your team is critical to your success. Motivate them with kindness and every kind of support during this crisis.

Rewarding Your Team

It's a great idea to boost your team's morale after it's just gone to bat for you during an online crisis. Going through an experience like this can bring your team much closer together. Trust has been earned. Reputations have been enhanced.

I suggest you take them all out to dinner or celebrate together somehow, or (if you can) maybe give your team members a little paid time off if they put in extra hours to handle the crisis. In the next few days when the fire's been extinguished, give them the kind of praise and recommendations that solidify their pride in working for an organization of integrity. This is a huge endorsement for your brand moving forward because it

- ✔ Demonstrates how cool your brand is, both internally and to the world around you
- ✔ Shows that your organization is about more than profits and that it has a code of ethics that includes embracing employees' humanity

Some practical ideas include

- ✔ Presenting and framing an award. It serves as a badge of honor.
- ✔ Posting a LinkedIn recommendation commending their cool-headed efficiency and resourcefulness under fire.
- ✔ Dishing some online love via your Facebook page and Twitter after the crisis.

Chapter 17

Promoting Goodwill

· ·

In This Chapter

▶ Making personal connections

▶ Staging delightful surprises

▶ Creating interactive fun and games

▶ Doing good in the world

▶ Juicing lemons into lemonade

· ·

Creating a strong, positive online reputation requires you to have a sense of purpose, a unifying outlook or viewpoint that ties together all your online creations. People instinctively pick up that kind of consistency, and they'll reward you with their time and attention. This is particularly true when your viewpoint reflects a positive and upbeat attitude. Cynical or negative views, particularly in the business world, repel more people than they attract.

Cultivate an optimistic online attitude. It's the best way to get to know people, for them to get to know you better, and for them to feel good about sharing you with their friends. Whether you are in a startup or are representing a Fortune 100 company, you need to "promote happiness" online. In this chapter, I show you the best ways to do it.

Promoting happiness is not only good for your business. It's great for your quality of life, too.

Making Personal Connections

Doing well in the online world requires more than being charitable. Sure, you can publish free tutorials, upload funny videos, or distribute rebates or coupons, but people won't necessarily appreciate you for it. After all, people tend to distrust strangers. If you're giving away something for free, people will naturally question your motives. They'll assume you're going to ask them for something in return.

This is why it's critical for you to make personal connections online. When people feel that they have a good sense about who you are and what you're about, they'll have less reason to be suspicious about you. You become a friend. And the next time you offer something online, odds are good that the people you've befriended will respond positively.

It's important for you to be upfront about

- ✔ Who you are
- ✔ What you do
- ✔ Whom you do it for
- ✔ What you expect to receive in return

Approach others online in a friendly, open way. Speak to them the same way you'd talk to your best friend. The best way to have a friend is to be a friend. Allow all your friendships to develop naturally.

Long-term emotional connections are the key to developing these kinds of relationships. I want you to cultivate a few different categories of personal connections online, and in this section, I show you how to explore them.

Developing connections with bloggers

The fastest and easiest way to connect personally with any blogger who is a thought leader in your industry is to read and comment on his posts. When you're a blogger, there's nothing quite as satisfying as getting lots of informed, insightful comments on posts you've researched and crafted with love. The more consistently you contribute to the discussion by commenting and sharing, the more likely somebody is to respond to you either in his blog or on a social network. You can begin to establish a rapport at a pace that feels comfortable to you both. Figure 17-1 shows some comments on a WordPress blog, complete with social media–sharing enabled. It's never been easier to spread your message like wildfire online.

Sometimes well-known bloggers in your area of expertise just don't have the time and space to include new people into their lives. I'm not the biggest new media and design blogger you'll ever meet, but I really make the effort to get to know people who reach out to me in a way that's comfortable to me online.

Figure 17-1:
Blog com-
ments with
Facebook
"Like"
enabled.

Developing connections with social media users

I try to always be positive and give you examples of something to do, but sometimes it's useful to look at what *not* to do in order to understand what makes sense. Just in case you are brand new to Twitter, Facebook, LinkedIn, and other social networks, here are a few activities to avoid using very often to reach out, unless you're engaging in a dialogue. I'll be surprised if you haven't seen somebody either overuse one of these terrific tools or indulge in one of the following relationship inhibitors. I show you which of the following are useful tools when used judiciously and which ones can put a strain on your relationships unless you already know the person you're contacting very well.

As you grow in popularity and influence online, understanding where the boundaries are helps you to function within your own happy bubble.

✔ Direct messaging on Twitter (tool)

✔ Private messaging (tool)

✔ Initiating chats via any backchannel, such as Facebook chat (tool)

✔ E-mails asking for free products or services (probable relationship inhibitor)

✔ Asking for "just a few minutes" of service (probable relationship inhibitor)

✔ Being confrontational just for attention (probable relationship inhibitor)

✔ Hijacking a conversation thread with one's own agenda (probable relationship inhibitor)

✔ Asking to use the other person's platform to post links and so forth (probable relationship inhibitor)

✔ Posting links without even asking (probable relationship inhibitor)

I bet you can add to this list with activities you've seen or experienced.

Developing relationships with clients

Hopefully, when you take your business online, you maintain a personal kind of connection with your past and present clients, and also build such a connection with future clients. The easiest way to do this is by providing them with a product or service that makes their lives better in a demonstrable way.

This is one of the easiest kinds of personal connections to maintain, because your clients already believe in you and in your business. Here are a few proven ways to keep up with your clients and continue to show them that they are special to you, that they rate a higher standard of TLC than someone who has never done business with you before:

✔ **Send them updates about your business or organization in e-mail newsletters.** If you decide you want to publish an e-mail newsletter, I suggest you use it to help your audience with valuable, relevant content such as

- *Maintenance tips:* For example, if you own a knitting-related brand, you can show people how to maintain (and store) different kinds of knitting needles. If the article's going to be long or involve more than a couple pictures, you can link to a blog post. This drives more traffic to your site and saves your newsletter subscribers from having large e-mail files cluttering up their computers.

- *Industry news:* Share the latest and greatest news trends for your industry. For example, if you have a knitting-related brand, you can make a big splash with Yak yarns, should they ever develop, by telling all about how they're made, what to do with them, and linking to Yak yarn patterns.

These days, there is a lot of talk about using e-mail newsletters to sell stuff for other people in exchange for including you on their e-mail lists when you release a product.

This is all good fun until somebody gets hurt. When someone else's product doesn't measure up and you've pitched it to your e-mail subscribers, many of whom are your strongest brand advocates, you'll be the one getting hurt. I don't want that to be you or your clients.

Carefully consider what offers you will share and guard the people on your list jealously. Signing up for an e-mail newsletter is a sacred trust with most people, and trust is really all you have when it comes to your reputation online. Take the high road and use your newsletter to do good in the world, make an occasional sale, and guard the privacy of your subscribers. They will love you for it.

✔ **When you're preparing a special promotion, send your clients invitations to participate in the promotion before anybody else.** Invitations can include

- Reduced pricing
- First crack at special features, such as a beta version of a software application you've been developing

✔ Send your clients occasional bonus products or services, just because these people have been your clients.

Your best sources for referrals and repeat business are the clients you already have.

Developing relationships with fans

When you reach out to make personal connections with fans, both old and new, keep in mind that going after demographics such as age or gender isn't going to get you nearly as far as looking at psychographics. (See Chapter 8 for more on psychographics.) Basically, psychographics refers to groups of people who share the same kind of thinking about a subject or product.

For example, if your company sells glow-in-the-dark Chia pets, your research may reveal that the people most interested in your products are people who are also interested in topics as diverse as

✔ Organic food

✔ Home decor

✔ Delightfully tacky retro stuff

✔ Gag gifts

When you know these groups of people constitute your fan base, it's a great idea to go where they hang out online and connect with them in those places. Be a fan anthropologist: Contact your fans. Have fun with them. Let them know who you are and why you do what you do. Study their languages and the way they refer to your products or similar products, and learn to respond in kind. And always treat them with respect.

Staging Delightful Surprises

Have you ever received a gift that turned out to be much better than you expected? How did it feel? Did you feel unusually connected to the person who gave you that gift?

When people go online to research a product or a service, they generally want to obtain information in the simplest and fastest way possible. When you can provide that information in an entertaining way, you give people more than they expect. You begin to create a personal connection.

Creating this effect is a powerful way to improve the reputation of you and your brand online. It's a fundamentally human thing.

Some of the ways you can do this are to

- **Create surprising and delightful experiences that evoke positive feelings.**

  This can involve

  - Genuinely fun contests

  - The chance to name a product

  Be creative. You can get downright theatrical when creating a genuinely delightful surprise for your present and future fans online.

- **Make sure your products and services are better than anyone has a right to expect.**

  Great products make great companies. They virtually speak for themselves, and people will associate the positive feelings those products engender with your brand. For example, you can inspire and entertain visitors about the glories of glow-in-the dark Chia pet ownership, but you need to take it one step further and make sure that your especially cool, glow-in-the-dark Chias are what people want to support. You can do this by

  - Improving your product or service. Incorporate fans' ideas!

  - Offer special discounts to longtime customers.

  - Allow fans to get involved: Host a forum where fans can share tips or information. Allow them to upload photographs of themselves with your product. Create an online fan hall of fame.

Being seasonally appropriate

I used to own and operate an upscale specialty boutique located in the trendy part of town. Many of the things that worked for me in retail apply equally well online, even though the dynamics can be very different.

One such trick is to time your product launches or special events so that they fit with the season.

Savvy shoppers are used to buying certain kinds of things at certain times. Tap in to those shopping rhythms — even if your business model doesn't seem very seasonal. When you give people a routine they already understand, they feel like they can relate to you and trust you. Our glow-in-the-dark Chia pet company, for instance, can offer

✔ Back-to-school specials:

- Special-edition glow-in-the-dark Chia pets wearing backpacks or holding a pencil
- Cooler weather growing tips

✔ Halloween:

- Best photo of glow-in-the-dark Chia pet in costume gets featured on the site and wins a year's supply of Chia seeds and fertilizer
- Seasonal slogan: "Growing Chia pets doesn't have to be scary . . ."

✔ Winter holidays:

- Go wild (or at least more than mild) with holiday fun by posting holiday themed pictures, videos, and music.
- Hold a Christmas costume party. Ask fans to upload photos of their glow-in-the-dark Chia pets in full holiday regalia.

You can cultivate relationships online by connecting with people in a way that's already familiar and enjoyable to them.

Working with serendipity

One of the smartest things you can do to connect with your audiences and to attract new people to your online community is to somehow piggyback who you are or what you do to current events.

At the very least, you can get inspired by events that are getting lots of main-stream press coverage and have fun with them.

For example, I'm writing this book in a U.S. presidential election year. Our glow-in-the-dark Chia pet company can use the occasion of an election to frame some new ideas. The company can hold elections, complete with online campaigns and posters supporting a new glow-in-the-dark Chia pet creation, or conduct polls that include cute, made-up biographies for each Chia candidate.

You wouldn't even have to conduct such a poll yourself. There are many different free survey and polling services online. Two of the trusty ones that I've field tested include

- ✔ PollDaddy (`http://polldaddy.com`)
- ✔ SurveyMonkey (`www.surveymonkey.com`)

Photo-editing or graphic art skills can come in handy here. If you don't have these skills or the budget to hire them out professionally, consider taking on a college intern who's eager for real-world experience.

Promoting events

Sometimes you need to publicize an event — not a seasonal promotion but an important change or updates you want to spread the word about online. Such events can include

- ✔ New product launches
- ✔ Adding a new service
- ✔ Announcing a change in leadership
- ✔ Notifying people about a change in direction

In order for you to make the biggest splash without sacrificing your personal relationships online, I suggest that you present these events in a one-to-one way as much as possible. Once you've thoughtfully considered the most exciting, informative, and respectful way to reach your community, the most common way to reach people one-on-one is to notify them via

- ✔ E-mail newsletters
- ✔ Community managers
- ✔ Fans sharing your news with their own audiences

People remember how you make them feel when you communicate with them.

When you're publicizing a large event online, be prepared to go with the flow instead of trying to control exactly how you want people to respond.

Creating Interactive Fun and Games

This is my favorite part of this chapter. This case study will give you a first-class start at creating something online that's truly remarkable and delightful. You won't have to try to push people to do anything to get close to your brand. Fans almost greedily pursue this level of engagement.

In 2011, HBO began airing *Game of Thrones,* a TV series based on *A Song of Ice and Fire,* the award-winning series of high fantasy novels by George R. R. Martin.

To help raise awareness about the series, HBO contacted Campfire NYC, a marketing agency specializing in "social storytelling." The novels are about swords, sex, and the quest for power at all costs. That's pretty exciting promotional material. Nonetheless, Campfire NYC's work was highly creative and wildly successful. Rarely has an ad campaign provided so many brilliant ideas and so much interactive fun for fans. Their experience can show you what's possible with your own campaigns.

Creating engaged communities is crucial to your long-term success.

Enticing via aromas

Campfire NYC sent influencers an elaborate "Maester's Path Scent Kit" intended to evoke the scents of key locations in the fantasy series. Each kit was a box crafted to match the design and art direction of the series, inside of which were yellowed scrolls and dusty, medieval-looking bottles. (See Figure 17-2.) The scents in the bottles were supposed to reflect the smells from places like Pentos and Winterfell, settings in the series. *Game of Thrones* bloggers went wild.

Within 48 hours, these key influencers were sharing this online via blog posts, YouTube, Facebook, and Twitter just because they were so overjoyed to be included in the launch and because the scent kits were so lovingly crafted. It made the fantasy world of *Game of Thrones* become real in a tangible way.

Figure 17-2:
Maester's
Path Scent
Kit.

Admittedly, this approach isn't for everyone. If you're a software developer, this may not work for you, but a restaurant can use this idea to appeal to an elite group of influencers online. Prominent food bloggers would probably be delighted to receive a well-presented, intricate scent experiment that involves the scents from your signature dishes. You can get wildly creative with how you present your experiment, too.

Presentation is everything. Make it special.

Creating immersive experiences

In the fantasy world of Game of Thrones, hanging out in a tavern and eaves-dropping on the scuttlebutt from all that political intrigue is tons of fun. In the *Game of Thrones* online "sound experience" created by Campfire NYC, many a dark conspiracy is overheard in a tavern you can move around within. The experience looks and feels like a sophisticated game and yet serves to whet the appetite for the *Game of Thrones* HBO series that is to come.

Also, the "Viewer's Guide" Campfire NYC created provides an informative map that features background information and a side panel that notes epi-sode landmarks, as well as the more strategically important major landmarks. Of course, each section can be easily shared via social media with "share this story" callouts and sharing icons for Facebook, Twitter, Google+, and Tumblr. (See Figure 17-3.)

More and more people are accessing the Internet via a mobile device, rather than sitting in front of a desktop. Where at all possible, make sure your web developers and designers create experiences that can be enjoyed online via all kinds of mobile phones and tablets.

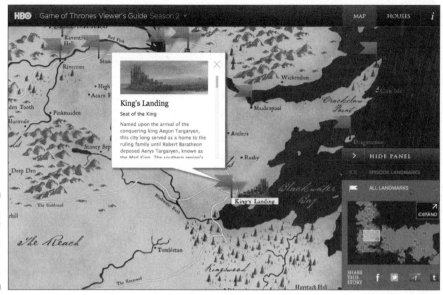

Figure 17-3:
Game of
Thrones
interactive
map.

Appealing via rich graphics

Using rich, textural graphics that captivate your visitor's imagination can heighten any online experience. Unless your brand wants to come across as being slick, modern, or highly engineered, consider using graphics that look more organic.

In *Game of Thrones,* a 700-foot-tall wall of ice separates the civilized "Seven Kingdoms" from the wilderness beyond. Men positioned in castles on the wall guard against attackers. Campfire NYC created a graphically rich "on the wall" experience that conveys a sense of being on this enormous wall. This online experience educates visitors with *Game of Thrones* background storylines and enables them to experience the sights and sounds of being a watcher on the wall. They experience the cold isolation of those who protect the Seven Kingdoms. As a visitor, you almost feel like this place is real and that you've been there, if only for a little while.

In an effort to spread the message and translate this fantasy experience into something that feels real, Campfire NYC goes so far as to create a local climate-based application on iTunes that reads the weather in your locations and shows which region of the *Game of Thrones* world your weather most closely resembles. This can be a lot of fun for travelers or during the change of seasons. It also shows the lengths Campfire NYC went to in order to sweep visitors up into an experience. Campfire NYC and HBO designed this promotion to be spread more like wildfire (instead of a controlled burn), and gave visitors every opportunity to share this amazing series of experiences with their audiences online.

Whenever you're stuck for ideas, ask yourself, "What would Campfire do?"

Tantalizing their taste buds

In a brilliant move, Campfire NYC partnered with a top chef to create dishes that might conceivably be part of the world shared in this fantasy series. Not only that, but it decided to create videos of the chef preparing *Game of Thrones* inspired food, explaining his recipes, and showing how it was to be served. It then shared them on YouTube and with traditional media outlets, such as TV news and radio.

Not satisfied with tantalizing the senses with some great food video and menu ideas, Campfire NYC sponsored food trucks to serve those dishes created by its chef and featured via video to prominent food bloggers at to-be-named locations in L.A. and New York City.

One featured menu includes squab with hot-spiced wine, nutmeg, raisins, leek and black bread pudding, served with sweet corn fritters and followed by lemon cakes. Of course, the menu was graphically represented in a medieval, *Game of Thrones* style in order to carry out the theme and a sense that visitors are indeed entering an entirely different dimension of experience — going where fantasy meets reality.

Traditional media outlets were going nuts interviewing fans and bloggers on the street as they waited for the food trucks and chatted with one another about the series and this shared experience. Every day had the atmosphere of a fan convention.

Each day's dish was announced via a preview video on YouTube, only to be shared with followers on Twitter and Facebook. It's a super clever way to build your following and train them to come back to you first, instead of the traditional media, for updates on where things are going next.

Going deeper

Campfire NYC leveraged all of this to take its more engaged fans much deeper into the fantasy world of *Game of Thrones*. Campfire NYC created free online games (see Figure 17-4) and community forums (see Figure 17-5). The games featured intricate puzzles and presented mysteries online that can only be solved with the help of other fans in the online communities. By the time this series had gotten ready to air, fans' excitement had risen to a fever pitch, and the series continues to be a success season after season.

Figure 17-4:
Game of Thrones free role-playing game.

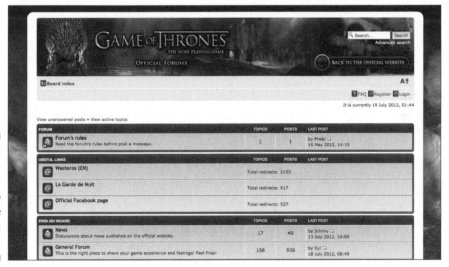

Figure 17-5:
Going deeper into the *Game of Thrones* community forums.

Being careful about the company share

Every time something is purchased via clicking on an affiliate link, a commission goes back to the person who posted and shared that link. If you do choose to create affiliate accounts with vendors, I can't stress enough how crucial it is for you to be positive that what they are doing is top-notch and ethical. Your reputation is on the line every time you endorse somebody else, especially for money. That's why I almost never share affiliate links. (An *affiliate link* is a special URL that contains the ID or username of an advertiser so it can track all traffic sent to the advertiser's site. People sign up with affiliate marketing programs in hopes of making money from the sales that they may generate for that advertiser.)

Doing Good in the World

In an old story, a man sees three construction workers wearing dusty clothes and working in the hot summer sun. He asks the first worker, "What are you doing?" and the man replies, "I'm laying bricks." When he asks the second construction worker what he's doing, that one says, "I'm building a wall." As the man approaches the third worker, he can hear that man humming as he works. Intrigued, the man asks, "What are you doing?" The third worker breaks into a smile and says, "I am building a cathedral."

Sometimes, you can make things easier just by changing your point of view. Whether you're a small-business entrepreneur or the interactive marketing director for a huge organization, creating an energizing vision for the people around you is one of the most important things you can do. When you create that vision, building and maintaining a vibrant online reputation will happen almost effortlessly.

Sharing valuable resources

One of the most powerful ways you can do good in the world for your fans and clients online is to publish informative or entertaining posts that can be easily shared. People come to the Internet for valuable information. When you supply information about your field you will gather a following as people find out about you. Don't worry about trying to supply all kinds of content to all kinds of people — that's impossible. It doesn't diminish your credibility at all to admit that you can't be all things to all people all the time. People appreciate your honesty and transparency.

They also appreciate your good taste and ability to qualify resources when you share links to products and services related to your area of expertise that are genuinely remarkable, reputable, and stand behind what they do. I especially appreciate service providers who willingly share out of the goodness of their hearts, and not because an affiliate link is going to make them money or enhance a highly influential relationship.

Promoting meaningful causes

It's a good idea to consider what meaningful cause stirs you. If you are representing a larger brand, consider what meaningful causes resonate with your brand's core values. There are a million different ways to implement this. I encourage you to expand your thinking about how to amplify your positive reputation online. Some examples of meaningful causes include

- ✔ Organic farming for a restaurant
- ✔ Going green for an architectural firm
- ✔ Literacy programs for a writer

Always do your homework when investigating any charity that your brand will be referencing online. Make sure what it says matches what it does.

Juicing Lemons into Lemonade

It's impossible for everything you do online to get a 100 percent "tickled pink" response. Even if you offered $1 million to the next five responders, you'd get criticized. It's just human nature.

Whether you're a seasoned hand online just looking to beef up your online reputation management and security, or a newcomer into this exciting space, I encourage you to keep doing, keep trying, and to pick yourself back up again if something goes amok. This is the only way you can get through the learning curve to where you want to go quickly.

Thankfully, the stakes tend to be pretty low when you're starting out online. You should always be experimenting, trying new things — and sometimes that translates into falling flat on your face. It's part of the experience. Oftentimes, people don't even notice your mistakes. They're too busy taking care of their own businesses to pay a lot of attention to what's going on with somebody else online.

No great plan that goes sideways online is ever a waste of time if you're appropriating valuable lessons from what did and didn't work. It's a process, not a formula.

Dealing with constructive criticism

Sometimes when you try something new and it doesn't work out as planned, people will be kind enough to point out what you could've done better. Feedback loops like these can help keep you on track, at least in terms of technical issues and community considerations that may never have crossed your mind otherwise.

It's pretty awesome to have free consultants sharing their best information and expertise with you. That happens a lot online when you put yourself out there with something new or different and the results aren't perfect. I have lots and lots of experience with not-perfect.

When you throw your heart into what you're doing, your positive energy shows and energizes the most surprising people, even total strangers, to

- ✔ Share their best tips
- ✔ Create graphics for you
- ✔ Solve technical problems for you
- ✔ Give you the benefit of their professional expertise
- ✔ Rescue some aspect of your project

Oftentimes, comments of this nature will come from goodhearted people who like you and just want to see you grow faster and thrive. The most important thing you can do when you experience complaints, suggestions, and what I call "wish lists" online, is to sincerely thank those people for caring enough to pay attention to what you're doing and share their perspectives with you.

When you thank a critic, you always look great. Specifically you

- ✔ **Demonstrate that you're trustworthy.** Responding with kindness demonstrates your humanity. Treating others the way you would want to be treated tends to come back to you in a good way. You receive more input from trustworthy people outside of your brand because they know that you will value their opinions and expertise. Even when the critic is wrong or is giving you awful advice, thanking him can create a loyal fan simply because you treated him with kindness.

> ✔ **Demonstrate your fallibility.** You don't know it all, and that's okay because nobody possibly can. There's such a rush of new information exploding at the seams every minute of the day that it's impossible to know everything. Admitting this makes you a lot more approachable and like the kind of person whom most people would want to have as a friend.

Identifying room to grow

Once people have been kind enough to reflect back to you constructive criticism online, you may discover that there's nothing that needs to be fixed per se but that they have identified room to grow. Sometimes the biggest mistake you can make in creating and expanding your online reputation is to forget about some areas of involvement that may well be crucial to your brand.

There will always be people who want you to do more (or fewer) videos, explore less popular social media networks, or write about their favorite subjects. Some people may contact you and object to your style or tell you that they absolutely love it and will stop paying attention to you if you ever change.

I encourage you to disregard these people and to plot your own course. Other people are often poor navigators. Have you ever watched a movie in which stranded people have to find their way out of a densely wooded forest without a compass? Even though every person will swear that he's walking in a straight line and heading toward his destination, he ends up walking in circles.

People, even Fortune 100 companies, sometimes do this with their online reputation management without realizing it.

The only way you can truly build a strong and positive reputation online is to stay true to those decisions about where you want to go and what you want to do. Sometimes you may get off-track or decide that you need to make a change. This isn't failure; it's a learning curve.

Sometimes meaningful feedback can give you just the wake-up call you need to identify room to grow. Embrace it with an open mind and evolve your strategy past this if the criticism holds up to research, critical thinking, and your best instincts.

It's a wild kingdom out there online, and nobody has all the answers. The best thing you can do when you discover that you've done something that wasn't all that well received or that people downright hated is to pick yourself up, research, think it through, and change your direction toward something that makes better sense for you. And always, always thank people who are kind enough to reflect back something honestly structured, even if it doesn't feel good.

Dealing with nonconstructive criticism

Occasionally, you may be dealing with somebody who attacks your brand, dismisses you, or just behaves like an outright troll. The more you choose to differentiate your brand from others online, the greater the chance you have of experiencing remarks like these.

On the plus side, you can take these actions as an indication that you're different from your competitors and that you're saying something provocative. After all, if you were better at blending in, you wouldn't receive comments like these. But success online usually requires getting noticed — noticed for the right reasons, of course — and blending in won't help you do that at all.

Part VI
The Part of Tens

The 5th Wave

By Rich Tennant

"Good news, honey! No one's registered our last name as a domain name yet! Helloooo Haffassoralsurgery.com!"

In this part . . .

In Part VI, I give you the time-honored, ever-popular *For Dummies* "Part of Tens." Chapter 18 gives you my top ten online reputation tips for special events. Here I "show" (pun intended) you ten ways to safeguard and make the most of your special events. In Chapter 19, I take the opposite approach by sharing ten time-tested ways to "faceplant" your online reputation. You get my top ten important ways to safeguard your reputation every day. And to top it all off, now that you will be your own online reputation management expert, I share my top ten ways to create happy fans online. Keep this by your bedside.

Chapter 18

Ten Online Reputation Tips for Special Events

So you have a special event coming up! As with any big shindig, there is a lot more planning than meets the eye in order to pull this off success-fully with your sparkling reputation intact and hopefully turbo-boosted. In this chapter, I give you ten solid online reputation tips for your face-to-face special event. Whether you're planning a conference, trade show, live prod-uct launch, or a 5K run/walk, I have tips for you to make the most of your online reputation before, during, and after your event. (And yes, I promise I can count: I just couldn't resist tossing in an extra tip for you!)

Special events can be the life or death of your brand's reputation online, depending on how you manage them. In this chapter, I show you how to channel positive feedback generated by your event into an improved online reputation.

Note that most of these tips apply to online events as well as face-to-face ones — events such as large-scale webinars, live courses, and live streaming presentations. Just apply what you can, and omit the obvious parts that relate to a physical location.

Getting Ready for the Big Event

The most important thing you can do related to your online reputation is to create what I call an online communications "central nervous system" for your event. Just as your body can thrive only with a healthy central nervous system, to communicate what's going on and what to do about it, your brand needs a specially designated system for your special event. Your special event's "central nervous system" needs to be more than one harried confer-ence director or assistant.

In this new electronic echo chamber called the Internet that we know and love, good news travels fast. The bad news is that bad news travels even faster. Your team has to know what's going on and what's being done about it in real time. This takes a lot of thought and collaboration on your part because there's no way that you can silence online negativity about a technical issue or what a speaker said. You simply have to respond transparently and quickly, acknowledging what's happening and keeping people informed about what's being done.

Once you all agree on how your "central nervous system" works, you need to

- ✔ Interview, select, and train extra social media team members.

- ✔ Consider hiring a PR agency to pitch in with your social media monitoring, leveraging that firm's media relationships, and distributing press releases.

- ✔ Practice, practice, and practice some more. I suggest you conduct "fire drills" in case there are negatives to address at your event in order to discover what works and what needs more refinement. If at all possible, doing advance dry runs of your event can be a lifesaver because they reveal issues that need refinement. Practicing like this will give your team a greater sense of confidence that they will do just fine during your actual event.

Now that I'm going on record with the most important thing you can possibly do for your online reputation, the rest of these tips function to promote your well-deserved and positive reputation online.

As long as you are doing right by people, being transparent, and letting people know what's going on, odds are good that your conference, trade show, workshop, or special event is going to be a success for your online reputation.

Sponsor Weekly Twitter Chats before the Event

One of the best things you can do before your special events like trade shows, conferences, and live workshops is to make sure as many people know about them as possible. There are people out there who want and need what your event supplies, but need to know it exists in order to decide whether they want to attend.

Many successful Twitter chats include a prominent guest speaker, where Twitter audiences at large ask questions. Create a designated hashtag for the event so that people can share and respond using that hashtag. This amps up the fun for all attendees because they can keep track of what's going on in the conversation just as well as you can.

Get Prominent Speakers to Feature Promo Videos

If your event hosts keynote speakers, ask them to create a promotional video, or better yet, a series of promotional videos that gives people a sneak peak into what the speakers will be talking about and why it's important to your audiences right now.

Host these promotional videos on the event page on your site as well as in a post. You can also share them on your YouTube, Facebook, Twitter, and LinkedIn channels if they will appeal to your audiences there.

Don't forget to ask your speakers to share these videos with their own audiences. This will go a long way toward building excitement and word-of-mouth about your great event.

Contact Industry Leaders Well in Advance

Depending on what kind of industry you're in, it's a good idea to contact your industry leaders well in advance of your event. Sometimes these people will sponsor a booth or send a speaker, but in terms of your online reputation ask them endorse your event and share it with their audiences. You can pre-write a blog post for them for possible inclusion on their sites.

You never know until you ask. There may be all kinds of behind-the-scenes activity that would make endorsing your event mutually beneficial.

Include Teasers and Early Bird Benefits

Promote video, picture, or interview highlights from last year. Tell what's new and share all of this via Facebook, Twitter, LinkedIn, and your brand's newsletter. If you have a presence on LinkedIn, that's a great place to share industry news with an entirely different audience.

Also consider embedding slide show presentations from last year's talks. Slideshare is a terrific service for hosting and sharing slide shows. When you upload presentations to a slide show and then embed a link to that post on your site, you exponentially increase your exposure online.

Some events, such as conferences, offer early bird benefits to people who sign up by a designated date. Often times, these discounts are quite significant and trigger online sharing because the people sharing them feel like they are giving their audiences something of value, too.

Offer Incentives to People Who Spread the Word

Speaking of people who share valuable stuff with their online audiences, I suggest you reward people who spread the word about your event online.

Earlier in this chapter, I suggest that you designate a hashtag for your event. Consider creating a reward structure so that people who spread the word once a day for a couple of weeks get a discount or awesome swag (fun giveaways like t-shirts, shopping bags, or toys). It's the best way I can think of to show your appreciation.

Host Select Live Portions for Free on Your Site

One of the coolest things currently happening online is hosting live events on places like Google+ hangouts and Ustream. I give you more detail about these venues in Chapter 13.

Some people simply won't be able to attend your event. Lots of those people would love to feel like they are participating in some way besides checking out the live tweets. Give them live footage of segments that you decide on in advance. You may even decide to give away an entire session for free, hosted live on a Google+ hangout via your brand page there or via Ustream.

You can even give online watchers a special hashtag in order to tweet and share their impressions as the presentation is happening. Consider acknowledging them during the presentation; that way, they'll feel more included.

Use foursquare to Create a Place for Check-Ins

Depending on what your audiences are like, they may enjoy using a geo-tagging service like foursquare to check in to your event. You can get details about adding your own specific venue on foursquare by visiting the Add Venue section of foursquare online.

If you do, be sure and offer them some kind of special swag, discount, badge (a virtual status symbol within foursquare), or recognition for participating. If you set up a foursquare check-in, be sure to monitor foursquare alongside your other social media channels. In Chapter 7, I show you how to add social media network streams to the media aggregator HootSuite. Foursquare is one of its supported channels, so adding foursquare to your dashboard is easy.

Prominently Display All Tweets with Your Event Hashtag

Nothing makes tweeting more fun for participants than seeing their tweets projected onto a huge display for all other attendees to see. Only tweets with your designated hashtag will show up, so this encourages everybody to stay on track so that you can monitor and respond to what's being said.

Note, however, that this can backfire if your social media isn't being monitored adequately by having a bunch of tweets advertising a problem where no solutions are being offered. If you're monitoring adequately, this is a good way to demonstrate that you're on top of things and are responding to issues in real time, which really contributes to how well people will perceive your brand. At some large conferences I attended, the huge leaderboard on their "Tweet wall" showed the names of the people who tweeted the most at the event at any given time. It adds to the energy of the event and demonstrates that they're being transparent. Get all the perspectives on this before you make your decision.

Feature and Link to Shared Pictures from the Event

Hire a photographer to wander around your event and take candid pictures of people enjoying themselves or being captivated by an informative presentation.

Featuring people's pictures that are taken during your event can also be a powerful way to generate excitement and interest online. Consider ways that attendees can submit their pictures to you for possible inclusion on your site, too. Offer them the opportunity to be a guest blogger in connection with their photos.

This is a great way to boost your visibility and enhance your reputation online, but only if your event is appropriate for this level of sharing. Even so, it's a good idea to ask conference attendees to sign something that gives the conference permission to use their images on all kinds of media for free.

If you plan to use attendees' photos from your event, keep your word by only posting photos of or from people who give you permission to use their images. It's an essential layer of good online reputation management.

Bonus Tip: Create a Narrative on Storify

Storify (`http://storify.com`) is a clever, little online tool that gives you the capability to piece together a stream of social media content from several different networks in order to tell the story about your event.

Storify gathers photos, videos, tweets, and more into a running, real-time narrative that you can embed into your website and share via your social networks. This is another resource that you can pull together for the people who were unable to attend your event. In Figure 18-1 I'm creating a story about those energetic, loveable rat terriers.

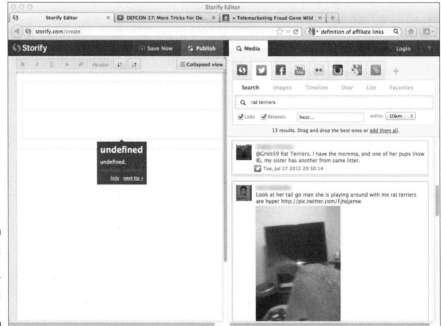

Figure 18-1:
Building a rat terrier story on Storify.

Chapter 19

Ten Ways to Faceplant Your Online Reputation

•••

Social media and blogging have revolutionized the way people communicate both online and in person. It's no longer cool to broadcast a one-way message that doesn't even pause to listen for an answer or gauge a reaction.

With social media, people can reconnect with old friends and coworkers, and make new friends who share their passions, even unusual passions. As I sit here in my office, I can see an antique cuckoo clock. Entire communities of people exist online who collect, repair, and otherwise love talking about antique cuckoo clocks. I love the way online communication brings people together in fresh and exciting ways.

Nowadays it's really easy to think of social media as a place where you can let your hair down and be the real you. If you let your guard down too much, however, you risk harming the reputation you've worked so hard to achieve. In this chapter, I present ten ways you can faceplant your online reputation.

Denying Issues

Before Google became a household phenomenon and people began looking for information online for just about everything, many organizations opted to deny developing issues in hopes that they could resolve them before the issue got so hot that it the mainstream press started to take notice. It's an understandable policy, but in today's world of instant information that kind of strategy can backfire badly.

It used to be a safe assumption that most people don't have the power of the media behind them. It's not as true anymore because social media networks and blogging leveled the playing field to a great extent. These days anybody can cultivate a large following online based on his sense of humor, status as a prominent player in a game-playing community, professional affiliations, college connections, or on any number of other characteristics.

If somebody wants to get covered via mainstream media, they can generate momentum online that gets noticed by news hungry traditional media organizations. Denying an issue that can be disproved via a picture of a receipt, letter, or compelling video being shared online can be more embarrassing than the original issue.

Deleting Comments

It's perfectly acceptable to delete irrelevant, spammy comments (such as "Buy homemade cookies from me, at MoreUselessCookies on Facebook!") when your brand has nothing whatsoever to do with cookies or food of any kind. You can also respond with something like "Really? We talk about commercial real estate in this community," for example, and then delete the comment.

But occasionally, as a heated situation escalates online, an organization will start to accumulate lots of comments from people who are new to the Facebook page or the blog community. It can be scary to watch these comments mount up and wonder what to do about them. Sometimes, in a misguided attempt to defray online tensions, administrators will choose to delete Facebook page comments and blog comments that are unflattering or angry instead of engaging with them appropriately.

Situations like this tend to escalate quickly and also migrate elsewhere online if they continue to be ignored, or worse yet, deleted.

Social media can't be stifled or simply ignored. If people are emotionally moved about a topic, they will find a way to share and discuss it online.

Allowing Issues to Flame

Delay tactics do nothing to smother the flames of outrage, particularly when you are managing the online reputation of a large, well-known brand. These tactics only feed the fire. Normally, there are two ways that issues can be successfully fanned into a full-scale online conflagration. They include

 ✔ Employing the "spin" tactic of delaying an announcement involving bad news. This becomes a huge problem as

  • Bad news leaks easily via the Internet and then spreads like wildfire via social media networks like YouTube, Twitter, and Facebook. You always want to be the one breaking your own bad

news so that you can frame the discussion, which gives you significant leverage in the discussion.

- It's a huge breach of trust, which only fuels the fire with fresh passion and new commenters.

✔ Dawdling in indecision because of

- Poor communication within an organization.

- Waffling on the part of the crisis team.

- Not enough information to make a proper statement, though in this
  case it's better to tell audiences that you are looking into the situation right now and will provide more information as soon as you
  get it.

People don't judge you for making mistakes nearly as much as they do if you
don't take responsibility for them. Own up and get on with it.

Being a Twit

With all this emphasis about being accessible online, creating community,
and sharing meaningful content, it's easy to get the wrong idea and start
tweeting or posting updates excessively.

Although it's true that reading a Twitter feed can be like trying to drink from
a fire hose, it's important to let up for air and give people a little bit of space
to miss you. Surely you'd prefer your audience to be glad to hear from you
instead of weary from constant updates. It's also true that some updates are
more attractive than others. Be careful what you post and be especially careful to note whether you're being

✔ **Confrontational:** It's easy to faceplant by being confrontational about
silly things that very few people care about. Go one step further by
dickering over something that really doesn't matter. If you aren't into
faceplanting your online reputation, I suggest you hold off on being confrontational unless you have a clear, cool-minded focus and genuinely
feel that justice is being served.

✔ **Unkind:** Ignoring people always helps faceplant your brand, but being
unkind ratchets that several notches higher on the faceplant scale.
Seriously, it takes only a moment to be kind and it's often appreciated.
Take the higher ground.

✔ **Selfish:** Share great content by and for other people. It's a great way
to contribute to the community. For faceplanting purposes, only

tweet your own stuff. Don't act like conversations are taking place and respond to people, either.

Also, I want to take a moment to point out these important details:

- *Don't be afraid to follow people back.* You won't look less cool. You'll look like a community member. If you want to pay closer attention to certain feeds, create lists. That's how I manage different groups of people. For example, I have foodie, creative, and "short list" lists where I follow some of my favorite people on Twitter.

- *Don't share insignificant updates like "Just finished breakfast. Oatmeal's good."* Unless you're a best-selling author who writes about different grades of oatmeal, it's something to avoid.

✔ **A copycat:** Retweets alone get boring, as does copying somebody else's tweets. Be an original.

Responding in a Rude, Angry, or Impatient Way

In April 2012, Ben Polis, (now former) CEO of the Australian utility monitoring company called Energy Watch, had a bad habit of making social media status updates about whatever was on his mind. His diatribes are too offensive to share here, but one of his tamer outbursts was, "Some days if you gave me a gun I would open fire and shoot half the muppets in my office . . . followed by a few shots at their offspring."

Even after media commentators called him out on his racist, sexist, drug-using, violent, rash, and offensive behavior, he responded flippantly with comments like, "I can't be racist, my cleaner is Asian, and I once dated a half-Aboriginal woman." Somebody fetch me a Pepto, won't you?

Being outrageous is a great way to get quick attention, but it is most certainly a disastrous way to maintain a strong and positive online reputation. Put a lid on inflammatory remarks, no matter what mood you're in or what time of day it is.

Once online, always online! If people are willing to dig for it, they can find everything you ever post online.

Keep your words tender and sweet. You may have to eat them someday!

Getting Your Wires Crossed

Online reputation management faceplanting 101 requires getting your wires crossed in a big way. For example, the band Metallica broke trust with its fans, igniting an online firestorm when it sent journalists and bloggers advance copies of it latest album for review. Metallica forgot to ask reviewers to sign a non-disclosure agreement, so when they began sharing their reviews online, Metallica blew a gasket. Suddenly Metallica's representation demanded for those reviews be taken down, even though the reviewers, having not signed that agreement, had been within their legal rights to leave them up.

This is a clear example of faceplanting your image online via getting your wires crossed. I don't know why Metallica suddenly changed tactics, but this is a good lesson in thinking your course of action all the way through and sticking with it so as not to confuse your audiences and reflect negatively on your good name.

Failing to Learn from Others' Mistakes

We are all collectively learning as we go. Mistakes that were overlooked last year are often detected once a crisis has arisen and after the subject has been discussed openly, those mistakes don't get overlooked again. Pay attention to others. See how they responded — what they did wrong, what they did right. Use their examples as models for your own responses.

Ignoring Potential Online Influence

Online communities, blogs, and social media have totally changed the dynamics of public influence. Some people have even called it a communications revolution. One of the biggest faceplants that people or brands can make to their online reputations is to forget that everybody they deal with may have large, influential audiences online. Mind your manners with whomever you meet, and if you find you're connecting more closely with somebody you don't know, check out that individual's profiles online and get an idea of whom you're talking to. You may be surprised (and there are two kinds of surprises: good and bad!). This extends to more than just online conversations, as the following case clearly indicates.

One Saturday afternoon, a Papa John's Pizza employee carelessly decided to give an Asian customer a rap-inspired nickname, and wrote "Lady Chinky Eyes" on her receipt. It never occurred to him that she may have a large, engaged social media audience to share this literary treasure with. She saw the name as a racial slur. When she tweeted "Hey @PapaJohns just FYI my name isn't 'lady chinky eyes," along with a picture of the receipt, Papa John's began to have a very bad day. Things got worse when

- The story spread like mad via Twitter.
- It got blogged by different individuals with large audiences.
- Huffington Post picked up the story after two or three hours (good job monitoring trends, Huffington Post!).
- All the major social networks exploded with this story.

Papa John's had to create a video apology featuring one of its top executives and release a statement saying that it never meant for its employees to abuse the ticketing system that way or to be racist in any way.

Publishing Lies, Damn Lies, and Statistics

People can say just about whatever they want online. Unless somebody is willing to dig deep to research what you are saying, odds are good that you may get away with inaccuracies now and then (not to say that I advise such behavior: read on!).

I worry about people who stretch the truth, however, though it is a face-planting favorite that likely will always stand the test of time. Here's where it becomes a faceplant for your online reputation. If you've ever watched reruns of any of those police shows, you've seen someone getting interrogated. That process involves asking the same questions again and again, watching to see if the answers change or stay the same.

The tricky thing about online communication is that it requires publishing lots of status updates, blog posts, pictures, and tweets. It would be enormously difficult to keep up a lie consistently over so many communications and not contradict the story.

The easiest way to faceplant your online reputation is to break trust with your followers. The easiest way to build a strong reputation online is to be authentic, share what you're honestly good at, and contribute to your community.

It's the kind of investment that gets paid back with interest. Build demonstrable integrity into your brand by

- ✔ Providing (actual) client testimonial videos.

- ✔ Provide (on request) a link to that person's site, if applicable, and contact information if somebody asks for a reference. (Of course, you need to be sure that your client has already given you permission to do so!)

- ✔ Posting before and after pictures, where applicable, with contact information for the client who's referring you.

Forgetting to Do Your Homework

It's simple: Before you ever publish a blog post with a funny name, please do yourself a favor and Google it first to make sure it isn't offensive or off-color in some way. Surprisingly, even prestigious public relations and marketing firms can sometimes forget to take a minute and do this important homework. In case you think I'm exaggerating, consider Nike's dreadful March 2012 "Black and Tan" public relations disaster.

Ironically enough, in celebration of St. Patrick's day, Nike actually named one of its running shoes the "FB Black and Tan quick strike," saying that it was celebrating the popular drink consisting of combining a dark beer with a light one so that you can see the layers of color. It claimed to have had no clue that Black and Tan also was the name of one of the most vicious, bloodthirsty, and widely feared groups that were sent into Ireland to make it a "hell for rebels to live in." The Irish haven't forgotten that tragedy, and emotions run high on the subject to this day.

After this "forgetting to do your homework" flavored faceplant where social networks and blogs angrily opined and shared, Nike issued an apology stating that no offense was intended, though it did remain silent on the topic for a period of time — the "allowing situations to flame" faceplanting scenario I describe earlier in this chapter.

Bottom line: Do your homework.

Chapter 20

Ten Ways to Create Happy Fans

● ●

*A*fter you've set up your listening tools, pulled together your online communications team, and worked through all your worst-case crisis scenarios, you've done a lot, but your biggest job still awaits you: Pleasing your audience. Robust online reputation is really based on clearly communicating who you are and what you do to the people who matter: your potential fans, voters, or clients.

This chapter offers a list of ten ways to create a happy fan base. The list is by no means exhaustive, but if you use these tips, you will be amazed by how quickly word spreads about the great work you're doing, both online and face-to-face.

Sending a Clear Message

Sometimes this takes getting alone with a notebook and just writing about exactly what you want your online reputation to be about. If you take your career online with the vague goal of being "popular," this may happen for you, but consider what you want to get out of it.

People will respond to you positively when you identify what you're doing in clear terms that they can understand almost right away. If you have to educate people about what you do, it takes a lot longer to gain traction online. That can be discouraging. Something amazing happens when you get super clear on what you want and what you have to offer. Suddenly the way you talk about it gets much clearer. Your blog posts are more focused because you're using your search engine optimization (SEO) keywords I show you in chapter 6, and people feel like they can share what you're saying because it's valuable and easy to understand.

Keeping Your Words Tender and Sweet

Keeping your words tender and sweet makes them taste much better if you end up having to eat them later. Every now and then, it's possible to receive a hurtful or irrational comment on a blog post or status update. I cover this in a lot more detail in Chapter 15, but the bottom line is to always keep a level head when if you respond. You may be surprised to discover how quickly your loyal fans will defend you via comments on your blog posts and status updates — even before you're aware of a criticism or complaint.

Save the drama for daytime television or reality shows. Keep your focus on contributing meaningfully to your communities. When you establish yourself as a positive (or at least entertaining in your snark) voice, people come to you again and again for your content.

You set the tone for your online communities. Rise above any pettiness that comes your way and move that conversation to a private channel, like e-mail.

Giving Freely

I don't mean you should give away the candy store, only that you should give generously with valuable insights, training, information, or even encouragement. It makes all the difference between having a few lukewarm followers or a growing fan base of genuinely happy and enthusiastic brand ambassadors.

Speaking of giving freely, every time you incentivize or recognize contributions from your community, you deepen the level of your relationship. You can reward contributors with something as simple as featuring them in one of your blog posts, giving them sneak peeks of your new products and services, or inviting them to special events. Let them know that they are VIPs in your world, because they are.

Maintaining Authenticity

There is a lot of confusion right now about what exactly it means to be authentic online without sharing information that compromises your privacy or offends people unnecessarily. Although there will always be exceptions, it's generally a good idea NOT to

- ✔ Use salty language online
- ✔ Comment on religious beliefs
- ✔ Opine about politics
- ✔ Share openly about your love life
- ✔ Share everything about your kids, if you have them
- ✔ Tell all about your financial successes or failures

Some people have built successful brands around being foul mouthed, shocking, and full of bedtime stories. And I don't mean the kinds of bedtime stories you read to your kids. This is perfectly legitimate if it is the kind of image that you want to cultivate online as part of your brand. Some people are doing very well with this approach and I applaud their success. But understand that if you go there, you should probably commit to it as part of your brand and not throw it in now and then, because it confuses your message.

Whatever part of your personality you choose to bring out online, own it and give people a clear message about your brand.

Visualizing Your Ideal Fan

When I say you should "visualize your fan," I'm not getting all Zen on you or leading you in a guided meditation. I only mean you should take some time to consider who your ideal fan or client really is. Ask yourself

- ✔ Who are some of your greatest clients, past or present?
- ✔ What do they tend to have in common?
- ✔ What's their education level?
- ✔ What do they love to do?
- ✔ What are they most afraid of?
- ✔ What do they value?
- ✔ What are their goals?
- ✔ How old are they?
  - ✔ Are they free to make spending decisions?

Once you have visualized your ideal fans, speak to them in your blog posts, your updates, and everything that you create online. You will attract the right people to you, and they, in turn, will share you with their audiences because they know you're a great find.

Staying Focused on Your Strategy

This may seem like a strange way to keep a happy fan base, but focusing on your overall direction and strategy takes care of the people you care about online. Maintaining clarity with your message, where you are, and where you want to go is the smartest thing you can do to keep your fan base happy and growing.

Think about it this way: If you're going somewhere different all the time, it's a rare person who will continue to follow you online.

Go through the system outlined in this book. Build your online reputation from the architecture of your site, to your SEO keywords, your social media and blog monitoring, and your sparkling, generous engagement online. Go through all the steps, and you will be amazed by how quickly your online reputation grows and will be able to sustain dramatic growth or crisis. People will trust you because you make your brand's message simple and clear.

Qualifying Your Representatives

Always remember: Even after you've successfully implemented your own online reputation management strategy, occasions may still arise when you need to hire a social-media monitoring service. When this happens, make sure you thoroughly communicate your strategy to that service so that it'll know what you expect of it.

This may sound like a no-brainer, but it's not. Many companies find that handing their businesses over to a social media consultancy results in . . . nothing much at all. Instead of implementing their strategies, these services will simply "babysit" their brands.

Give your fans and your own organization the best representation by carefully qualifying your representatives. You can't expect them to give you what you want until you're sure they *know* what you want.

These days, social media "experts" are popping up like flowers after a rainstorm, but the vast majority of these so-called experts don't have the experience needed to develop a deep understanding of the tools, and they really won't know the best ways to spread your brand's message, achieve your goals, or (*gulp*) manage a crisis. This goes for large agencies as well as small, surprisingly enough. Many PR agencies are getting on the social media bandwagon without getting fully qualified first.

Don't gamble with your online reputation management by letting somebody with an impressive-sounding sales pitch get behind the wheel of that gorgeous, sleek Ferrari that is your brand-in-the-making online. Get lots of references that talk more about measurable results than how cool that person or agency is or how many friends it has online. Where the rubber meets the road, your fans can most definitely tell the difference. They deserve the very best you can give them, and it's often at the same price or less than what wannabe "experts" charge.

Blogging Like a 5-Star Restaurant

Once you've determined what your message is, consider serving up tastefully informative and sharable blog posts as if you were a five-star restaurant. Think about it: If you serve snackable content and delicious meals of meaningful, entertaining information, you will quickly build a happy fan base that will share you with their audiences. Keep in mind

- ✔ **Consistency:** Obviously, if your brand is about golf clubs, don't go off on a tangent and talk about golf carts. Stay tightly focused and go deep, rather than wide, with your messaging.

- ✔ **Freshness:** Reading about what happened at a conference two months ago isn't nearly as much fun (and doesn't rank nearly as well) as reading about it extremely close to the actual time it occurs. Stay in front of the trends as much as possible with the tools I share in this book.

- ✔ **Seasonality:** Tie in seasonal interests to your posts. For example, seasoned tax preparation experts can present a series on tax preparation in the months of February when it's on everybody's minds. In September, it's a lot harder to get excited about taxes. I frankly never get excited about taxes, so February is definitely the best month to get my attention on this taxing subject. Yes, I went there.

- ✔ **Chef's own individual flair:** This is where your personality and authentic engagement sparkle come into play. Own who you are and what you're doing so that what you express comes from a place of authenticity. (Refer to the earlier tip, "Visualizing Your Ideal Fan," for more spot-on advice about creating a happy fan base online.) This stuff works!

Expending your online reputation isn't using another traditional marketing channel. It's a fresh, new communication platform that has to be two-way and personal.

Connecting as a Friend

One of the fastest ways you can cultivate happy fans online is to connect with them as a friend instead of as an authority figure. Even if you really do know your topic better than everybody else, people will love you for approaching them as an equal or as an expert in their own field.

Cultivating mutual respect is one of the most rewarding and enjoyable activities that you can engage in to promote your reputation online. People gladly share you with their own audiences when they feel as though they can trust you to respect them.

Telling Your Story

The reasons why people get into business are often compelling. People like to know what fuels your passion and creativity. These stories add meaning to their experience with your brand. For example, when I owned an upscale specialty boutique, I shopped relentlessly for the best-quality, most deliciously indulgent soaps and lotions I could find, and in the process, discovered something absolutely astonishing.

My customers, many of whom were extremely well educated and well-to-do, didn't care about the quality of the item as much as how it was packaged and the story that went behind the product. I'm still wrapping my mind around this one, but I swear to you that it's true and that every successful wholesaler and retailer told me the same thing.

One particular line of baby soaps we carried had excruciatingly cute packaging. On the packaging was an engaging background story about how the soapmaker created this soap — its scent, its look, even its name. The soap itself was indeed good quality, but it was nothing revolutionary or life changing. Still, the packaging, and particularly the background story would touch my customers deeply.

On the other hand, another soap we carried was indeed revolutionary and life changing: It was an effective treatment for eczema. Some of my customers, people who had spent thousands of dollars on dermatologists and got unsatisfactory results, found that this soap could cure their eczema. It was a great product, perfect for sensitive skin. It was packaged nicely, too. But it had no background story to go with it.

Probably you already know which soap sold more. Even though both soaps were priced the same, and even though I told my customers about the effectiveness of the second soap, the cute soap with the background story was the big seller. It astonished me. It showed me that a great background story and cute packaging are everything. My takeaway from this example: Provide first-class value in your packaging (meaning your brand's look and story), and your fan base will race to share you with all their audiences.

Index

• G •

• H •

• I •

• *K* •

• *Y* •

• *Z* •